£5

39/24

1c

Econ/
Bus

CW01496568

Dilemmas in Economic Theory

Dilemmas in Economic Theory

Persisting Foundational Problems
of Microeconomics

Michael Mandler

New York   Oxford

Oxford University Press

1999

Oxford University Press

Oxford   New York
Athens   Auckland   Bangkok   Bogotá   Buenos Aires   Calcutta
Cape Town   Chennai   Dar es Salaam   Delhi   Florence   Hong Kong   Istanbul
Karachi   Kuala Lumpur   Madrid   Melbourne   Mexico City   Mumbai
Nairobi   Paris   São Paulo   Singapore   Taipei   Tokyo   Toronto   Warsaw

and associated companies in
Berlin   Ibadan

Copyright © 1999 by Oxford University Press, Inc.

Published by Oxford University Press, Inc.
198 Madison Avenue, New York, New York 10016

Oxford is a registered trademark of Oxford University Press

All rights reserved. No part of this publication may be reproduced,
stored in a retrieval system, or transmitted, in any form or by any means,
electronic, mechanical, photocopying, recording, or otherwise,
without the prior permission of Oxford University Press.

Library of Congress Cataloging-in-Publication Data
Mandler, Michael.
    Dilemmas in Economic theory : persisting foundational
problems of microeconomics / Michael Mandler.
        p.   cm.
    Includes bibliographical references and index.
    ISBN 0-19-510087-5
    1. Value.   2. Microeconomics.   I. Title.
HB201.M3985   1998
338.5—dc21   98-5437

1   3   5   7   9   8   6   4   2

Printed in the United States of America
on acid-free paper

Preface

Neoclassical economics advances a distinctive understanding of the social world. In its first decades, this fact was well understood; early versions of neoclassicism explicitly maintained that the market offers consumers and firms manifold opportunities for choice and that individuals select actions so as to maximize the quantity of pleasure they experience. In detailing this vision, economists of the late nineteenth century liberally applied the preferred mathematical technique of their day, the differential calculus, and brought about the marginal revolution. Much of the theory they invented still guides empirical applications and is taught to undergraduates.

Both the conceptual worldview and the mathematical particulars of neoclassical economics were sharply criticized as the theory rose to dominance. Partly in response, economists since the 1930s have tried to construct a more plausible theory of markets that does without the assumptions and tools that drew analytical fire. Calculus, marginal productivity, hedonistic decision theory, and utilitarianism were excised. This book evaluates the attempt to purge neoclassical economics of its reliance on these controversial precepts. I argue that the endeavor exposes the characteristic dilemmas of economic theory and does not achieve a trouble-free gain in generality.

Like most students, my introduction to economics in college contained an ample dose of early neoclassical orthodoxy. I learned, for example, that marginal productivity is analytically indispensable to economics, and therefore, since the assumption that factors have well-defined marginal products is an empirical claim, that neoclassical theory is committed to a substantive view of economic reality. Consequently, I was astonished in graduate school by the generality of the Arrow-Debreu account of economic equilibrium. Many of the questionable and empirically dubious features of early neoclassical theory had been eliminated. Particularly in its more refined versions, the general equilibrium model assumes that individuals obey only the most limited dictates of rationality and does away with the entire apparatus of marginal products. The discrepancies between these two images of economic theory led me to write this book.

I have pared the mathematical prerequisites of the book to a minimum. Although some claims require more complex tools to be demonstrated in full generality, all of the key arguments presented here employ techniques that are no more complicated than counting equations and unknowns. Any first year graduate student in economics and a good many upper-level undergraduates can grasp the entirety of the book. Still, I have explicitly or implicitly cordoned off the more formal material; the main ideas can be understood without it. My aim is not only to address an audience beyond the readers of specialist journals in economic theory; debate on the principles of economics ought to accommodate any member of the profession.

Many people generously took the time to discuss the ideas underlying this book with me or to read drafts of various chapters. Let me single out Alberto Alesina, David Cass, Patricia Craig, John Geanakoplos, Shira Lewin, Stephen Marglin, Andreu Mas-Colell, Ben Polak, Robert Pollak, Mark Steitz, Philip Steitz, and Paul Wendt. Herbert Scarf was instrumental in communicating the mathematical core of much of contemporary economic theory to me. Claudia Goldin first suggested that I write on welfare economics; chapter 6 of this book ultimately issued from this encouragement. Jane Ransom closely edited several chapters; her counsel led to a more transparent and forceful book. Jennifer Oser carefully and tirelessly proofread the manuscript. Several classes of graduate students at Harvard University listened to early, less systematic versions of the ideas presented here. Their reactions pushed me to greater precision and to avoid pointless convolutions. I have also been favored with unusually thoughtful referees. Even those who remain anonymous will recognize the impact they had on the finished manuscript. Finally, I am grateful for the early confidence and subsequent patience that Herbert Addison and Kenneth MacLeod, of Oxford University Press, showed in this project.

I dedicate this book to my parents, whose influence on this work, though indirect, is all pervasive.

Contents

Dilemmas in Economic Theory

1

Introduction

The Transformation of Economic Theory

While much has been written about the breach between classical and neo-classical economics, an equally significant divide lies within neoclassical theory, separating the "early neoclassicism" of the late nineteenth–early twentieth centuries from the general equilibrium models predominant since World War II. An exploration into this divide reveals foundational problems paved over rather than solved, whose irresolution weakens contemporary economic theory.[1]

Not only mathematical form but the very content of economics shifted. Utilitarianism in preference theory and welfare economics was overturned, replaced by an ordinal theory of rational choice and Pareto efficiency, and the marginal productivity theory of distribution was supplanted by a set-theoretic model with no allegiance to the differentiable, "neoclassical" production function. The earlier camp's highly specific accounts of technology, economic psychology, and social welfare had exposed neoclassical economics to damaging criticism. By dropping the previous commitments, contemporary theory claims to be less restrictive than, and hence superior to, early neoclassical theory.

As we will see, postwar theory does not adequately address the problems the discarded concepts were designed to solve. Difficulties at the core of economic theory therefore appear: factor markets may well be unable to determine factor prices or even operate competitively, and agents cannot be expected to obey the rationality assumptions of neoclassical preference

1. Although the "general equilibrium" label may seem misleading in that the key postwar innovations began outside of formal general equilibrium theory, it was the Arrow-Debreu model that combined the changes into a unified theory. For historical analyses of the rise of modern general equilibrium theory, see Ingrao and Israel (1987, chap. 7) and Weintraub (1985, chap. 6).

theory. But I also argue that logically adequate sufficient conditions for factor price determinacy can be specified, and that while some rationality assumptions lack convincing rationales, others are well grounded. When these and other problems are given due consideration, economic theory becomes more analytically satisfying.

1.1 Three transitions

To examine the two eras of neoclassical economics more closely, consider a representative work from each period. The first volume of the Swedish economist Knut Wicksell's *Lectures on Political Economy* both marks the consensus of the early twentieth century and is unrivaled in clarity and precision.[2] From the postwar Arrow-Debreu tradition, Debreu's own *Theory of Value* remains authoritative.

The most conspicuous difference between these works, of course, lies in the mathematics employed. Where Debreu's book, cast in the language of Bourbaki, is a treatise in applied mathematics, Wicksell's *Lectures* rarely go beyond simple applications of the calculus, and explicit mathematics is relegated to small-print asides. But the *Theory of Value*'s technical sophistication does not simply present the same content with greater rigor; the content itself differs markedly.

Wicksell took the psychological experience of utility to be the basic object of the theory of individual behavior, whereas Debreu treats individual preferences between pairs of alternatives as primitive. Following tradition, I refer to the Debreu approach as the *ordinal* model of preferences.

Wicksell and Debreu also differ in their choice of welfare criterion. Although he spent relatively little time on welfare issues in his *Lectures*, Wicksell was an unabashed utilitarian, summing the welfare of different individuals and explicitly rejecting Pareto's criterion of optimality. He thereby endorsed a variety of egalitarian social policies, even arguing (though in this he was a little unusual) that utilitarianism justifies systematic departures from laissez-faire, including price manipulations that redistribute wealth from rich to poor. Debreu, on the other hand, makes no use of utilitarian reasoning. Although he does not directly address policy issues, Debreu uses Pareto efficiency to evaluate markets, stating and proving the two fundamental theorems of welfare economics: competitive equilibria are Pareto optimal, and any Pareto optimum can, with appropriate redistributions of income, be "decentralized" as a competitive equilibrium.[3]

---

2. I choose Wicksell in part because of Schumpeter's imprimatur: "consolidation took place between 1890 and 1914, and a theoretical system of apparatus emerged which is embodied in the standard works of A. Marshall and K. Wicksell." Indeed, Schumpeter called the early twentieth century consensus the "Marshall-Wicksell system." Schumpeter (1954, p. 1142). Marshall's *Principles* itself sometimes waffles at difficult junctures.

3. For consumer theory, see Wicksell (1901, pp. 29–43) and Debreu (1959, chap. 4); on welfare economics, see Wicksell (1901, pp. 72–83) and Debreu (1959, chap. 6).

In production theory, Wicksell invariably described technology with differentiable production functions, and even seems to have been the first to use the Cobb-Douglas functional form.[4] Debreu's model, by contrast, describes feasible input-output combinations with arbitrary convex sets that are not assumed to be differentiable on the boundary. For example, even when it is possible to describe an Arrow-Debreu production set with a production function, the latter is never required to be differentiable. Debreu's theory therefore does away with the traditional mechanism of marginal productivity.

These three elements of the transition from Wicksell to Debreu—the move to ordinalism, the rise of Paretian welfare economics, and the rejection of marginal productivity—(and a fourth change in interest rate theory discussed in section 1.5) are my primary focus. The transition does not just replace older theories with new, more accurate ones; contemporary work drops several structural assumptions of early neoclassicism, thereby claiming to offer a more general theory that supersedes the past.

This contention is easiest to see in producer theory. The Arrow-Debreu model, while it does hold to convexity, imposes no other substantive requirements on how technology is described. Moreover, its central theorems on the existence, optimality, and determinacy of equilibrium hold regardless of marginal productivity's differentiability requirements. The Arrow-Debreu approach therefore appears to be more general than early neoclassical theory; older, seemingly interminable debates about the validity of marginal productivity's factor substitution assumptions apparently can be put to rest.

In preference theory, ordinalism holds that utility as a psychological entity can be dispensed with, thus bypassing Jevons's and Edgeworth's questionable introspections into the mechanics of pleasure. Indeed, some ordinalists contend that all psychological components of decision theory can be eliminated. Modern work instead makes direct assumptions—of completeness, transitivity, convexity, etc.—on preferences. Since preference orderings do not presuppose cardinal judgments of satisfaction intensity, and since agents may well form their preference rankings through entirely nonhedonistic means, ordinalism is more general than a utility- or pleasure-based approach. Thus, in the ordinal view, a utility function conveys no pertinent information beyond the preferences it summarizes; it carries no psychological meaning or interpretation and serves merely as a mathematical convenience.

The case for the superiority of Paretian welfare economics, although less clear-cut, ultimately rests on the same rejection of hedonist psychology. The fact that a multiplicity of utility functions can represent a single

---

4. Wicksell (1901, p. 128). One of Wicksell's most distinctive contributions to microeconomics—his demonstration of the connections between constant returns to scale and free entry—lies in production theory, but for our purposes his adherence to marginal productivity theory is more important.

preference ordering implies that a utilitarian summing of individual utility functions can be conducted in multiple ways; indeed, partly for this reason, the early neoclassicals themselves often appealed to efficiency measures supposedly free from interpersonal welfare comparisons. Pareto efficiency foregoes any aggregation of utilities—it does not use utility representations at all—but still manages to dispense policy advice. Given access to wealth redistributions, the new approach argues that policymakers should remove any preexisting distortions—excise taxes, for example—and institute a Pareto-improving competitive equilibrium. The Pareto criterion appears to cut through the conflict of individuals' goals; no matter how the satisfactions of different agents are weighted, social welfare orderings always recommend Pareto-improving policies over a distorted status quo.

Postwar theory thus accuses traditional neoclassicism of making needless and questionable assumptions on technology and individual psychology. Avoiding such blunders, it is said, allows a more believable and general theory to emerge. But in fact, although the early neoclassical postulates were difficult to defend and sometimes embarrassing, to simply discard them raises several intractable problems. For instance, the Arrow-Debreu model's weakened requirements on production sets can cause factor prices to be indeterminate. Indeed, the original purpose of the differentiable production function—as well as an array of substitute mechanisms that Arrow-Debreu theory also eliminates—was to rule out just this indeterminacy. Factor prices in contemporary general equilibrium models can also vary dramatically as a function of market participation; the assumption that agents act as price takers therefore becomes implausible.

Likewise, Pareto efficiency does not in fact generate the clear policy advice promised by the welfare theorems. The difficulty is not the well-recognized problem that governments only have a limited set of policy tools. Rather the problem is that any proposed policy reform will, in reasonably general settings, be rejected by some legitimate social welfare function. Far from doing without interpersonal comparisons of utility, the Pareto criterion requires them.

Finally, ordinalism, although undeniably more general than early preference theory, sidesteps the primary purpose for which hedonism and utility theory were devised, namely, to provide psychological rationales for assumptions on economic behavior. Although ordinalists vaguely suggest that individual self-interest coincides with the standard assumptions of rationality (completeness and transitivity), contemporary hostility to theorizing "going beyond behavior" has prevented the elaboration of supporting arguments for assumptions on preferences and hidden the difficulties of assembling them. Hedonism once performed this role, but shorn of psychological content, ordinalism does not and cannot provide justifications for each of the neoclassical rationality axioms.

It would be foolhardy to deny the manifest implausibility of utilitarian psychology and of at least the crude versions of marginal productivity; early neoclassicism deserved criticism and reform. But the postwar renunciation of older ideas either opens theoretical holes or reintroduces difficulties that earlier economists had been trying to solve. Where early theory often recognized and grappled with long-standing problems, postwar theory, isolated from the past, has overlooked the same dilemmas.

1.2 The timing of the transitions

Although most of the postwar innovations were foreshadowed early on, the division of economic theory into early neoclassical and contemporary eras is broadly accurate.[5] Notwithstanding minor overlap, each era had its own distinctive consensus. While the contemporary consensus is more obvious, early neoclassical economists were also surprisingly uniform in their thinking. The twin principles of utilitarianism and marginal productivity were widely adhered to in the early twentieth century; the consensus was particularly plain in Marshallian England, but, as the example of Wicksell shows, it attained international reach. There was opposition, of course, but dissent was met by imaginative defense, reinforcing confidence in received wisdom. Critics were deflected by assurances that utility theory could do without narrow forms of hedonism and that marginal productivity could be made more palatable. Critical debate fueled the creativity of economic theory and put early neoclassicism on firmer footing.

The overthrow of early neoclassical theory was unmistakable and decisive. Encouraged by Lionel Robbins's *Essay on the Nature and Significance of Economic Science* (1932), which disavowed utilitarian psychology, John Hicks and R. G. D. Allen's papers of 1934 argued that consumer theory could forsake hedonism and cardinality without sacrificing any valid theorems on economic behavior.[6] Hicks and Allen met only tepid resistance, and by the 1940s, the ordinalists had become the establishment. Robbins's *Essay* also challenged the scientific status of traditional policy recommendations, sparking the transition in welfare economics as well (1932, chap. 6). Robbins's apparent rejection of normative economics did not take root, however; economists were unwilling to relinquish their traditional role as policy advisors. Efforts soon began to establish an alternative welfare economics, which, given the new intellectual climate, could not simply resurrect utilitarianism. Although the "new welfare economics" of the 1930s and

5. The claim that no cardinal significance should be attached to functions representing preferences dates at least to Irving Fisher's doctoral dissertation (1892); Pareto's optimality criterion achieved a modest notoriety following its presentation in his *Manual of Political Economy* of 1909; and Walras in the first edition of his *Elements of Pure Economics* in the 1870's (prior to the invention of marginal productivity) described technology with fixed coefficients.

6. Robbins (1932), Robbins (1935), and Hicks and Allen (1934). See Hicks (1939b, p. 18), on the advantages of leaving utilitarian psychology behind.

1940s took various forms—from the Bergson social welfare function to the Hicks-Kaldor compensation criteria—all variants stressed the importance of satisfying the necessary conditions for Pareto optimality.[7] Crowned by Arrow's and Debreu's independent proofs of the welfare theorems in 1951,` a new orthodoxy based on Pareto efficiency took hold.

Meanwhile, a new generation of mathematicians rewrote the rules of producer theory, apparently rendering marginal productivity obsolete. Although the general equilibrium literature of the 1930s employed fixed coefficients rather than differentiable production functions, the general production set point of view arose only after the study of linear programming and activity analysis during World War II. Research developed rapidly in the late 1940s and early 1950s, capped by a volume on activity analysis edited by Tjalling Koopmans in 1951. When the general equilibrium models of the mid-1950s were constructed, linear activities or arbitrary convex production sets became the consensus description of technology.

In sum, economic theory underwent a twenty year reformation, marked at one end by mid-1930s ordinalism and at the other by the general equilibrium models of Arrow and Debreu and Lionel McKenzie in the mid-1950s.

1.3 Theory versus practice

The transition has often been described as a revolution in mathematical technique; and the gap in mathematical proficiency between early and late twentieth-century economic theory is undeniable. But focusing on the revolution in technique obscures the equally dramatic—but separate— revolution in content. Moreover, the ideas that were discarded are not intrinsically incompatible with today's mathematical rigor. Although ordinalism was developed using new techniques of constrained maximization, those tools could as easily have been applied to utility functions assumed to have cardinal or hedonic significance. In producer theory, the more careful mathematical depictions of the profit-maximizing firm that appeared in the 1930s used differentiable production functions; initially, therefore, greater mathematical rigor continued, and did not break with, pre-existing theory. Finally, the mathematically formalized Bergson-Samuelson social welfare function (particularly in its Harsanyi form) furthered the utilitarian tradition of welfare analysis and was not simply a tool for characterizing Pareto optimality. Indeed for Paul Samuelson, a leading attraction of the social welfare function was that it could be used to charge the new welfare economics with inconsistency.[8] The greater use and sophistica-

7. Bergson (1938), Kaldor (1939), and Hicks (1939a). Hicks's article actually proposed a straightforward Pareto optimality test.

8. Samuelson (1947), pp. 249–252. For Harsanyi's model of utilitarianism, see Harsanyi (1955) and chapter 6 in this book.

tion of mathematics therefore did not hardwire content; the onward march of technique could have remained faithful to the substance of early neoclassicism.[9]

In fact, much of that substance survives in practice, despite having been ruled out of theoretical court. Although the Arrow-Debreu model has become a staple of the graduate curriculum, it and many other postwar innovations remain curiously restricted to the domain of pure theory. Even if the norm in general equilibrium models, production sets have not displaced differentiable technologies within the broader orbit of economic theory. Particularly in macro and growth theory, the neoclassical production function rules undisturbed. In day-to-day applications of welfare economics, cost-benefit analysis continues to sum agents' dollar gains and losses; notwithstanding the Paretian window dressing it is sometimes given, this practice lies squarely in the Marshall–Pigou tradition of the utilitarian calculus. (Sporadic revivals of utilitarianism have also occurred in theoretical welfare economics but have not, so far, threatened the Paretian consensus.) And in consumer theory, although no self-respecting economist would defend cardinality on theoretical grounds, every student of economics is nevertheless taught the intuition of diminishing marginal utility. But diminishing marginal utility, since it is not an ordinal property of preferences, should not, according to strict principle, be admitted as a primitive assumption.

The split between precept and practice, now reaching the half-century mark, shows no signs of abating. Why not? Discussion of this question is meager, but perhaps the most common answer blames the impracticality and mathematical complexity of postwar theory. The tractability of differentiable functions, it is said, outweighs the generality of production sets; and in welfare economics, Pareto improvements may be achievable in principle but not in the real world, where only a limited menu of policy tools is available.

These explanations fall short. Economists' long-standing loyalty to the neoclassical production function provides an illustrative clue to the rest of the story. Despite official theory, many believe that marginal productivity cannot be safely generalized away and that a diversity of production techniques is theoretically indispensable; the neoclassical economic problem, after all, involves allocating scarce means among *competing* ends. So far, this belief only amounts to an intuition. But as we will see, the continuing hold of older ideas in fact stems from the failure of contemporary theory to take on successfully the functions that early neoclassicism tried to perform.

---

9. Philip Mirowski has argued extensively that mathematization per se does not rigidly determine content. See, e.g., Mirowski (1991). I am not claiming that postwar theorists were uninfluenced by a desire to use certain types of mathematics, or that mathematics has not shaped the content of postwar theory.

1.4 Where early neoclassical theory fails

Rather than finding early neoclassical ideas superior, my aim is to illuminate those structural problems that persist and yet are oddly difficult to see. Indeed, contemporary theory far surpasses its predecessor in technique and in substantive areas particularly suited to mathematical analysis.

For instance, postwar theory has produced comprehensive and elegant analyses of the existence of equilibrium, thereby exploring the basic consistency of Walrasian theory. Only a few early neoclassical economists addressed the subject; and, even given their limited mathematical know-how, their work is primitive compared to postwar work. Any comparison between, say, Walras's study of existence and Debreu's would reveal little but a catalog of the earlier treatment's inadequacies. Furthermore, no difference of economic principle separates the early neoclassical from the contemporary approach; the latter simply completes Walras's program. Similarly, contemporary study of the uniqueness of equilibrium in exchange economies is encyclopedic, whereas older work sticks to examples. And contemporary conclusions roughly conform to early neoclassical thinking; that it is unexceptional for exchange economies to have multiple equilibria was understood by earlier writers—certainly by Walras, and also more generally.[10] (Concerning production economies, on the other hand, the early neoclassical study of factor price determinacy differs substantially from the contemporary approach; a fortiori, these differences affect the uniqueness of equilibrium.)

Contemporary work also far outshines early neoclassicism in the analysis of aggregate consumer demand and excess demand functions. Early neoclassical thinkers typically presumed that aggregate demand obeys a variety of intuitively plausible conditions—for example, that consumer demand for a good decreases in its own price—as economists still assume outside of general equilibrium theory. Contemporary theory, however, has shown that virtually no restrictions on aggregate demand can be inferred solely from the assumption that agents are utility maximizers.[11] Although the early neoclassicals routinely recognized the possibility of paradox (witness the Giffen good), the contemporary understanding of the seriousness of the problem goes far deeper. Indeed, contemporary work challenges early neoclassical theory's ability to provide an adequate foundation for its account of the aggregate economy and calls into question the very method of taking the characteristics of individual agents to be arbitrary. Perhaps early neoclassical theorists, like many contemporary thinkers, would have regarded the entirely negative character of the aggregation literature with suspicion. But it is doubtful that any interesting rejoinder can be extracted from their writings.

---

10. Wicksell again provides a convenient example: Wicksell (1901, pt. 1, chap. 3).
11. See Shafer and Sonnenschein (1982) for a survey.

This brief list is meant to be illustrative, not exhaustive. As a general rule, when the aims of research have not shifted, the contemporary claim to progress has a prima facie plausibility.

1.5   Interest theory: a further blindspot

In interest rate theory, on the other hand, research aims have shifted markedly. From the earliest writings in economic science through the early neoclassical era, theorists tried to explain why interest rates are normally and substantially positive; but on the contemporary scene, although economists still presume that interest rates are positive, the job of explaining this fact has disappeared as an active theoretical question.

Like the other transitions, the change leaps out of a comparison of Wicksell's *Lectures* and Debreu's *Theory of Value*. A dedicated follower of Austrian capital theory, Wicksell invoked elaborate and ingenious arguments for why real interest rates are strictly positive in competitive equilibrium. Nothing remotely parallel appears in Debreu's work. Debreu distinguishes between commodities according to the date at which they appear; since relative prices at different dates therefore need not be equal, a single interest rate between dates is not even defined. But even if we overlook this fact, say by concentrating on steady-state equilibria, at which relative prices are constant through time, Debreu's model still does not address Wicksell's concerns. The sign of an interest rate is determined by the ratio of the prices of earlier-date goods relative to later-date goods, and there is no more reason for later-date goods in the Arrow-Debreu model to be cheaper than earlier-date goods than for any arbitrary pair of goods to have a particular price ratio.[12]

The change in theoretical agenda is attributable, once again, to the Arrow-Debreu urge to build a more general theory. Early neoclassical theorists gave future commodities special, distinguishing features, in terms of preferences and technology, relative to current goods; postwar general equilibrium theory removes these features, and consequently is silent on the sign of interest rates.

Contemporary economics is divided on how to study intertemporal issues, with many literatures continuing to use models where positive interest rates arise. Though rarely an end in itself, positive interest rates are needed for many models to be well behaved; the usual stopgap remedy is to assume that agents psychologically discount future utility. Originally a cornerstone of early neoclassical interest rate theory as well, used in both the Austrian and Anglo-American schools, discounting today appears

---

12. The refinement of the definition of commodities is a distinguishing trait of Arrow-Debreu economics; in this dimension too, contemporary work breaks with the early neoclassical past. As we will see—sections 2.8 and 4.12—the separation of goods by date and by state of nature, though one of the great innovations of postwar theory, introduces new difficulties into production and preference theory.

in theories of optimal economic growth and market-equilibrium models with infinitely lived agents. The steady states of these models indeed display positive (implicit or explicit) interest rates.[13]

The separating insight of early neoclassical capital theory was the realization—expounded forcefully by the Austrian Eugen von Böhm-Bawerk—that discounting by itself need not lead to positive real interest rates: the time distribution of assets can induce agents to save large portions of their wealth, pushing interest rates down to or below zero. Current-day models deriving a positive interest rate are subject to the same problem; only when agents or the planner allocate wealth over an infinite horizon is a positive interest rate guaranteed. Böhm-Bawerk, and later Wicksell, responded to the limitations of discounting by arguing that intertemporal transfers of resources that span relatively large amounts of time necessarily have greater productivity. Despite the obscurities of Austrian capital theory, particularly in Böhm-Bawerk's presentation, a coherent version of the positive-interest rate argument can be constructed.

Even if internally consistent, Austrian capital theory's account of positive interest rates is ultimately unconvincing. Thus, once again, I do not intend to rehabilitate early neoclassical theory. In fact, Austrian theory commanded an irregular following even in the early twentieth century; many economists made casual reference to the greater productivity of "round-about" technologies, but few were willing to commit themselves to the details of Austrian doctrine.

Rather, my purpose is to uncover the part that Austrian theory and its alternatives once played in economic theory. The unquestioned pursuit of an explanation of why interest rates are positive—and the appreciation of its challenges—underscores the distinctiveness of the Arrow-Debreu agnosticism on interest rates. The early neoclassical concern is absent from contemporary general equilibrium theory, making the Austrian depiction of technology—like the differentiable production function, psychological hedonism, and cardinal utility—appear to be another pointless complexity. In fact, like the other dismissed concepts, Austrian theory was geared to a specific, coherent theoretical goal.

Even if bewilderment at Austrian capital theory is an anachronism, the unresolved puzzle of why interest rates are positive does not directly jeopardize Arrow-Debreu theory. Contemporary theory readily acknowledges that many results that economists regard as intuitive—including nice properties for aggregate demand functions, mentioned in section 1.4—do not hold in models of any generality. Consequently, both the Austrian capital theorist and the general equilibrium economist can grant that positive

---

13. See, e.g., Böhm-Bawerk (1889) and Fisher (1907) for representative early neoclassical usages. Optimal growth theory is voluminous; for a survey, see McKenzie (1986). For the general equilibrium theory of infinite-horizon economies, see Bewley (1972), and for a model generating steady states, Bewley (1982). Infinite-horizon models with discounting are also used extensively outside of general equilibrium theory.

interest rates need not arise in models that treat the present and future sym-metrically—though they might differ on whether such models are flawed. Furthermore, current theory does not ban adding structure to intertempo-ral economics; it too could legitimately explore the demand or technologi-cal restrictions that guarantee positive interest rates. (Contemporary preference theory, in contrast, objects in principle to adding extra-ordinal theoretical structure.) Still, it is not clear that appealing restrictions exist; indeed, the travails of early neoclassical capital theory show just how difficult it is to build a microeconomic account of why interest rates are positive.[14]

1.6 Why the history of economic theory?

This book contends that the transition to contemporary economics has been misunderstood, and that, as a consequence, some current theories are mis-guided. Much of the argument is laid out historically, as part of an account of the development of economic theory. Yet I do not champion past doc-trines. At least as they were originally issued, the ideas rejected in the 1930s and 1940s deserved to be jettisoned; and if there are any exceptions, they could always be recast in contemporary language. Rather, the need for his-torical analysis arises from the fact that the evaluation of ideas cannot be separated from their past usage. This principle holds particularly true for economic theory, which cannot resort to an immediately empirical refer-ence. Economic theory explores the logic of assumptions and models that seem natural. These constructs are not invented anew with each article and monograph, but are partly conventional; they derive their plausibility from the past practices, or perceived practices, of the discipline. Consider the commonplace that neoclassical economics characteristically takes prefer-ences and technology to be exogenous. This program, far from being justified with every theoretical exercise, is simply assumed to be the right point of departure; on occasion, it is deemed inappropriate, but only in the face of pressing analytical need. Nor is this starting place tested empirically; the explanation of economic events in terms of preferences and technology *constitutes* sound neoclassical theorizing.

The dependence on the past explains why theories are so often judged by their generality. Unable to assess theories directly, economists try to build theories that are as parsimonious as possible and judge a theory with fewer assumptions that achieves a larger number of analytical goals to be superior to its competitors. This methodology dominates the literatures of economic theory and was pivotal in the triumph of postwar general equi-librium theory.

But comparisons of generality need not be applied only to the most recent theoretical work. Earlier judgments of which assumptions are

14. For another area in which contemporary theory studies different questions without claiming to supersede earlier work, see the analysis of stability theory in Weintraub (1991).

plausible and which theoretical goals are coherent are just as pertinent. For instance, contemporary economists (though not general equilibrium theorists) often hold that the differentiable production function accurately describes technology. But as we will see, when differentiability assumptions came under criticism in the past, many defenders of marginal productivity conceded that if factors of production include industry-specific or highly specialized inputs, then differentiability loses its credibility. They argued that the core idea of factor substitutability could nevertheless survive if applied instead to aggregated factors or if a longer run equilibrium concept is used. Since this episode broadens the set of judgments of which assumptions on technology are natural, the historical record directly pertains to contemporary production theory. Even the firm advocate of marginal productivity can then see how to make factor substitutability a more credible doctrine.

In preference theory, the ordinalists' rejection of hedonism and cardinality is easy to defend when understood as a proposal to broaden the set of psychological principles that can be used to justify assumptions on preferences; nonutilitarian psychologies can often serve with equal or greater plausibility. But the larger goal of early neoclassical utility theory—to provide rationales for assumptions on preferences—stands unthreatened by this reasoning; economic psychology therefore still merits a foundational role in preference theory. The case for providing explicit rationales for assumptions can of course be made without mentioning early neoclassical utility theory or the specific arguments the ordinalists directed against that theory. But recognizing the priority that early neoclassical thinkers attached to psychological foundations—and the limitations of the ordinalist indictment—makes the case more powerful.

The history of economic theory also reveals a disturbing pattern in which flawed positions are cyclically revisited. In producer theory, economists have at various times resorted to an extreme marginal productivity theory requiring that each production function be differentiable; interspersed with these phases, others have gone to the opposite pole of prohibiting factor substitution altogether, and still others to a variety of intermediate positions. As the doctrines cycle, each stage is justified in finding conceptual or empirical flaws with the preceding position. Of course, if some definitive resolution were available, historical analysis would be unnecessary; but the cycling is itself a sign of unsolved theoretical problems. Hence, to grasp fully the dilemmas of producer theory, one must take a bird's-eye view of the subject. The evaluation of assumptions by current practice alone, by contrast, will only confirm the preconceptions of the moment and, in a longer span, perpetuate the churning of inadequate alternatives.

The discontinuity between current and prewar economic theory makes the need for historical perspective particularly acute. Postwar mathematical economics has tried to put economic theory on a new footing, deliberately leaving aside earlier work and beginning de novo. A methodological change compounds the problem. Earlier theory attempted to show how it supplanted its predecessors; consequently, analytical reconstructions of the past were integral to the great treatises of the early twentieth century—from Wicksell's *Lectures* to Hicks's *Value and Capital*. The retrospective dimension of economic theory has since receded. Although the claim to displace the past persists, major postwar theorists have consigned historical reconstructions to the occasional postscript or to self-contained explorations in the history of economic thought;[15] more recently, even these explorations have come to a near halt. As a consequence, the danger of sidestepping rather than resolving long-standing problems or of unintentionally reintroducing older difficulties looms large.

This book is divided into three self-contained segments: chapters 2 and 3 on production and factor price theory, chapters 4 through 6 on preference theory and welfare economics, and chapter 7 on interest rate theory. In addition, most of the narrowly historical issues are considered in chapters 3 and 5; a strict analytical reading of the book can omit them. Also, chapter 6 on welfare economics can be read with only a quick glance at the relevant sections—4.6, 4.7, and 4.9—of the primary preference-theory chapter.

This book is an internal commentary on economic theory, not a history. Historical figures and their ideas are mined opportunistically as the needs of evaluation dictate. Widely held interpretations and judgments of plausibility, including those occurring in the past, are germane to the assessment of contemporary theory, but the exact attitude of past thinkers to their own creations—which contributions were most important, how models should be understood—is not. Furthermore, given the internal nature of this book, my explications of the past must embody—if only for the sake of argument—a contemporary view of what constitutes theoretical coherence. Ideas are evaluated from this stance, not from the standpoint of earlier conceptual systems or of hypothetical neutrality.

15. Samuelson's explorations of the history of economic theory are voluminous; in Arrow's case, see Arrow and Starrett (1973).

2

Marginal Productivity and the Indeterminacy of Factor Prices

2.1 Introduction and overview

Economists customarily view production processes as differentiable functions of the inputs employed. Indeed, it has been 100 years since Philip Wicksteed first used the constant returns to scale differentiable production function to present a complete marginal productivity theory of factor pricing and distribution. But accompanying this century-long tradition have been steady complaints that the extensive possibilities for factor substitution implicit in marginal productivity theory are unrealistic; critics have insisted that factors may be combined productively in only a handful of discrete ways.

Although the "neoclassical" production function remains the leading description of production, arguments over how to characterize technology seem mysterious today. Considerable effort, after all, has been devoted to showing that the most wide-ranging model of competition—the Arrow-Debreu model of general equilibrium—is well behaved whether the boundaries of production sets are differentiable or not. Bygone debates over the scope of factor substitution thus seem to turn on an irrelevancy. To contemporary eyes, the problematic neoclassical assumption on technology is convexity (weakly diminishing marginal productivity), which is indispensable for the conclusion that firms are price takers and that supply correspondences are continuous; but both sides of the factor substitution debate can concur on convexity.

The Arrow-Debreu claim of freeing economic theory from its earlier confusions is in fact mistaken. Early worries about factor substitution were well justified: in the absence of sufficient substitutability, factor demand will be inelastic and factor prices can be indeterminate. Indeed, the contemporary general equilibrium model, far from eliminating a superfluous depiction of technology, creates an ideal environment for factor price indeterminacy; the current agnosticism about technology therefore reintroduces a long-standing and once well-known problem. Indeterminacy, moreover, is not just a technical nuisance; it undermines the price-taking assumption of competitive models. Since arbitrarily small manipulations of factor supplies can dramatically increase a factor's price, factor owners will not take prices to be parametric.

I begin the chapter with a quick look back to see what precisely marginal productivity originally accomplished. The neoclassical view that factor demand is geared to the expected profitability of factors does not automatically determine how a firm or an industry's aggregate revenue is parceled into factor payments: either the demand for or the supply of factors must vary as a function of factor prices. Marginal productivity chooses the first option: it posits enough choice of technique so that any variation in factor prices alters the set of profitable production activities and thereby changes the demand for factors.

But if factors are concrete, specialized inputs, technology will inevitably be characterized by fixed coefficients, or at least by a limited number of factor substitution possibilities. This objection was often mooted, most trenchantly in the interwar years; and in response, new defenses of traditional marginal productivity and innovations designed to avoid factor substitution assumptions emerged. Debate was sparked by the Swedish economist Gustav Cassel's general equilibrium model, introduced in 1918, which used fixed coefficients to describe technology. Cassel's work did not itself venture far into new terrain, but it popularized Walras's general equilibrium theory and inspired an extraordinary legacy of original theorizing. Most famously, it was Cassel's model that led to the initial investigations into the existence of general equilibrium. Simultaneous with this research, a sustained, international examination of whether Cassel's use of linear activities could adequately replace the differentiable production function was also pursued.

Cassel concurred with the limited factor substitution critique of marginal productivity theory and acknowledged that industries face sharp limits on the number of techniques they have at their disposal. He was content to make this revision, moreover, since he believed that the determinacy of factor prices could nevertheless be maintained. Cassel reasoned that the potential of sectors to use factors in different proportions provided a substitute logic for the elasticity of factor demand: if a factor price is raised from its equilibrium value, for example, those consumption goods that intensively use that factor also rise in price, leading to a substitution away from those goods and hence from the factors that produce them.

Cassel's position was roundly criticized, most incisively by the German economist Heinrich von Stackelberg (1933)—later famous for his oligopoly theory—who pointed out that Cassel's reasoning depended on factors being used by a sufficiently large number of industries. When such a condition fails, as it is sure to when factors are disaggregated, Stackelberg argued that factor prices in Cassel's model will be indeterminate. Although

Stackelberg's indeterminacy assertion has since been criticized, most prominently by Arrow and Debreu, his reasoning is sound. Stackelberg concluded
that marginal productivity could not be so easily disposed of. But for economists not willing to apply the differentiability assumption to specialized
factors, Stackelberg's criticisms of Cassel left the determinacy question
unsettled.

An alternate strategy, most carefully articulated by John Hicks and D.
H. Robertson in the early 1930s, was to advance a long-run version of
marginal productivity, which was in fact the intent of some of the original
formulations of the doctrine. Hicks and Robertson acknowledged that
the prices of specialized factors of production could be indeterminate in
the short run. But even with little or no variety in the way given stocks of
factors can be combined, there may be a rich array of potential specialized
factors that in time can be produced and used in substitute activities.
Hicks and Robertson viewed specialized factors as "intermediate" products
ultimately produced by the underlying "basic" factors of capital, land,
and labor. In the long run, the prices of specialized factors are determined
by the prices of the basic factor inputs needed to produce them. Consequently, if the prices of basic factors were to move away from an equilibrium configuration, the impact on the prices of specialized factors would
likely change the profit-maximizing choice of intermediate inputs; the
derived demand for basic factors will therefore also change, throwing the
markets for basic factors out of equilibrium. As we will see, these ideas
can be made rigorous—without relying on questionable aggregation
assumptions—by a long-run definition of equilibrium. In fact, as Hicks
recognized, long-run equilibria are determinate even when there is no
choice of technique.

Hicks and Robertson brought the course of factor price theory back to
the long-run arguments that classical economists had once used to establish determinacy. Although more sophisticated and complete than classical
treatments, Hicks's and Robertson's analyses apply only to models in which
relative prices are constant through time. Since, strictly speaking, relative
prices are constant only in steady states, the ultimate explanatory value of
long-run equilibria is limited.

Astonishingly, Arrow-Debreu general equilibrium theory repudiates
each of the above mechanisms for determinacy. A key premise of the theory
is its generality, and its freedom from differentiable technologies in particular; the original Wicksteed form of marginal productivity is thus analytically prohibited. The theory is also highly disaggregated, allowing any given
set of factors to be used by only a few industries, thwarting the Cassel argument for determinacy. And finally, in an attempt to free intertemporal analysis from the straightjacket of earlier, long-run equilibrium concepts, the
Arrow-Debreu theory systematically distinguishes commodities by the
dates at which they appear, allowing prices at different dates to vary independently. Taken together, these innovations are tailor-made to allow factor
price indeterminacy to emerge.

The early years of postwar general equilibrium theory saw attention directed away from determinacy and toward the existence and stability of equilibrium; the study of determinacy only reappeared in the 1970s with the development of regularity theory. This literature does not resurrect traditional arguments for determinacy; in particular it continues the Arrow-Debreu custom of allowing technology to be described by fixed coefficients or linear activities. Consequently, regularity theory acknowledges the possibility of the factor price indeterminacy discussed by previous generations; but it argues that indeterminacy only occurs when endowments of resources appear in unlikely, "nongeneric" configurations. Hence, although possible in principle, indeterminacy occurs only for a small proportion of potential models; the remaining economies are determinate. We will see that this argument is fatally flawed. The endowments where indeterminacy occurs systematically arise through time and therefore cannot be dismissed; the Arrow-Debreu model is thus fully subject to the dilemmas of factor price theory.

The disjunction between contemporary general equilibrium theory and earlier theoretical work leads to confusion when economists using an older idiom encounter current mainstream thinking. As we will see, the fierce but confusing arguments in the 1960s and 1970s between Sraffian and neoclassical theorists provide a model example. Although some amendments are necessary, Sraffa's use of linear activities rather than neoclassical production functions creates a natural environment for factor price indeterminacy; indeed, Sraffa can be understood as reproducing the standard early neoclassical case that models without differentiable production are indeterminate. Unfortunately, contemporary theorists, unaware of what hinges on the specification of technology, simply presume that general equilibrium completions of Sraffa's model must be determinate. On the other hand, Sraffians cast their claim in a long-run setting in which relative prices are constant through time; in this environment, as my analysis of Hicks and Robertson will show, Sraffa's indeterminacy argument will not stand. Thus, each side of the Sraffa controversy backs an equilibrium concept inimical to the determinacy result it hopes to establish.

2.2 Marginal productivity theory

Marginal productivity theory, as pioneered by J. B. Clark, Wicksteed, Marshall, Wicksell, and others, provided an original and powerful explanation of the factor demands of both individual firms and the economy as a whole. Though the classical analysis of differential rent was an antecedent, the neoclassicals proposed a unified theory: all of a firm's demands are derived, by way of the calculus, from the single mathematical problem of maximizing profits. It is difficult to exaggerate the importance of marginal productivity. Without a general theory of production and distribution, neoclassical economics would never have displaced classical thinking; it would have remained an intriguing application of calculus to consumer decision making, applicable only to such artificial environments as the exchange economy.

Marginal productivity met two long-standing goals of factor price theory. First, if the supply of some factors to firms is fixed, diminishing marginal productivity explains why the demand for each of the remaining factors is well defined and a decreasing function of the factor's own price. Second, marginal productivity offered a clear rationale for why factor prices are determinate, a problem that had particularly vexed late nineteenth-century economists.

Both of these points are elementary, but a brief recapitulation of the logic of the determinacy argument will be helpful. Imagine an economy with a single output and m factors, where each firm has a constant returns to scale technology. Aggregate factor demand can then be seen as stemming from an aggregate production function, $F(k)$, where $k = (k_1, \ldots, k_m)$ is the vector of factor usage levels (demands). Let $e = (e_1, \ldots, e_m)$ be the endowment of factors, which I assume are inelastically supplied; let $w = (w_1, \ldots, w_m)$ denote the m factor prices and p the price of output. Aggregate profits therefore equal $pF(k) - \Sigma_{i=1}^{m} w_i k_i$.

The pivotal assumption is that F is differentiable. Profit maximization then requires, for each i, that

$$p \frac{\partial F(k)}{\partial k_i} = w_i. \qquad (2.2.1)$$

If F is concave, equation 2.2.1 is also sufficient for profits to be at a maximum. It is immediate that factor prices are determinate at a competitive equilibrium: market clearing requires $k = e$ and therefore, for each i,

$$\frac{\partial F(e)}{\partial k_i} = \frac{w_i}{p}. \qquad (2.2.2)$$

Since there is an equation 2.2.2 for every i, each factor price is determined.

As long as more than one factor can be productively employed—that is, if F is strictly increasing in more than one of its arguments—the assumption that F is differentiable implies that there are an infinite number of factor combinations producing the same level of output. An arbitrarily small expansion in the employment of one factor can be counterbalanced by a reduction in the usage of a second factor; hence, the ratio of any two productive factors used to produce a given output level can be locally increased or decreased.

2.3 Initial criticisms of marginal productivity theory

Marginal productivity quickly established itself as the leading neoclassical theory of factor demand. Even today, despite the postwar innovations, it remains the backbone of textbook explanations of the distribution of income; and neoclassical histories of production theory routinely portray the differentiable production function as the solution against which earlier, flawed theories of factor pricing should be compared. But even as it rose to theoretical dominance, marginal productivity theory was criticized for its assumption of extensive factor substitutability. When factors are specialized or adapted to particular production processes, the differentiability assumption rapidly becomes implausible; the ratio of nuts to bolts cannot be varied continuously. Was the adoption of marginal productivity then only due to its mathematical elegance and the theoretical role it filled?[1]

Historical accounts often associate these doubts with the work of the English social scientist J. A. Hobson in the early 1900s. Hobson criticized the idea that a specific amount of output can be attributed to a separate, marginal "dose" of a factor of production. After defining a marginal product as the amount of output lost by the withdrawal of a discrete unit of a factor, Hobson pointed out that the marginal products of all of the factors involved in a production process could collectively be too large; that is, if factor prices equal marginal products, as Hobson defined them, then total factor payments could be greater than the value of total output [Hobson (1900, chap. 4)].

It is true that if a production function is differentiable and constant returns to scale and if factor prices are set to Hobsonian marginal products (defined using infinitesimal factor units), then total factor payments will exactly exhaust the value of output. But when production is of the linear activities type—where, say, a_1 units of one factor and a_2 of a second are required per unit of output—Hobson's conclusion can be correct. If the quantities of factors used in production, $k = (k_1, k_2)$, are such that

$$\frac{k_1}{a_1} = \frac{k_2}{a_2}, \qquad (2.3.1)$$

then the production function, which has the Leontiev form $\min[k_1/a_1, k_2/a_2]$, is not differentiable at k. Consequently, marginal products in the sense of derivatives are not defined. In Hobson's sense, however, marginal products *are* defined; they are equal to $1/a_1$ and $1/a_2$. Furthermore, using these marginal products as factor prices, total factor payments equal twice the quantity of output. Hobson's claim is affirmed.

This compatibility between the nondifferentiability of the production function and Hobson's conclusions has made it easy to read Hobson as a nondifferentiability critic of marginal productivity theory. But unequivocal interpretations of Hobson are difficult; an absence of differentiability may not capture what he had in mind. Hobson thought it relevant that very large decreases in factor inputs could yield marginal products (in his sense) that are too large, as for example when all of a factor is withdrawn from production. With discrete, noninfinitesimal withdrawals of inputs, however,

---

1. Stigler (1941) remains the archetypical marginalist history of production theory. True to his theoretical camp, Stigler (e.g., p. 380) dismissed the possibility that there might not be ample opportunities for factor substitution.

even a differentiable production function will typically yield Hobsonian marginal products that are greater than production function derivatives. Furthermore, Hobson often agreed that increments to output vary smoothly as a function of factor inputs; in fact, in Hobson's most famous example, marginal increments to output are eventually diminishing.[2] Hobson's main target was the idea that the change in output stemming from the hiring of an additional factor can be seen as the "separate" product of that factor, an idea that he may have gleaned from John Bates Clark's unfortunate formulation of marginal productivity theory. It is unclear, however, what Hobson meant by a factor's separate product or, more importantly, what its relevance is. As a result, Hobson left himself open to easy rebuttal; Edgeworth (1904), for example, correctly scolded Hobson for using large rather than small factor increments in his calculations of marginal products.

Still, the nondifferentiability criticism became more persistent with time and its logic never escaped the more perceptive thinkers. Even before Hobson, Pareto, using simple examples of linear activities, had pointed out that production functions might not be differentiable, although he did not link the phenomenon to any larger problem in factor price theory.[3] And Marshall, as we will see, was both alert to the implausibility of differentiability and aware that without it marginal productivity was not a complete theory of factor pricing.

2.4 Nondifferentiable production and indeterminacy

The primary difficulty introduced by nondifferentiable production functions is that factor prices need not be determinate. Indeed, the example illustrating Hobson's criticisms of marginal productivity can readily be interpreted as a sample instance of indeterminacy. Assume that the industry under consideration produces the only output in the economy, as in section 2.2, and that the two factors are supplied inelastically. Also, suppose that factor endowments, $e = (e_1, e_2)$, are consistent with full employment of both factors, that is, that e satisfies $e_1/a_1 = e_2/a_2$; otherwise, one factor or the other will be in excess supply and have a zero price. Given equation 2.3.1, at full employment the production function will not be differentiable.

In order for the single activity to make zero economic profits, the condition

$$w_1 a_1 + w_2 a_2 = 1 \qquad (2.4.1)$$

must be satisfied. For convenience, I have let output be the *numéraire* and set $p = 1$. Under our assumptions, neither the demand for nor the supply

2. See the appendix to chapter 5 of Hobson (1909).
3. See Pareto (1897, sec. 714 and 717). Unfortunately, Pareto linked limits on factor substitutability to the fact that some factors are in fixed supply, thus conflating variability of factor demand with variability of factor supply.

of factors will vary if w_1 and w_2 are altered in such a way that 2.4.1 remains satisfied. Since 2.4.1 is only one restriction and there are two factor prices, the equilibrium value of factors in terms of output is indeterminate. In the differentiable case, in contrast, parity between the number of factor prices and the number of factor price equilibrium conditions (the equations 2.2.2) always obtains. Nondifferentiable technologies are therefore not mere inconveniences; they can undercut the determining force of supply and demand.

This example is extreme in that there is only one activity; indeterminacy is therefore guaranteed when both factors have a positive price. A general model with multiple activities introduces more possibilities. Suppose there is a set of activities, with each activity i denoted (a_{1i}, a_{2i}). In equilibrium, no activity can earn positive economic profits; hence,

$$w_1 a_{1i} + w_2 a_{2i} \geq 1 \qquad (2.4.2)$$

must hold for all i. And for activities j that are used in equilibrium,

$$w_1 a_{1j} + w_2 a_{2j} = 1. \qquad (2.4.3)$$

Generally, only one or two activities will in fact be used. If one activity is used and the remaining unused activities make strictly negative profits, then w_1 and w_2 can again be varied at least slightly while allowing the inequalities in 2.4.2 and the single equality 2.4.3 to remain satisfied. The earlier indeterminacy argument therefore generalizes. If two activities are in use, on the other hand, two 2.4.3 equalities must be satisfied, which then uniquely determine w_1 and w_2. I discuss whether the determinate or indeterminate case is more likely in sections 2.6 and 2.8; for the moment, just note that although determinacy is possible, it does not always occur when there are multiple activities.

There is no rigid conceptual divide between differentiable production functions and models with a broad range of possible activities. In the latter case, technology can be viewed as approximately differentiable: indeterminacy will still occur when only one activity is in use, but very small variations in factor prices will cause one of the inequalities in 2.4.2 to be violated. Hence, the magnitude of factor price variations consistent with equilibrium is highly constrained. Marginal productivity does not therefore hinge on the absurdity of an infinite number of activity choices; but it does depend on there being a considerable diversity of choices.

2.5 Alternatives to differentiable production

Early neoclassical economics relied on other mechanisms besides the differentiable production function to ensure factor price determinacy. The most obvious alternative was simply to assume that the consumption of factors provides direct utility to agents and that factor supplies therefore vary as a function of price. Given the neoclassical tradition of focusing on the exchange of consumption goods as the paradigmatic economic model, such an approach seemed natural. Walras, for instance, whose *Elements of Pure Economics* relied exclusively on linear activities prior to the invention of marginal productivity, insisted on the direct utility of factors as a general economic principle [see Walras (1874, lesson 20)]. In a genuine production economy, however, the presence of capital goods and raw materials and apparent examples of inelastic labor supply render any universal assumption that factor supplies vary with price highly implausible.

Marshall made some headway with his concept of the *net product* of a factor. Marshall acknowledged that many production processes are characterized by fixed coefficients, and in fact his sharpest example of smoothly varying factor proportions—the use of hops and malt in producing beer—involves changes in product quality rather than different methods for producing a single output. Marshall therefore defined the net product of a factor as the increase in value yielded by an increment of the factor *less* the value of other inputs purchased in conjunction with that increment. Marshall hoped that this device would ensure that marginal products are always well defined, whether considering differentiable technologies, quality changes, or fixed coefficients.

Marshall's definition of a factor's net product is hardly trouble-free since he did not specify which accompanying inputs are purchased. But at the very least Marshall intended to include enough complementary inputs to guarantee that the entire increment of the factor is in fact used in production. Thus, in the two-factor example, an extra unit of factor 1 entails that a_2/a_1 extra units of factor 2 be purchased. Letting p_a rather than 1 now be the price of output, the net product of factor 1 is therefore

$$\frac{1}{a_1} p_a - \frac{a_2}{a_1} w_2. \qquad (2.5.1)$$

That w_1 in equilibrium must equal its net product therefore just reproduces the fact that the activity makes zero profits (equation 2.4.1). For a complete theory of factor pricing, therefore, some other principle is needed to determine the prices of complementary factors—here w_2. Marshall himself remarked that net productivity "is not, as some have thought, an independent theory of wages, but only a particular way of wording the familiar doctrine that the value of everything tends to be equal to its expenses of production." Furthermore, "in order to estimate 'net produce' [of a marginal worker], we have to take for granted all the expenses of production of the commodity on which he works, other than his own wages."[4]

Marshall's idea does provide the beginnings of a more thorough analysis. If a second "*b*" industry—with production coefficients b_1 and b_2—uses the same two factors, a second equilibrium condition,

---

4. Marshall (1890, p. 548) and Marshall (1891, p. 568). For more on the limitations of net productivity, see Robertson (1931) and Samuelson (1947, p. 75).

$$w_1 = \frac{1}{b_1}p_b - \frac{b_2}{b_1}w_2, \qquad (2.5.2)$$

must be satisfied. As long as $a_1/a_2 \neq b_1/b_2$ it will not be possible to vary w_1 and w_2 while satisfying 2.5.1 and 2.5.2 and maintaining output prices at fixed values of p_a and p_b. A change in output prices, on the other hand, generally will change the composition of consumption demand and therefore will alter the quantities of factors used by the two industries. For example, if industry a uses factor 1 relatively intensively (that is, $a_1/a_2 > b_1/b_2$) an increase in w_1/w_2 will raise p_a/p_b. This in turn will decrease the demand for good a and thus indirectly decrease the demand for factor 1. Substitution in the consumption of outputs can thereby replace the technological substitution of factors as a reason for factor demand to vary in response to factor price changes.

2.6 Fixed-coefficients theory and its critics

Although the above output substitution mechanism was implicit in Walras and developed more fully by Wieser and Marshall, it was Gustav Cassel's *Theory of Social Economy* that expressly used this line of reasoning to argue that determinacy of equilibrium could be achieved without resort to marginal productivity.[5] Cassel's analysis, although flawed, led to an intensive investigation of whether the fixed-coefficients model could fully supplant the differentiable production function.

Output substitution can lead to determinacy but only if each set of factors in the economy is used by a sufficiently large number of industries. For instance, as we saw in sections 2.4 and 2.5, if two factors are employed only in a single industry, indeterminacy is possible, but if two factors are used by two industries, equilibria will usually be determinate. I call the general determinacy requirement the *Cassel condition*: factor prices will typically be determinate if each subset of m inelastically supplied factors is used by at least m industries. Thus, although Cassel's theory of distribution does not provide a general solution to the indeterminacy problem, it delineates the circumstances under which indeterminacy arises.

Our formal model uses the following notation. There are ℓ consumption goods and m factors of production. The production technology, or activity, that produces good i is described by a vector $a_i = (a_{1i}, \ldots, a_{mi})$ of the inputs necessary to produce one unit of good i. Letting y_i be the quantity of good i produced, the demand for factor j is $\sum_{i=1}^{\ell} y_i a_{ji}$. Let e again denote the inelastically supplied stock of factors, p the prices of the consumption goods, and w the prices of the m factors.

5. See Wieser (1884, 1888). Wieser's work unfortunately contains little formal detail and neglects the interdependence between output and factor prices.

Cassel's formal model simplifies Walras's original general equilibrium model a little by having consumers derive their income from their initial holdings of money rather than from endowments of goods. The demand for consumption good i therefore is not a function of w and can be represented as $x_i(p)$. Equilibria are then solutions (p, w, y) to the equations:

$$x_i(p) = y_i, \qquad i = 1, \dots, \ell, \tag{2.6.1}$$

$$\sum_{i=1}^{\ell} y_i a_{ji} = e_j, \quad j = 1, \dots, m, \tag{2.6.2}$$

$$p_i = \sum_{j=1}^{m} a_{ji} w_j \quad i = 1, \dots, \ell. \tag{2.6.3}$$

The first two sets of equations require the markets for consumption goods and factors to clear, and the third requires that activities make zero profits. Cassel argues for the determinacy of this system by noting that the number of equations above, $2\ell + m$, is equal to the number of unknowns—the $\ell + m$ prices, and the ℓ production levels.[6]

An equality of equations and unknowns does not by itself imply that a system of equations has locally unique (determinate) solutions. Intuitively, determinacy requires that any given subset of factors is used in a sufficiently large number of production processes; otherwise, factor prices can vary without necessitating any change in output prices.

This gap and other difficulties were soon identified by the German literature that appeared in response to Cassel's book. Neisser (1932) and Stackelberg (1933) criticized Cassel's use of fixed coefficients, arguing that traditional marginal productivity theory using differentiable production functions could not be so easily dispensed with. This work is usually viewed as addressing the existence of equilibria in the Cassel model, a problem that is then solved using a "complementary slackness" definition of equilibrium in which goods in excess supply are assigned a zero price. In fact, Neisser and Stackelberg were pursuing more substantive problems. Neisser pointed out that if a factor's endowment were sufficiently large, a negative price for that factor might be necessary in equilibrium, a possibility that is indeed an artifact of Cassel's requirement that demand exactly equal supply. But Neisser would no doubt have found the contemporary device of letting a zero price clear factor markets just as unsatisfactory; the ability of the economy to fully employ resources at positive prices was the question at stake. The lack of equilibria with positive factor prices is not, however, inherently related to fixed production coefficients; as Neisser more or less understood, equilibria with nonpositive factor prices can arise when production functions are differentiable.[7] Perhaps Neisser can be

---

6. Due to Cassel's assumption that consumers begin with initial holdings of money, there is no redundant equation in 2.6.1–2.6.3. For the same reason, demand will not be homogeneous of degree zero; hence, we cannot set a *numéraire* without restricting the set of equilibrium production levels.

7. See also Neisser (1942) on this point.

interpreted as arguing that with differentiable production, zero price equilibria are in some sense less likely.

Stackelberg developed a more comprehensive and ultimately sounder critique of Cassel's model. He first observed that if $m > \ell$, 2.6.2 contains more equations than unknowns, and thus, for typical values of e, there can be no solution for 2.6.2 and hence for the entire system. Stackelberg concluded that in these cases, $m - \ell$ factors must be in excess supply and therefore free in equilibrium; Stackelberg thereby took the first steps toward the modern, complementary slackness definition of equilibrium.[8]

But Stackelberg did not dismiss cases where $m > \ell$ and an equilibrium in the sense of Cassel (i.e., not using complementary slackness) does exist. He argued that the system of equations 2.6.1–2.6.3 is then indeterminate. To see why, note that 2.6.3 is a set of ℓ linear equations in the m unknowns w and hence generates a continuum of solutions (of dimension equal to at least $m - \ell$). Furthermore, w does not appear in 2.6.1 or 2.6.2. (Indeed, the absence of w in 2.6.2 is due to the fact that factor demand and supply are inelastic.) Consequently, if we fix p and y at equilibrium levels, 2.6.1 and 2.6.2 remain satisfied as w varies. The existence of a continuum of w's solving 2.6.3 thus implies that the entire system is indeterminate.

Stackelberg's indeterminacy argument has been widely misinterpreted. Arrow and Debreu (1954), for instance, dispute the indeterminacy claim, arguing that the Cassel model is determinate when 2.6.2 has no solution. But this fact is irrelevant since Stackelberg was considering the case when 2.6.2 is solvable.

To recap, Stackelberg's analysis implies that for typical endowment levels Cassel's model has no equilibrium (in Cassel's sense); but if an equilibrium does exist, it will be one of a continuum. Given the latter result, Stackelberg concluded that Cassel's model provides an inadequate account of an economy with more scarce (i.e., positively priced) factors than consumption goods. Since, moreover, he could see no a priori economic rationale why there should be at least as many consumption goods as scarce factors, Stackelberg concluded that Cassel had failed in his attempt to rid economic theory of marginal productivity foundations.[9] Stackelberg also rejected elastic factor supply as an argument for determinacy, on the grounds of empirical implausibility.

Stackelberg's argument generalizes the indeterminacy example discussed in section 2.3; in fact, Stackelberg used the same example to illustrate his argument. To see the parallel, observe that when there are two

---

8. See also Schlesinger's (1935) follow-up to Stackelberg as well as the independent articles of Zeuthen (1933), and, in a different context, von Neumann (1936). For commentaries, see Koopmans (1951b), Arrow and Debreu (1954), and, for a detailed history, Weintraub (1985).

9. As will be clear in section 2.8, if more than one activity is available to produce some of the consumption goods, indeterminacy is not a necessary consequence of $m > \ell$ factors having a positive price. But since indeterminacy is still possible with multiple activities, Stackelberg's assessment of the Cassel model extends to more general models.

factors and one consumption good, equation 2.6.3 reduces to equation 2.4.1 (if we set $p = 1$). Stackelberg's argument that Cassel's model will typically not have an equilibrium (in Cassel's sense) can also be easily seen in the two-factor, one-output case. In order for factor demand to exactly equal factor supply, e_1 and e_2 must be such that

$$\frac{e_1}{a_{11}} = \frac{e_2}{a_{21}} \qquad (2.6.4)$$

(which then ensures that at full employment the production function is not differentiable). Since this single equation contains two endowment parameters, 2.6.4 will not be satisfied for most values of e_1 and e_2. One factor or the other will be in excess supply and have a zero price; the other price is determined by 2.6.3.

Stackelberg's results can be extended in a number of ways. First, one of the idiosyncrasies of Cassel's formal model, that factor prices only enter the model in the zero profit conditions and do not affect consumption demand, is easy to repair. As Stackelberg more or less understood, we can use the standard formulation of consumer demand and allow agents to obtain their income from the sale of endowments. Let the demand for consumption goods now be represented by homogeneous-of-degree-zero functions $x_i(p, w)$ obeying Walras' law (i.e., $\sum_{i=1}^{\ell} p_i x_i(p, w) = \sum_{j=1}^{m} w_j e_j$). An equilibrium is then defined as before except that $x_i(p)$ is replaced by $x_i(p, w)$:

$$x_i(p, w) = y_i, \qquad i = 1, \ldots, \ell, \qquad (2.6.5)$$

$$\sum_{i=1}^{\ell} y_i a_{ji} = e_j, \qquad j = 1, \ldots, m, \qquad (2.6.6)$$

$$p_i = \sum_{j=1}^{m} a_{ji} w_j, \qquad i = 1, \ldots, \ell, \qquad (2.6.7)$$

Due to Walras' law one of the demand equals supply equations is redundant, and due to homogeneity only the $\ell + m - 1$ relative prices are of economic significance.

Stackelberg's indeterminacy argument is now slightly more complicated. Suppose there is an equilibrium and $m > \ell$. Then there are only $2\ell - 1$ independent equations in 2.6.5 and 2.6.7, which is fewer than the $\ell + m - 1$ relative prices. Therefore, if we fix y at its equilibrium value, a continuum of solutions to 2.6.5 and 2.6.7 will typically exist (with dimension $m - \ell$).[10] Since p and w do not appear in 2.6.6, solutions to 2.6.5 and 2.6.7 are equilibrium prices. The feedback of factor price changes on the distribution of income and thus consumption goods prices means that the indeterminacy is no longer of factor prices alone, but the current indeterminacy nevertheless springs directly from Stackelberg's original argument. In fact, inde-

---

10. Since equation 2.6.5 is nonlinear, a regularity condition must be satisfied before the implicit function theorem can be used to prove that the model is indeterminate. This was unnecessary in Stackelberg's original model, where only the linear equation 2.6.3 was relevant.

terminacy in Stackelberg's two-factor example is virtually unchanged. Agents now acquire the income for their demand for the single consumption good from sales of their factor endowments, but we can consider the market-clearing equation for the consumption good as the redundant equation and set p equal to 1. The analysis of indeterminacy then proceeds as before; when 2.6.4 is satisfied and a Casselian equilibrium exists, there remains a single equation, $w_1 a_{11} + w_2 a_{21} = 1$, to determine both w_1 and w_2.

Stackelberg's reasoning can also be applied to a subsector of the economy rather than to the economy as a whole if there is some subset of m' factors such that the number of activities that use these factors, say ℓ', is less than m'. Suppose that we fix these ℓ' production levels and eliminate from the system 2.6.5–2.6.7 the m' market-clearing equations in 2.6.6 that correspond to the specified subset of factors. We are left with a smaller number of equations than the number of remaining endogenous variables (that is p, w, and the other $\ell - \ell'$ production levels), thus typically leaving a continuum of equilibria. We therefore arrive at the general condition guaranteeing that Stackelberg's indeterminacy argument fails; as mentioned at the beginning of the section, let us say that a model satisfies the *Cassel condition* if it has no equilibrium where a subset of scarce factors is such that $m' > \ell'$.[11]

Stackelberg's argument that for most endowments an equilibrium with more scarce factors than consumption goods will not exist also applies to the above extension to subsectors. Violations of the Cassel condition require that endowments are such that a set of m' equations in 2.6.6 with fewer than m' endogenous variables (the ℓ' production levels) has a solution; for most values of e this will be impossible.

Can we not be satisfied that at most endowment levels indeterminacy does not arise? Stackelberg, as I indicated, thought it absurd that economic theory should impose a restriction on the relationship between the number of scarce factors and the number of industries using them. He therefore considered his argument that the Cassel condition is typically satisfied to be a criticism of Cassel's model; differentiable production functions, after all, impose no restrictions on the number of scarce factors.

Moreover, when endowments are themselves the outputs of production processes originating in the past, not all endowment levels are equally likely. Producers of a capital good, for example, will not in equilibrium manufacture quantities large enough to cause their product to be in excess supply and its price to fall to zero. Market forces can therefore work to ensure that endowments occur in specific configurations. Thus, although Stackelberg's argument can be applied legitimately to factors such as land whose endowments are determined by nature, his argument does not apply directly to

---

11. Stackelberg's indeterminacy argument can be extended to general linear activities models in which there is a choice of technique and activities can have multiple outputs; the Cassel condition must then be modified somewhat. See Mandler (1995).

produced factors. I discuss the likelihood of the endowments generating indeterminacy more extensively in section 2.8, when considering contemporary generalizations of Stackelberg's argument.

2.7 Long-run theories

Models with fixed production coefficients or linear activities will only be determinate if the Cassel condition is satisfied, that is, if sufficiently many industries use each subset of factors. Furthermore, when specialized capital goods are analyzed as distinct commodities, it will be easy for the Cassel condition to be violated. Although British economists of the interwar years used less formal models than their German counterparts, they were well aware of this and other dilemmas in factor price theory. John Hicks, in a paper in 1932, acknowledged that neither direct marginal productivity nor the Cassel approach could be applied fruitfully to the short-run pricing of what he called "intermediate products."

Together with a slightly earlier essay by D. H. Robertson, Hicks's paper marked the high point of the pre–World War II understanding of the dilemmas of factor price theory. Although they disagreed on some points, Hicks and Robertson both concluded that there could be no short-run solution to the indeterminacy problem. Still, even if it is impossible to determine the prices of given stocks of inelastically supplied factors, they argued that persistent deviations of factor prices from their long-run equilibrium values will be inconsistent with market clearing.

Hicks (at this stage of his career) and Robertson worked within a tradition that viewed commodities as transmuted forms of a small number of "basic" factors of production, namely capital and various types of land and labor.[12] Each good was seen as the output of a vertically integrated industry that uses only basic factors as inputs. Competitive equilibria could then be analyzed in a reduced form that considers only the demand and supply for basic factors—with the prices of final outputs and intermediate inputs derived ex post from the value of the basic factors necessary to produce them.

Narrowly construed, the basic factor technique determines only the prices of intermediate inputs produced currently and in the future. But Hicks's and Robertson's long-run view of equilibrium did not treat the prices of initial stocks of goods as independent variables. As a long-run equilibrium unfolds, the prices of each period's historically given stock of intermediate inputs are required to equal the prices of intermediate inputs currently being produced; hence, they are tied indirectly to basic factor prices. The prices of intermediate inputs, both current and future, are thereby eliminated as independent variables, reducing the number of free

---

12. See also J. B. Clark's original formulation of marginal productivity theory, for example, Clark (1899, pp. 113–115, 159–160).

factor prices dramatically. The difficulty of the determinacy problem eases accordingly.

The use of long-run equilibria marked a partial return to classical theory, in which, wherever possible, the producibility of factors was used as an argument for determinacy. Such an approach requires explanations of the prices of nonproduced factors—most prominently labor. As we will see in chapter 3, classical economists struggled with wage rate determination, alternately trying to construct a theory of labor demand and resorting to the Malthusian interpretation of labor as a produced good; neither option was viable in the neoclassical era. To fill this gap, Hicks and Robertson turned to economic mechanisms similar to those used in the static theories we have already considered. Specifically, they argued that long-run changes in basic factor prices will eventually change the demand for basic factors through a substitution of techniques, a mechanism that Robertson conveniently dubbed the "principle of variation." For instance, when long-run wages rise, specialized factors requiring relatively large amounts of labor will become more expensive and hence be less likely to be used as inputs; consequently, the demand for labor will ultimately fall. When the principle of variation could not be applied, Hicks and Robertson invoked the Cassel output substitution theory. A permanent change in basic factor prices will in the long-run raise the relative prices of consumption goods whose production (directly or indirectly) requires large amounts of the newly expensive factors; substitution away from these goods then changes the long-run demand for basic factors.

These mechanisms make far more sense in long-run settings than in static formulations. It strains credibility to imagine that specialized intermediate inputs can be combined in arbitrary proportions, but it is plausible that basic factors—due to the very fact that they can be used to create diverse intermediate inputs—will show the needed flexibility. As for output substitution, Stackelberg's argument that at most endowment levels indeterminacy will not occur can be applied validly: endowments of intermediate capital goods are endogenously determined, but natural endowments of land and labor are exogenous and therefore can be taken to be random.

Long-run equilibria do not achieve the impossible: at any given point in time, current-period prices of the available stocks of basic factors and intermediate inputs can still be indeterminate. But if long-run equilibria are in fact determinate, a sustained change in factor prices will in the end be inconsistent with equilibrium.

A formal model

At first glance, the Hicks (1932) and Robertson (1931) papers seem to be fatally compromised by a suspicious aggregation of inputs into basic factors. In fact, although Hicks and Robertson did not provide formal treatments, a simple model will show that their key conclusions can survive disaggregation. Unfortunately we must interpret the long run as a steady-state equilibrium in which, in addition to goods having the same relative prices through time, the quantities of goods produced and consumed remain fixed. There is little choice in the matter; changes through time in quantities will generally be inconsistent with stable relative prices. An alternate but ultimately similar modeling procedure would be to analyze economies in which resources and outputs grow proportionately. Either choice has obvious limits to its applicability.

When possible we keep to the notation of the static Cassel model of the previous section. The first change is to partition the m inputs into two classes, m_β basic factors of production (various types of labor and land, but *not* capital) and m_γ intermediate factors of production. The intermediate factors are produced, as are the ℓ consumption goods. There will be J activities, each activity still having a single output, but now J_i activities are available to produce each good i. Each activity j is described by the m_β-vector β_j and the m_γ-vector γ_j, specifying the basic and intermediate factors needed to produce one unit of one of the $\ell + m_\gamma$ producible goods. The level at which activity j operates is y_j. We assume that at least one entry of β_j is positive for each j. The total output of consumption good i and intermediate good i are given by q_i^c and q_i^γ, respectively; each is the sum of the production levels of the J_i activities producing that good. Output appears one time period after inputs are applied.

We could in principle distinguish among the prices of a good according to the date at which the good appears, but since our interest is only in equilibria with constant relative prices, we do not do so. Let w denote the prices of basic factors, p^γ denote the prices of intermediate goods, and p^c denote the prices of consumption goods. The interest rate earned on investments made for one time period is given by r. The discounted profit earned by activity j when it is run at the unit level is therefore

$$\pi_j = \frac{1}{(1+r)} p_i - \sum_{k=1}^{m_\beta} w_k \beta_{kj} - \sum_{k=1}^{m_\gamma} p_k^\gamma \gamma_{kj},$$

where p_i is the price of the good (either consumption or intermediate) produced by j. In equilibrium a *zero profit condition* must hold:

$\pi_j \le 0$, for each activity j,

$$(2.7.1)$$

$\pi_j = 0$, if $y_j > 0$.

We complete the model with a *steady-state demand function* for each of the ℓ consumption goods, $x_i(r, w, p^c)$, homogeneous of degree zero in (w, p^c), and the *steady-state endowment* of basic factors, e.[13] A *long-run*

---

13. If microfoundations are desired, think of the demand function as arising from an overlapping generations model. If each generation lives n periods and $x^i(r, w, p^c)$ is the demand for consumption goods of agents in their ith period of life, $x(r, w, p^c) = \sum_{i=1}^{n} x^i(r, w, p^c)$. The demand function is not a function of p^γ since (in a steady state) intermediate goods are not among any agent's initial endowments.

equilibrium is then a (r, w, p^c, p^y, y) such that the zero profit condition, 2.7.1, is satisfied and such that the demand for factors and consumption goods is no greater than their supply, that is,

$$\sum_{j=1}^{J} \beta_{kj} y_1 \le e_k, \quad k = 1, \dots, m_\beta, \tag{2.7.2}$$

$$\sum_{j=1}^{J} \gamma_{ij} y_1 \le q_i^y, \quad i = 1, \dots, m_y, \tag{2.7.3}$$

$$x_i(r, w, p^c) \le q_i^c, \quad i = 1, \dots, \ell, \tag{2.7.4}$$

and where the complementary slackness condition that goods in excess supply have a zero price is assumed to hold. We restrict ourselves to cases where each $q_i^c > 0$ and 2.7.4 holds with equality.

Viewing long-run equilibria in terms of the demand and supply for the basic factors is accomplished as follows. Fix an arbitrary interest rate r and positive basic factor prices w, which—given that (w, p^c, p^y) can be rescaled without changing the set of equilibrium quantities—constitute m_β relative prices. Given values for these variables, there are consumption goods prices, p^c, that must occur in any equilibrium where all of the consumption goods are produced and intermediate goods prices, p^y, that can always serve as prices in any equilibrium.[14] Since we know p^c and therefore $x_i(r, w, p^c)$, we can associate with w and r the set of activity-level vectors $y = (y_1, \dots, y_J)$ that obey 2.7.3, 2.7.4, and the zero profit condition, 2.7.1. For any qualifying y we can calculate the resulting long-run demand for basic factors, $\sum_{j=1}^{J} \beta_{kj} y_j, k = 1, \dots, m_\beta$. Thus, beginning only with the m_β relative prices w and r, we can calculate the set of possible demands for the m_β basic factors; if these amounts are less than or equal to e (and complementary slackness holds), we have a complete equilibrium. Note that in equilibrium some of the intermediate goods will be inputs only in activities that earn negative profits; these goods are therefore not produced.

Though we have not yet suggested why w and r should be determinate, we can already see that the basics of a long-run equilibrium markedly reduce the scope for indeterminacy that occurs in Cassel's theory. Consider the troublesome case in section 2.6 where many inputs are required by only a small number of industries. Indeed, to take an extreme example, imagine that for some consumption good i, each activity j that produces i uses several completely specialized intermediate inputs; that is, no other activity in the economy uses those inputs. When considered in isolation, the static equilibria of one period of such an economy will usually be indeterminate since the Cassel condition is obviously violated. With a long-run

14. That is, given an equilibrium $(r^*, w^*, p^{c*}, p^{y*}, y^*), p^{y*}$ may be replaced by the specified p^y. This result follows, fairly straightforwardly, from Mirrlees (1969) and a suggestion in Arrow and Starrett (1973). See also Samuelson (1961) and Morishima (1964). The assumption that each activity has only one output is important but can be weakened somewhat. Also, unlike standard nonsubstitution theorems, the multiplicity of primary goods can make it necessary for more than one activity per produced good to be used in equilibrium.

equilibrium, however, as the economy proceeds through time the prices of each period's preexisting stocks of intermediate inputs cannot be changed independently of the output prices of those inputs. In fact, as we have indicated, once w and r are specified, p^γ is determined.[15]

What economic mechanisms were suggested for the determinacy of w and r? The first and most obvious, following J. B. Clark's marginal productivity theory, was to apply the principle of variation. Hicks and Robertson suggested that with a sufficient diversity of activities even very small changes in w and r would, by changing p^γ, also change the set of zero-profit activities. When firms switch activities, the derived demand for basic factors then changes. So, for instance, when the price of basic factor k falls, a shift is liable to occur to activities that employ those intermediate inputs that are produced with a relatively intensive use of factor k. By this indirect route, the long-run demand for k can rise. The principle of variation works independently of any change in the composition of consumption demand. That is, if the $x_i(r, w, p^c)$ and therefore, in any possible equilibrium, the q_i^c happen to remain fixed in response to the change in w and r, the demand for basic factors, $\Sigma_{j=1}^{J} \beta_{kj} y_j, k = 1, \ldots, m_\beta$, can still change due to a shift in the y_j that the zero profit condition dictates must be chosen.

This long-run version of marginal productivity theory differs markedly from the static theory in which outputs are simple differentiable functions of inputs; here, the short-run production of output can be carried out with rigid fixed proportions among inputs. But, as economic theory has learned since the 1930s, the pattern of activities adopted in the face of long-run factor price changes can be complicated and counterintuitive. Consequently, the long-run demand for factors can be badly behaved functions of factor prices. Worse still, both Hicks and Robertson, again following J. B. Clark, applied the long-run principle of variation to changes in the interest rate: they claimed that a fall in r causes production to shift to more "capital intensive" intermediate inputs. But it is perfectly coherent to claim, and no notion of capital aggregation is involved, that if w and r change significantly from an equilibrium configuration, then any of the resulting possible values for the $\Sigma_{j=1}^{J} \beta_{kj} y_j$ will violate 2.7.2. The principle of variation works as an argument for long-run determinacy insofar as the set of zero-profit activities shifts in response to factor price changes; it is not necessary that newly adopted activities use cheaper factors more intensively or that production is more capital intensive when r falls.[16]

---

15. More precisely, the prices of those intermediate goods that are produced in equilibrium are determined. If some intermediate good is both not produced and is not an input into any zero-profit activity, its price can obviously be lowered slightly without disturbing equilibrium. But such indeterminacy would not affect any agent's welfare.

16. The current description of technology closely resembles the putty-clay model of factor demand; see Salter (1960) and Solow (1962) for example. Much of the putty-clay literature, however, by continuing to rely on some form of economy-wide aggregation, has obscured the fact that a long-run definition of equilibrium is necessary for determinacy.

While it is coherent to claim that technology permits only small variations in w and r, such a position begs familiar questions. If the possibilities for factor substitution turn out to be meager, are there other mechanisms that can assure determinacy? A second strategy, advocated by Hicks but not Robertson, is to employ a long-run version of output substitution. Hicks imagined that each industry ultimately uses only a small number of basic factors; he therefore presumed that changes in basic factor prices are bound to change consumption goods prices and thus (indirectly) affect the long-run demand for basic factors. (Note that in contrast to the earlier Clarkian reasoning, this argument requires that consumption demand be sensitive to output prices.)

To look at the issue a little more closely, we return, only for simplicity, to the assumption of section 2.6 that there is only one activity per produced good; with no possibilities of factor substitution present, this is the most propitious case for indeterminacy. We can then model the economy as containing only integrated industries, and equilibria are described very simply. For each q_i^c, there is now only one possible vector of derived demands for the basic factors (namely, the basic factors directly used to produce i plus the basic factors indirectly utilized to produce the intermediate inputs needed for i). We represent the unit requirements of basic factors as $(\alpha_{1i}, \ldots, \alpha_{m_\beta i})$; see the appendix to this chapter for a derivation. Market clearing for basic factors is then

$$\sum_{i=1}^{\ell} \alpha_{ki} \, q_i^c \leq e_k, \quad k = 1, \ldots, m_\beta. \qquad (2.7.5)$$

The zero profit condition also reduces to a simple functional form,

$$p_i^c = \sum_{k=1}^{m_\beta} \alpha_{ki}(r) \, w_k, \quad i = 1, \ldots, \ell, \qquad (2.7.6)$$

where $\alpha_{ki}(r)$ is a function, derived in the appendix, that depends on the time pattern of input usage, and where the equality indicates that we are considering only equilibria where all consumption goods are produced. We reproduce the market-clearing condition for consumption goods, now explicitly requiring that consumption goods are not in excess supply,

$$x_i(r, w, p^c) = q_i^c, \quad i = 1, \ldots, \ell. \qquad (2.7.7)$$

In the background there are market-clearing conditions for the intermediate inputs and zero profit conditions for p^y (see the appendix), but only the above three conditions are needed to determine p^c, w, r, and the q_i^c.

As in the general model, we can interpret equilibria in terms of demand for and supply of basic factors. Indeed, deriving the reduced form is now much simpler. Once w and r are specified, p^c is determined from 2.7.6; from 2.7.7 we then know the q_i^c and hence the factor demands $\sum_{i=1}^{\ell} \alpha_{ki} \, q_i^c$. Factor demands can then be compared to factor supply, e; these m_β equilibrium conditions are ultimately functions only of the m_β relative prices w and r.

The current model is almost identical to the Cassel model of section 2.6 (see equations 2.6.5–2.6.7), the only essential differences being the presence of the variable r and the fact that Walras' law cannot be used to eliminate one of the equilibrium conditions. Given our earlier analysis of the Cassel model, we know that determinacy is not guaranteed by a simple equality of equations and unknowns. In particular, we can still expect indeterminacy if the Cassel condition is violated, that is, if there is a subset of m' positively priced basic factors used by $\ell' < m'$ activities. In the current context, however, since the endowment of basic factors, e, is determined arbitrarily by nature, it is entirely appropriate to use Stackelberg's argument that the endowment levels that allow the relevant m' conditions in 2.7.5 to be satisfied with equality are unlikely. In general, therefore, if technology happens to be such that some subset of m' factors is used by only $\ell' < m'$ industries, then $m' - \ell'$ of these factors will have a zero price; determinacy is not threatened.[17]

Although the above arguments do not formally establish the determinacy of the long-run model, it is possible to do so. For typical choices of parameters (including the endowments, e, of basic factors), the long-run model described by 2.7.1–2.7.4 has locally unique equilibria. The integrated-industry method used for 2.7.5–2.7.7 is not necessary for determinacy; it is also unnecessary to assume, as we have above, that each activity has only one output.[18]

Finally, consider a concrete instance of how the argument for determinacy works. Robertson usually focused on the most aggregated case, where there is one output and one basic factor, labor. Could it somehow be that a continuum of values for r can serve as equilibrium interest rates? Robertson reasoned that even if a deviation in r from equilibrium induced no substitution of techniques, a change in the level of savings would still occur. A fall in r, for example, would lead savings—the "supply of capital"—to decrease. On the other hand, given fixed coefficients and an inelastically supplied stock of labor, the equilibrium level of investment—the "demand for capital"—is fixed. Changes in r are therefore inconsistent with markets clearing.

Robertson's argument is translated into the language of our model as follows. Assume that both the consumption outputs and the basic factors are one-dimensional. Then, assuming that the basic factor (labor) is not in excess supply, the model reduces to the equations

$$\alpha \, q^c = e, \qquad\qquad (2.7.8)$$

$$p^c = \alpha(r) \, w, \qquad\qquad (2.7.9)$$

$$x(r, w, p^c) = q^c, \qquad\qquad (2.7.10)$$

---

17. Hicks did not explore the possibility of Stackelberg-style indeterminacy in his integrated-industry interpretation of the Cassel model. Given that he thought of the number of basic factors as small, this omission is not of great significance; the Cassel condition is then likely to be satisfied.

18. A general proof technique is in Mandler (1997).

in the three endogenous variables, q^c, w/p^c, and r. (Once again, any required intermediate inputs are in the background, incorporated into α, which gives both the direct and indirect labor needed to produce a unit of consumption.) Consumption output q^c is determined by the labor endowment e, given 2.7.8. Equations 2.7.9 and 2.7.10 then jointly determine r and w/p^c. In words, a change in r generally will change steady-state net savings, which must be zero in long-run equilibrium, just replacing the amount of capital consumed in each period. Equivalently, changes in r will usually cause steady-state consumption demand $x(r, w, p^c)$ to deviate from steady-state supply, e/α—either directly or via w/p^c, which, by 2.7.9, is affected by r.

Robertson's reasoning effectively returns to the classical or Marxian emphasis on the capacity of decreases in the profit rate to diminish the accumulation of capital; I discuss these theories in chapter 3. Undoubtedly Robertson would have stressed that intertemporal preferences lie behind the impact of the interest rate on savings—unlike Marx's reasoning but akin to the classical emphasis on abstinence. But on any interpretation, Robertson's equilibrating mechanism reproduces a key classical argument for determinacy. The reversion is not surprising since Robertson, partly for the sake of argument, was specifically excluding the mainstay of neoclassical factor price theory, the principle of variation, in either short-run or long-run form; with marginal products absent, no other options were available. For this reason, in the end Robertson emphasized long-run marginal productivity, along the Clarkian lines described above, as the primary force assuring determinacy. (This is yet a second return to classical thinking; as I earlier remarked, the use of long-run equilibria replicates the classical use of relative prices that are constant through time.)

2.8 Factor pricing in contemporary theory

There is a clear break, in both tools used and questions asked, between early neoclassical theories and the postwar general equilibrium model. The triumph of the Arrow-Debreu approach is its generality; it places fewer restrictions and none of the controversial differentiability assumptions on consumers and technology that dogged earlier theory. Using the theory of convex sets, the new approach describes a firm's technology in a remarkably general yet simple way as a set of feasible net outputs, with no "smoothness" requirements imposed on the set's boundary. The theory does not require differentiable production functions, or even production functions at all.[19]

Postwar general equilibrium theory initially concentrated on the existence of equilibrium and neglected the traditional concern with

19. The first comprehensive general equilibrium models cast in the new mold were, of course, Arrow and Debreu (1954) and McKenzie (1954).

determinacy. Using the complementary slackness definition developed in Germany in the 1930s, existence was established under a wide range of circumstances; the only substantial restriction on technology was that production sets be convex. Differentiable production functions, the fixed-coefficients model of Walras and Cassel, and general models of linear activities all obey this requirement. From the vantage point of the new theory, therefore, it seemed as though nothing hinged on earlier debates over the nature and plausibility of the neoclassical production function.

Another remarkable aspect of postwar economic theory is that the intellectual forerunner to the Arrow-Debreu model, linear programming, showed that even without the *assumption* of differentiable production functions, linear activities will nevertheless guarantee that production functions are differentiable—and marginal products therefore well defined—at most points in their domain.[20]

The canonical linear programming problem maximizes a linear function of an *n*-vector x, say $\sum_{i=1}^{n} c_i x_i$, subject to the nonnegativity constraints, $x_i \geq 0$, and the resource constraints

$$\sum_{i=1}^{n} a_{ji} x_i \leq e_j, \quad j = 1, \ldots, m. \qquad (2.8.1)$$

The quantity $\sum_{i=1}^{n} c_i x_i$ is the level of output produced by the *n* activities running at level x, $a_{ji} x_i$ is the amount of resource j needed by activity i to run at level x_i, and $e = (e_1, \ldots, e_m)$ is the exogenous quantity of resources. In resource allocation contexts, it is natural to assume that each a_{ji} is non-negative.

The production function $F(e)$ associated with a given set of activities is derived by solving the above programming problem as the value of e varies. With the exception of a small set of e—the *degenerate* endowments, which have measure zero—the derivatives of $F(e)$ are well defined and equal to the Lagrange multipliers of the resource constraints. At the nondegenerate endowments, often called *generic*, activity analysis can therefore prove rather than assume that production functions are differentiable. Programming problems of the above type can always be interpreted as simple market economies with one consumption good and *m* factors of production, where agents derive their income from selling their share of the *m* factors. Since Lagrange multipliers for the programming problem are equilibrium prices for the factors (when output is the *numéraire*), differentiability assumptions seem to be unnecessary even for the key early neoclassical theorem that factor prices equal marginal products!

An example of the isoquants generated from a linear activities model is pictured in figure 2.1, in which one output is produced by two factors and two activities. The activities have production coefficients (a_{11}, a_{21}) and (a_{12}, a_{22}). If the endowment e is *not* on the lines with slope a_{21}/a_{11} or a_{22}/a_{12}—that is, if either both activities are in use or one of the resource constraints is

---

20. For a history and exposition of linear programming, see Dantzig (1963). Much of the important early work on activity analysis was included in Koopmans (1951a).

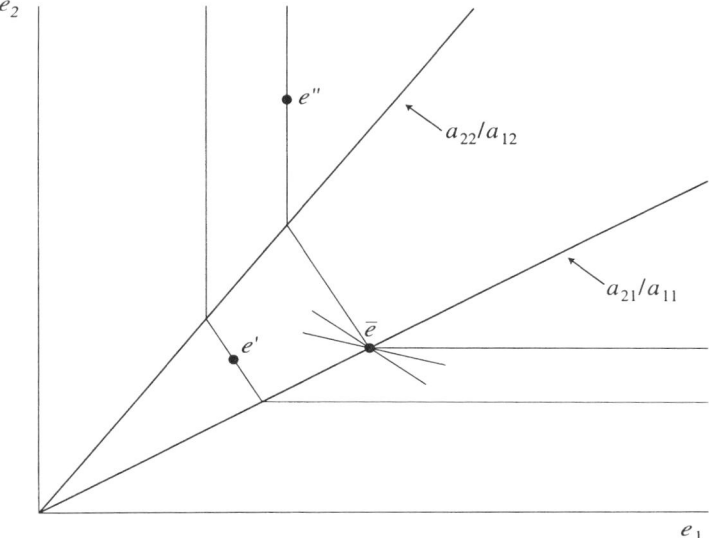

Figure 2.1 Isoquants in the linear activities model

slack—the production function is differentiable.[21] Lagrange multipliers for the constraints, or equivalently, the market prices of the resources, are also uniquely defined in these cases, as can be seen from the fact that at points such as e' or e'' the isoquant has a unique supporting price line. In fact, when both activities are in use, the earlier analysis of the equations 2.4.3 has already shown that factor prices are uniquely specified.

What about the exceptions? The degenerate endowments occur on the positively sloped lines in figure 2.1. At these points, the derived production function F is not differentiable and consequently factor prices or Lagrange multipliers are indeterminate; geometrically, the indeterminacy appears as a multiplicity of supporting price lines, for example, at $\bar{e}$. The apparent unlikeliness of degenerate endowments is easy to visualize: the endowment points on the positively sloped lines form a negligible subset of the set of all positive endowment points. Hence, if we begin at a degenerate (e_1, e_2), the slightest variation in either endowment variable will move us to a differentiable point in F's domain. To use slightly different language, the combination of the parameters (e_1, e_2) that yield nondifferentiability form a one-dimensional subset of a two-dimensional parameter space.

21. In the first case, the activity levels $x = (x_1, x_2)$ must solve the equations $a_{11}x_1 + a_{12}x_2 = e_1$ and $a_{21}x_1 + a_{22}x_2 = e_2$; since the solution values of x_1 and x_2 change differentiably as a function of e, output also changes differentiably. In the second case, say where the e_2 constraint is slack, output is given by the differentiable function $x_1 = e_1/a_{11}$.

The degenerate case occurs when there is a solution to a programming problem with a subset of m' binding resource constraints—j's where 2.8.1 is satisfied with equality—such that the number of activities that consume positive amounts of these resources—i's such that $a_{ji} > 0$—is less than m'. Degeneracy is considered unusual, since these m' binding resource equalities have fewer than m' activity level variables. (The remaining x_i appear in these equalities but they are multiplied by $a_{ji} = 0$.) Hence, for most values of e, the hypothesized m' conditions in 2.8.1 cannot be solved as equalities; at least one of the constraints must be slack. Although we are currently considering multiple activities to produce a single output, this reasoning is virtually an exact duplicate of Stackelberg's argument that Cassel's model (with the original Cassel definition of equilibrium) cannot be solved when the number of factors in the economy is larger than the number of consumption goods.

The claim that degenerate endowments are unlikely forms the core of the contemporary general equilibrium case for the determinacy of factor prices. Before turning to the determinacy literature, we must first see why modern equilibrium theory can no longer rely on the long-run arguments for determinacy discussed in section 2.7. Beginning in the 1920s and 1930s, intertemporal economics has increasingly considered goods appearing at different dates to be distinct commodities; this innovation provides a welcome alternative to the rarely applicable long-run equilibrium concept, where present and future prices are constrained to be equal. Dated commodities treat markets for current and future goods symmetrically, allowing intertemporal models to be analyzed as static equilibria. The breakthrough application of dated commodities appeared in *Value and Capital* (1939), where Hicks used the device in his theory of *simultaneous trading*. In Hicks's model, markets for present and future goods operate concurrently, permitting the prices of goods at all dates to be determined simultaneously.[22] An equilibrium of the simultaneous-trading model can then be interpreted as a perfect foresight equilibrium in which agents trade sequentially and where agents unanimously anticipate that the prices of future goods will be the prices that rule in the simultaneous-trading equilibrium. Not surprisingly, Hicks viewed both the simultaneous model and its perfect foresight interpretation as convenient theoretical gambits rather than literal descriptions. He assigned more significance to his theory of *temporary equilibrium*, in which agents trade sequentially and are permitted to have divergent expectations of future prices, and where consequently some agents' beliefs turn out to be incorrect.[23]

Postwar theory has followed Hicks's lead: merely by remarking that goods can be interpreted as appearing at different dates, static general

---

22. Hicks (1933) credits this idea to Hayek (1928); see also Milgate (1979) for a detailed history.
23. See Grandmont (1982) for subsequent developments in temporary equilibrium theory.

equilibrium models effortlessly provide a theory of intertemporal econom- ics [e.g., see Arrow and Debreu (1954)]. As it was for Hicks, the simultane- ous-trading model (or its translation into a model of perfect foresight) remains an intellectual idealization, useful, for example, as an analytical benchmark against which other intertemporal models can be tested. Although most topics in postwar equilibrium theory have first been analyzed with simultaneous-trading models, this research strategy is borne out of convenience, not a conviction that complete markets exist or that all agents' expectations of future prices coincide.

The move to dated commodities seems to furnish yet another instance of postwar theory repudiating a needlessly constraining early neoclassical assumption; intertemporal economics appears to have been freed from the confines of long-run equilibria and their implicit reliance on steady states. But treating the prices of commodities at different dates as independent variables leaves the prices of stocks of resources produced in the past untied to the prices of factors currently under production. The resulting degrees of freedom in factor prices—along with the Arrow-Debreu permissiveness about technology—opens the door to indeterminacy. The only alternative is to resort to Stackelberg's argument that the endowments generating in- determinacy are unlikely, precisely the tack taken by general equilibrium theory in the last 25 years.

Given the prominence of the determinacy issue in prewar economic theory, it is remarkable that the determinacy of the Arrow-Debreu model was not subjected to formal scrutiny until the 1970s. First and foremost, the delay was a symptom of the sharp divide between prewar and postwar the- oretical research. Early postwar general equilibrium theory concentrated on existence and other questions for which calculus techniques were unnec- essary; indeed the avoidance of differentiability assumptions was thought to be a sign of progress. This technical bias hampered the study of deter- minacy, which must treat equilibrium conditions as differentiable functions. In the 1960s, however, tools in differential topology placing calculus tech- niques on sounder footing were popularized, giving economists mathemat- ical foundations for differentiability assumptions and access to weaker (and hence less painful) forms of differentiability; calculus again became a math- ematically respectable tool. Second, the importance of determinacy was obscured in the early postwar years by attempts to argue for the unique- ness of equilibrium. Only in the 1960s did it become clear that this project could not succeed in any generality; determinacy could then reemerge as a subject in its own right.

The formal study of the determinacy of the general equilibrium model began with a paper by Debreu (1970) which showed that indeterminacy in an exchange economy, although possible, is very unlikely; only if the para- meters of the model are precisely arranged in an unlikely way will there be a continuum of equilibria. The "regularity" literature developed rapidly; results similar to Debreu's were ultimately established for constant returns to scale production economies and for models of linear activities in particular.[24] As in Debreu's original paper, indeterminacy is not impossible, just unlikely: if economies are indexed by a sufficiently rich set of parameters, indeterminacy occurs only at a negligible (zero measure) subset of parameters. These last results seem to demonstrate that differentiable technologies are as superfluous for determinacy as they are for existence.

I examined the logic of generic determinacy conclusions in my discussions of linear programming (earlier in this section) and Stackelberg's critique of Cassel (in section 2.6). In fact, since the programming problem considered earlier can be interpreted as a simple general equilibrium model, applying the results of the regularity literature to this case just reproduces the generic differentiability of the production function F. More complex general equilibrium models cannot be translated into programming problems. In particular, the endowments generating indeterminacy cannot be described as a system of linear equations; and consequently, Stackelberg's counting of equations and unknowns argument for generic determinacy cannot be invoked. But by using tools that apply to nonlinear equations, the regularity literature manages to tackle these cases. Thus, although they do not pioneer a new economic logic, contemporary arguments for generic determinacy represent one of the great technical feats of postwar microeconomics and genuinely advance on their 1930s predecessors.

Is the argument that most endowment levels produce determinate equilibria sufficient cause to dismiss indeterminacy? No internal mathematical problems trouble the regularity literature; the question hinges on the logic of dismissing the endowments inducing indeterminacy as virtually impossible. The endowments of natural resources are indeed arbitrary—and hence any particular configuration can be taken to be improbable. If, therefore, agents at the beginning of economic time trade once and for all for current and future delivery of all resources and consumption goods (as in the simultaneous-trading model), the generic case for determinacy is internally coherent. But once economic activity is under way, and assuming that agents trade again as time proceeds, endowments of capital goods and skilled labor will be determined by past decisions and therefore arise in specific patterns. Endowments yielding indeterminacy then appear systematically, as I demonstrate in the following simple general equilibrium model.

Example

I use the model of sections 2.3 and 2.4, where a_1 units of e_1 and a_2 units of e_2 are needed to produce one unit of output. To endogenize the endowment

24. The earliest papers on the determinacy of production economies are Fuchs (1974) and Smale (1974). Linear activity analysis economies are treated in Mas-Colell (1975) and Kehoe (1980); the first also can accommodate other types of constant-returns models. For a general approach and an overview of the regularity literature, see Mas-Colell (1985).

of one of the factors, suppose that e_1 is produced with factor inputs at a prior time period: specifically, let each unit of e_1 be produced at the cost of sacrificing one unit of a sole consumption good that appears in an initial period. The endowment of factor 2, e_2, is exogenous. Let the first-period consumption good be the *numéraire* and let p be the price of the second-period consumption good. Agents in the first period decide on their savings levels, the sum of which is e_1, based on their intertemporal preferences and their expectation of the price that e_1 will sell for in the second period in terms of second-period consumption, that is, w_1/p. When we arrive at the second period, we have the general equilibrium version of the two-factor model: agents have endowments of the two factors and sell them for income which they use to buy the second-period consumption good.

The important feature of this two-period economy is that degenerate endowments, that is, e satisfying

$$\frac{e_1}{a_1} = \frac{e_2}{a_2}, \qquad (2.8.2)$$

can occur robustly, leading to indeterminacy in the second period. This possibility is easiest to see if agents have unanimous and correct expectations of w_1/p. Observe first that w_1/p is the gross return to sacrificing first-period consumption in terms of second-period consumption and that the sum of factor costs must equal the output price of the second-period consumption good:

$$w_1 a_1 + w_2 a_2 = p. \qquad (2.8.3)$$

If $e_1/a_1 > e_2/a_2$, factor 1 will be in excess supply in the second period and therefore $w_1/p = 0$, while if $e_1/a_1 < e_2/a_2$, $w_2 = 0$ and therefore, by 2.8.3, $w_1/p = 1/a_1$. On the other hand, if 2.8.2 is exactly satisfied, 2.8.3 allows w_1/p to assume any value between 0 and $1/a_1$. Since, for a wide range of agents' intertemporal preferences, equilibrium will require the anticipated value of w_1/p to be one of these intermediate values, it will not be unusual for e_1/a_1 to equal exactly e_2/a_2.

If there is a single consumer, the fact that 2.8.2 will be satisfied systematically can be visualized easily. Letting x_f and x_s denote the aggregate levels of first- and second-period consumption, the shaded area in figure 2.2 is the set of feasible consumption bundles; the intersection of the feasible set and the single agent's indifference curve occurs at the kinked point, where 2.8.2 is satisfied. Clearly, perturbations of the agent's preferences (or of e_2 or of the maximal quantity of x_f) leave the intertemporal equilibrium at the kinked point.

The appearance of the endowments consistent with indeterminacy does not present the *simultaneous-trading model* with any difficulty. In the example, if agents trade only once in the first period, exchanging their endowments from both dates for consumption goods at both dates, the present values of the two second-period factors are determinate: if $\tilde{w}_1$ and $\tilde{w}_2$ are the present-value prices of the factors and $\tilde{p}$ is the present-value price

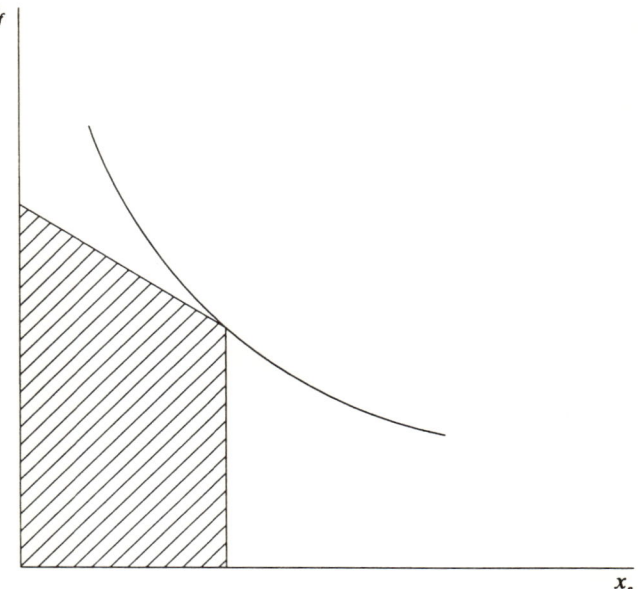

Figure 2.2 An intertemporal equilibrium generating indeterminacy

of the second-period consumption good, then in order for the activity to make zero profits,

$$\tilde{w}_1 a_1 + \tilde{w}_2 a_2 = \tilde{p} \qquad (2.8.4)$$

must hold in equilibrium. Since e_1 (when traded for in the first period) must exchange one for one with the first-period consumption good, $\tilde{w}_1$ must equal 1 (the price of first-period consumption). The gross return to saving is now $\tilde{p}$; the requirement that intertemporal marginal rates of substitution equal $\tilde{p}$ and 2.8.4 jointly determine $\tilde{w}_2$ and $\tilde{p}$.

But if trading is sequential—and if 2.8.2 is satisfied—equilibria in the second period are indeterminate. Even if agents unanimously expect a certain value of w_1/p to rule in the second period, any other value of w_1/p between 0 and $1/a_1$ can also serve as an equilibrium price for factor 1. Hence, once we arrive at the second period of this example, the primitives of the economy—its endowments, preferences, and technology—are not enough to pin down equilibrium prices.

Moreover, even if the anticipated value of w_1/p could somehow be selected, factor markets would not be able to function in a decentralized, competitive manner. Changes in the endowments of factors will have a large influence on market price; any withdrawal of either factor $i = 1$ or $i = 2$ from the market, no matter how small, will leave the other factor in excess supply, sending w_i/p from its anticipated value to $1/a_i$. Since the return to such market manipulations is so great, it is highly implausible that agents would view factor prices as parametric.   ■

This example generalizes: when there are linear activities, multiperiod perfect foresight equilibria can generate, in their later periods of operation, indeterminate equilibria.[25] Degenerate endowments only seem unlikely given the naive supposition that any resource level is plausible; once the dynamics of capital accumulation are accounted for, they become routine. The breakdown of the price-taking assumption also generalizes; since equilibrium factor prices change discontinuously as a function of market participation, agents will manipulate their factor supplies to influence prices, thus violating the rules of competitive markets.

Of course, for degenerate endowments to yield indeterminacy, the right equilibrium concept must be in place. If endowment production is ongoing and stocks of resources are required to have the same price as the same physical goods currently being produced—if, that is, equilibria are long-run—indeterminacy will not occur. In the example, e_1 is produced for use in the second period; if the same resource were produced during the second period, and its price had to equal w_1, the additional restriction on factor prices would prevent indeterminacy. The Arrow-Debreu practice of treating prices at different periods as independent variables is thus a crucial ingredient of the indeterminacy problem.

It is tempting to argue that factor price indeterminacy can be resolved by requiring that factor prices anticipated in the past become actual market prices. In some respects, this proposal extends the logic of long-run equilibria. In steady states, agents also form expectations about what prices stocks of factors will sell for, and despite the absence of a pure market mechanism to enforce their expectations, agents anticipate that factors will sell for their long-run equilibrium prices. In the long-run approach, therefore, as well as in contemporary general equilibrium theory, nonmarket institutions must both ensure that expectations made in the past rule in the present and prevent market manipulations (such as the endowment withdrawals discussed in the example) from occurring. But the predicaments confronting contemporary models are much more serious. In long-run equilibrium, observations of past prices make the assumption that agents' expectations coincide plausible. But when equilibria are not long-run, there is no obvious way to coordinate expectations of future factor prices. Moreover, if agents' expectations diverge, as in the temporary equilibrium model, whose anticipated prices should rule as the market prices? In the example, market equilibrium can be consistent with any of the conflicting values of w_1/p predicted in the first period.

Once the endowments yielding indeterminacy are not dismissed as unlikely, the dilemmas facing the Arrow-Debreu theory loom large. The use

---

25. I demonstrate this claim in a broader setting in Mandler (1995).

of general convex technologies and the rejection of long-run equilibria eliminate the two most powerful methods for guaranteeing factor price determinacy. Given the defects of the regularity argument for determinacy, however, there seems to be little choice but to adopt or adapt one of the analytical strategies of the past. Indeed, the failure of the attempt to do without differentiable technologies supports those who have insisted that factor substitutability is a cornerstone of sensible economic modeling. Some writers, such as Paul Samuelson, have argued as a matter of theoretical principle that activities are available in enough variety to justify the approximate truth of the neoclassical production function [e.g., see Samuelson (1962)]. From the Arrow-Debreu point of view, such a claim is a puzzling anachronism. But even if Samuelson's and kindred positions are empirically incorrect—and there is ample room for doubt—factor substitution has not yet been superseded as a rationale for the determinacy of equilibrium.

2.9 Factor-price indeterminacy revisited: Sraffa and general equilibrium theory

Contemporary economic theory has not recognized the difficulties of factor pricing. Indeed, as the pure theory of value unified around the Arrow-Debreu model in the 1950s and 1960s, the content of competitive price theory seemed increasingly settled. The developments still to come, such as the theory of regular economies, would further this analytical uniformity. The unity provided by general equilibrium theory, never experienced in earlier eras, has delivered considerable advantages. The internationalization of the content and methods of economic theory could never have occurred without the Arrow-Debreu model as a point of common reference. And general equilibrium theory seems to consign ideological controversy to the past; the theory of value is now the province of disinterested research. At the same time, the postwar consensus has unintentionally buried critical problems and insistently avoided contact with the theoretical past. Consequently, on the rare occasions when contemporary theory has had to confront reappearances of earlier theoretical impasses, the outcome has been more chaotic than illuminating.

With regard to factor price theory, the confusion is strikingly illustrated by the baffling debates surrounding Piero Sraffa's influential 1960 book, *Production of Commodities by Means of Commodities*. But when viewed in light of the history of factor price theory, the sources of the disagreement, and the confusion, become clear.[26]

Sraffa questioned the neoclassical tradition of viewing output as a differentiable function of the aggregate factors of labor, land, and capital. Like many other interwar economists, Sraffa presumed that at the industry level, at least, technology is best described by linear activities. In fact, through

---

26. I discuss Sraffa's model in more detail in Mandler (1997).

most of his book, Sraffa assumed that each of his model's n outputs is produced by only one activity. Each activity uses some subset of the same n goods as material inputs; after the passage of one time period, one basic factor—labor—is combined with the material inputs to produce one of the outputs. Sraffa's model is easily adapted to fit our notation: let p_i represent the price of a representative good i, r denote the single-period rate of interest, and w denote the wage. The activity producing i is described by the input requirements $(a_{1i}, \ldots, a_{ni}, a_{li})$. Sraffa assumed that each activity i should earn r on its capital investment. Hence,

$$p_i = (1 + r)(p_1 a_{1i} + \ldots + p_n a_{ni}) + w a_{li}, \quad i = 1, \ldots, n. \tag{2.9.1}$$

Since there are $n + 2$ prices—$p_1, \ldots, p_n$, w, and r—and only $n + 1$ equations—2.9.1 plus one setting a *numéraire*—Sraffa concluded that competitive price systems are indeterminate.

Although there is more to Sraffa's book than the indeterminacy argument, it is this claim that stands in sharpest contrast to postwar mainstream theory. In response, general equilibrium theorists contend that Sraffa committed two key mistakes.[27] The first is a failure to distinguish commodities by the date at which they appear. Sraffa illegitimately used the same variable, p_i, to represent the price of good i when it is an input at one date and when it is an output at a later date: the same p_i appears on both the right- and left-hand sides of equation 2.9.1. Unless the endowments and preferences of the economy are chosen in particular ways, it will not be possible to find an equilibrium where input and output prices are equal. To address this criticism, consider a simple two-period economy that uses a given stock of n material inputs in an initial period and labor in the subsequent period to produce n final outputs; we then have n new price variables. The new prices, of course, only expand the number of variables without reducing the number of equations. But by general equilibrium rules, this excess of variables over equations is an artifact of a second error, the omission of demand functions and market-clearing conditions. If these two shortcomings are corrected, general equilibrium critics of Sraffa claim that determinacy of equilibrium is restored.[28]

Are these criticisms persuasive? First, if we distinguish commodities by date and require markets to clear, Sraffa's theory is actually an ideal setting for indeterminacy. In the two-period interpretation of the Sraffa model discussed in the preceding paragraph, n industries use $n + 1$ factors. Consequently, if the factors are supplied inelastically and no factor is in excess supply, the Cassel condition of section 2.6 is violated and indeterminacy typically obtains. Despite the standard Arrow-Debreu criticisms, therefore, a rigorous completion of the Sraffa model can confirm the indeterminacy

---

27. Hahn (1982) is the classic Arrow-Debreu indictment of Sraffa.

28. This conclusion, if not the general equilibrium model itself, is broadly accepted by both sides of the debate. See Harcourt (1974), for example.

claim. The fact that Sraffa stipulated some but not all of the preconditions for indeterminacy deserves emphasis: there is no mention of inelastic factor supply in Sraffa's book, and allowing physically identical commodities to have different prices at different dates contradicts Sraffa's model explicitly.

Second, Sraffa's use of constant relative prices, far from being an oversight, was a product of his long-run view of equilibrium. Sraffa would likely have defended his approach on the grounds that endowments adjust through time in such a way that market-clearing relative prices can remain unchanged through time. Given that Sraffa began to write his book in the 1920s, his choice of equilibrium concept is hardly surprising. But if Sraffa's equilibria are long run, the determinacy arguments of long-run neoclassical models come into play. Indeed it is striking that Sraffa neither mentioned nor critiqued these arguments. If the n goods of Sraffa's model can be divided into mutually exclusive sets of intermediate inputs and consumption goods, and if labor is paid at the beginning of production rather than at the point of sale, Sraffa's economy would be an instance of the long-run Cassel model of section 2.7. (See equations 2.7.5–2.7.7, which, as a reduced form, suppress the price and market-clearing conditions for intermediate goods.) Furthermore, since Sraffa's model has only one basic factor and the Cassel condition is therefore satisfied, even the nongeneric possibilities for indeterminacy discussed in section 2.7 are absent. Hence, if we incorporate preferences and demand into Sraffa's long-run framework, the neoclassical mechanisms for determinacy will close the model: if w, r, or goods prices were to deviate from an equilibrium configuration, the long-run demand for labor would change, violating market clearing. In fact, as I pointed out at the end of section 2.7, in aggregative cases of the model the classical and Marxian argument that savings are a positive function of the interest rate is alone enough to establish long-run determinacy. Sraffa was the twentieth century's most penetrating scholar of classical economics; it is hard to fathom his failure to consider these rebuttals to indeterminacy.[29]

Confusion reigns on both sides of the debate. If we leave a long-run environment and allow relative prices to vary through time, Sraffa had the beginnings but not the entirety of a coherent case for indeterminacy. Most importantly, he grasped the fundamental connection between linear activities and indeterminacy. In the long-run setting that Sraffa preferred, however, the neoclassical and classical cases for determinacy stand unchallenged. Each side of the Sraffa debate has presumed that its equilibrium

---

29. Some work in the Sraffian tradition, for instance Garegnani (1976), does not consider long-run equilibria in which economies reproduce without growing to be legitimate. But long-run equilibria can accommodate growth if basic factor endowments all expand at the same rate or under certain forms of technical progress. Furthermore, if these uncomfortable extensions are rejected, Sraffians must confront the fact that equilibria with constant relative prices generally do not exist. Unless preferences, endowments, and technology are stable through time, market-clearing relative prices cannot remain unchanged.

concept supports its desired conclusion (determinacy for the neoclassicals, indeterminacy for the Sraffians). The opposite is true.

2.10 Conclusion

No single theory of factor pricing can stand on its own. The original formulation of marginal productivity, while ingenious, hinges on an extreme degree of factor substitutability. But simply replacing differentiable production functions with linear activities often leads to indeterminacy, particularly when factors are disaggregated. Long-run theories remedy the defects of crude marginal productivity, establishing determinacy with only a modest scope for factor substitution (and in fact can be extended to complete agnosticism about the nature of technology). Their drawback, of course, is the narrow usefulness of long-run equilibria.

Postwar theory has tried to begin anew. Although the flexibility of the set-theoretic model is ideal for establishing the optimality of competition and the existence of equilibrium, wiping the slate clean has allowed indeterminacy to return unnoticed. That factor prices can fail to be determinate when production functions are not differentiable was a commonplace in the early twentieth century; in fact, as we will see in chapter 3, effectively the same indeterminacy had earlier been pivotal in the demise of the classical school. Modern investigations into the theory of value nevertheless began by concentrating on the linear model of production, where nondifferentiabilities abound; when placed in models of market equilibrium, linear activities lead to indeterminacy. But determinacy was a dead letter in the 1950s; even when mining the German literature on Cassel, postwar theorists paid attention only to the literature's implications for existence, ignoring the economic content of what was being debated.

By the time the formal study of determinacy resumed in the 1970s, discussion of the dilemmas of factor pricing had long disappeared from formal economic theory. Obscured by the mathematical smoke screen of assuming that all possible endowment configurations are plausible, the indeterminacy associated with linear activities went unobserved. But unless it resorts to earlier theoretical devices or posits a mechanism by which agents' expectations of factor returns are translated into market prices, the contemporary general equilibrium model can escape indeterminacy only under the wildly improbable notion that trading for all goods occurs at a single point in time prior to the accumulation of capital. Postwar theory therefore does not adequately explain how competitive factor markets function.

Still, the weaknesses of particular episodes in the history of distribution theory contain an implicit account of how factor price theory can achieve analytical progress. Along with defects I have mentioned, an accompanying list of sufficient conditions for determinacy emerges: differentiable technologies, elastic factor supply, the Cassel condition, long-run equilibria, and the simultaneous-trading model all guarantee that markets can pin down factor prices. The history of the subject thereby illuminates when and why determinacy can be expected to obtain.

The dilemmas of factor pricing warrant reevaluation of long-standing differences over what constitutes the core of neoclassical thinking. Although most contemporary work outside of general equilibrium theory continues to impose differentiability assumptions, opinions differ on the reason for this fact. For some a key feature of neoclassicism is the assumption that economic agents always face a plentiful array of options; firms therefore should be modeled as choosing from a rich diversity of factor combinations. For others, the expression "the neoclassical production function" is a marketing error; differentiability is only a matter of tractability and convenience, not theoretical fundamentals. My arguments support the former camp. Rejecting the differentiable production function not only leads models to be mathematically less concise, but the resulting indeterminacy makes comparative statics—the prediction of unique equilibrium responses to small changes in parameters—impossible. Optimization, price taking, and market clearing are not the sole essential features of neoclassical economics; in the absence of a long-run equilibrium concept, empirical claims about the scope of factor substitution are just as important.

Appendix

I now fill in the details of the model behind equations 2.7.5 and 2.7.6. Exclude from the model any intermediate input not used, either directly or indirectly, in the production of any consumption good. Let A_β^c (respectively, A_β^γ, A_γ^γ, A_γ^c) be the $m_\beta \times \ell$ (respectively, $m_\beta \times m_\gamma$, $m_\gamma \times m_\gamma$, $m_\gamma \times \ell$) matrix whose ith column is the vector of basic (respectively, basic, intermediate, intermediate) input requirements for consumption (respectively, intermediate, intermediate, consumption) good i. Let q^γ be the quantity of intermediate goods produced, which I assume is positive in each component. Along with equation 2.7.7, which needs no further explanation, the following market-clearing conditions must hold:

$$A_\beta^c q^c + A_\beta^\gamma q^\gamma \le e,$$

$$A_\gamma^\gamma q^\gamma + A_\gamma^c q^c = q^\gamma.$$

Combining, we have

$$(A_\beta^c + A_\beta^\gamma [I - A_\gamma^\gamma]^{-1} A_\gamma^c) q^c \le e.$$

Hence α_{ki} in 2.7.5 is the kth row and ith column entry of $A_\beta^c + A_\beta^\gamma [I - A_\gamma^\gamma]^{-1} A_\gamma^c$.

To produce all consumption goods in positive quantities, all activities must be in use. Consequently, profit maximization requires that the following zero profit conditions hold:

$$p^c = (1 + r)(w A_\beta^c + p^\gamma A_\gamma^c),$$

$$p^\gamma = (1 + r)(wA^\gamma_\beta + p^\gamma A^\gamma_\gamma).$$

Solving for p^c, we have

$$p^c = (1 + r)w(A^c_\beta + (1 + r)A^\gamma_\beta[I - (1 + r)A^\gamma_\gamma]^{-1}A^c_\gamma).$$

Hence $a_{ki}(r)$ in 2.7.6 is the kth row and ith column entry of

$$(1 + r)(A^c_\beta + (1 + r)A^\gamma_\beta[I - (1 + r)A^\gamma_\gamma]^{-1}A^c_\gamma).$$

3

The Prehistory of Distribution Theory

The Wage Fund and the Invention of Marginal Productivity

3.1 Overview

Economics embraced marginal productivity as essential at the turn of the twentieth century, only to dismiss it as superfluous after World War II. As we have seen, this dismissal invited back the indeterminacy problem that the early neoclassicals had solved primarily by using marginal productivity. Indeed it was precisely this solution that earlier had brought conceptual order to the clutter of nineteenth-century distribution theory, thus allowing neoclassical economics to establish itself as a full-fledged replacement to the classical school and guaranteeing its future as the dominant voice of economic analysis.

Confusion plagued the theory of labor demand and wage rate determination from the late 1860s through the 1880s. The bedrock principle of classical price theory had held that in the long run the price of a produced factor gravitates to its cost of production. Economists made intermittent attempts to fit labor into the produced-factors model, but failed because the inaccuracies were too glaring and the wage issue too politically charged. Instead, the most prominent theory of labor demand—the so-called wage fund— derived the price of labor by dividing a predetermined stock of wage goods by the number of workers employed. The theory met a multitude of criticisms beginning in the 1860s, the most enduring of which called for the logic of factor demand to be rethought. According to these critics, employment does not involve advancing consumption goods to tide workers over during the course of production; instead, the decision to hire factors should be seen as a function of the prospective profitability—and hence, in the end, productivity—of the factors employed. Although many have claimed otherwise, the wage fund is perfectly consistent with modern views of factor pricing; but it does not answer the questions asked by the prospective profitability model.

It was several years before the prospective profitability view took hold; indeed only in the wake of marginal productivity theory did all competitors vanish. Until then, the profitability model unacceptably left wage rates indeterminate. William Thornton, whose work in the late 1860s set off the debates over the wage fund, pointed out that changes in wages need not induce any variation in either the supply of labor to the market or in demand. Just as critics of marginal productivity would argue in the early twentieth century, Thornton reasoned that market forces alone do not suffice to pin down the wage.

The disintegration of the wage fund theory spawned a welter of competing and inconsistent approaches, lasting from 1870 until marginal productivity's triumph at the end of the century. Many economists during this era tried to explain factor pricing from the prospective profitability perspective, but they did not yet have the crutch of the differentiable production function to rely on. A cross section of writers—from Marshall among the neoclassicals to J. E. Cairnes, the dying gasp of classical thinking—recognized the short-run indeterminacy of factor prices, but held that the interest sensitivity of investment could guarantee that permanent wage changes ultimately produce disequilibrium. This reasoning foreshadowed the later, more refined use of long-run equilibria by Hicks and Robertson in the 1930s, who had differentiable production functions at their disposal but tried to make do without them.

Counterposed to the postclassical muddle, the power and ingenuity of the marginal productivity theory of the 1890s shines clear. The theory argued that variations in factor prices lead to factor substitution, thereby giving demand an elasticity with respect to price changes. Confusion subsided; for example, the tortuous defenses of the wage fund, which persisted through the end of the nineteenth century, could be permanently retired. A new theory now decreed how to think about factor demand.

3.2 Factor pricing in classical economics

The classical theory of value rested on the principle that the prices of produced goods tend toward their long-run costs of production. Classical theorists also provided the outline of a short-run equilibrating mechanism. For example, an unexpected increase in the demand for a good increases the good's price, raising short-run profits and drawing capital into the industry; in time, increases in supply return price to its long-run equilibrium value. The completeness of the classical account depends on whether long-run production costs are themselves adequately determined. Despite occasional (and awkward) attempts to use the labor theory of value to this end, the basic classical strategy since Adam Smith was to explain a good's cost of production in terms of the money value of its constituent inputs. Since classical economists for the most part took physical factor requirements as given, the theory hinged on its ability to determine factor prices.

Unable to provide a unified theory, classical economics gave diverse explanations for the pricing of different types of factors. Classical theorists explained the prices of produced inputs by invoking the same cost of production principle used to price any produced good. At least in the long run, no additional theory of capital goods pricing was thought necessary. Nonproduced factors required other explanations. The only such account to meet with complete success, the theory of differential rent, explained rental rates by the requirement that capital invested in different types of land (or in production processes of different land intensity) earn the same rate of return.

The theory of wages proved far more troublesome. Although workers are not produced and sold for a profit, classical economists sporadically attempted to squeeze labor into the model of produced goods. Ricardo and others used Malthusian population theory to argue that wages above subsistence rates would induce increases in population and labor supply; for a given level of capital, and thus the demand for labor, these increases in labor supply push down wage rates, eventually leading to a long-run—a very long-run—equilibrium in which wages provide workers with a standard of living just equal to subsistence. A similar equilibration process was assumed to work in reverse when wages fall below subsistence.

Subsistence typically was defined as the standard of living that induces zero population growth; classical economists made no rigid claims about the minimum biological or social necessities of life. Classical theory thus did not (as is sometimes presumed) rely on a wholly implausible demographic thesis. The true difficulty of Malthusian wage theory was the time frame—decades at the least—in which it operates and its assumption that the demand for labor adjusts more slowly than population. Consequently, classical economists by and large regarded the subsistence theory as a distant theoretical construct rather than as a concrete prediction; they believed, for instance, that capital accumulation can systematically outstrip growth in labor supply, leaving wages quasi-permanently above the zero population growth wage rate. Since Malthusian theory did not tie down wage rates over practical time spans, the need arose for a precise short-run theory. Unfortunately the initial classical treatments of Smith and Ricardo offered little detail on how "capital" translates into a demand for labor at a point in time or how the short-run demand for labor varies, if indeed it does vary, with the wage rate. They asserted that increases in capital relative to a given population raise wages, and that increases in the working population at a given level of capital lower wages, but these two claims came close to exhausting the Smith-Ricardo short run.

A short-run theory is necessary even if one accepts, for the sake of argument, that labor and produced capital goods are supplied elastically in the long run and have adjusted to all short-run disturbances. What short-run market force guarantees that factors earn their long-run rates of return? Classical economists finessed this question by presuming that if the price of a produced input is above its long-run equilibrium value, then increases in the supply of the input eventually result. But those increases in supply arrive at a later date, and only then if the price increase is not deemed temporary. This point did not trouble classical writers in the case of capital inputs. For the classicals—and as we saw in our analysis of long-run equilibria in chapter 2, for many early neoclassicals as well—it would be odd to consider changes in price not initiated by some disturbance to supply or demand; in the absence of exogenous shocks, prices were simply assumed to be constant and equal to their long-run equilibrium values. (It is only from the contemporary vantage point of seeing current stocks of factors as conceptually distinct from future factors that the absence of a theory of short-run factor pricing is so conspicuous.) But since the time span between factor price disturbance and supply response is so long in the case of labor, the short run in wage theory could not be ignored; pointing to the long-run Malthusian supply response simply was not credible.

3.3 The wage fund

In the face of this pressing need, classical economics groped for a theory of short-run labor demand. The wage fund, which invoked yet another analytical principle, was the best they could do.[1] In the classical view, capital consists not only of physical machinery but also of wealth spent on any other factor prior to the completion of production. In particular, advances made to workers are part of capital and were known as the wage fund. In its crudest form, used primarily for expository purposes, the wage fund was conceived as a physical stock of "corn" that workers receive as payment prior to the sale of their product. If the size of the fund is physically fixed, a rise in the corn wage must lower the number of workers employed. Classical economists thereby arrived at an elastic demand curve for labor, and thus, it was thought, at a determinate theory of wages.

From this common beginning, the wage fund was developed in various directions. In some hands, the stock of wage goods was translated into a homogeneous sum of value that capitalists devote to wage payments. If the wage bill comprises the whole of capital and if total capital is fixed, increases in wages will still lower employment. In fact, as one of the later proponents of the wage fund, J. E. Cairnes, pointed out, even if part of capital must be used to purchase other inputs, say raw materials, the same qualitative conclusion holds: higher wages will lower the volume of workers *cum* materials that can be purchased with a fixed sum of wealth.[2] The difficulty with this account is that presumably total capital will vary with the wage; for example, an increase in wages will lower the rate of return on investment

---

1. It is revealing that the theory was expounded in the most detail by the lesser figures of the school. See Marcet (1816, chaps. 8–9), McColluch (1825, pp. 326–334), Senior (1836, pp. 207–209), and Fawcett (1865, p. 120), for a sampling.

2. Cairnes (1874, pt. 2, chap. 1, sec. 8). Hollander (1985, chap. 6) provides a nice model.

and is therefore likely to diminish the amount of wealth invested as capital.[3] There is then no analytical moment at which the wage is determined by a fixed stock of capital divided by the number of workers.

Relying on the fixity of the physical stock of wage goods at a point in time therefore seemed to be the more sound theoretical move. No analysis of investment incentives or even of the prior accumulation of wage goods by capitalists is necessary; if wage goods are distinct from the consumption goods of other social classes, any agent can own the stock of wage goods ex ante. For an ironclad derivation of the wage fund relationship between real wages and employment, two further assumptions—neither particularly plausible—are also necessary: workers must spend all of their wages on consumption and wage goods must be perishable, disappearing prior to the completion of current production. The per capita consumption wage will then equal the preexisting stock of wage goods divided by the number of workers. Along with the distinction between wage goods and other consumption items, I call this bundle of assumptions the *wage goods rigidity thesis*.

The wage fund is a theory of workers' consumption; it does not explain how labor hiring decisions are made or what relationship holds between employment and the expected revenue labor generates. (The profitability of hiring decisions of course played a major role in classical thinking, but not in the theory of aggregate wage determination.) The wage fund therefore does not constitute a theory of labor demand in the sense the term is used today. Indeed, the wage goods rigidity thesis does not explain labor demand at all; it merely explains the equilibrium quantity of consumption goods that aggregate wages exchange for.

To see this point in more detail, suppose that firms hire labor and other factors at time t in order to produce output at $t + 1$. Let C^t indicate the stock of goods consumed by workers at time t, p_C^t the price of corn at t, w^t the money wage of workers hired at t, and L^t the number of workers hired at t. The wage fund theory at the least asserts that

$$w^t L^t = p_C^t C^t \qquad (3.3.1)$$

must hold. Note that 3.3.1 is not quite an "identity"; it requires, following the wage goods rigidity thesis, that workers save none of their wages. A stronger version of the wage fund theory asserts that C^t is exogenously specified—presumably because consumption output at t is determined by production decisions made prior to t and only workers consume wage goods. We then arrive at a one-to-one relationship between w^t/p_C^t and L^t; if L^t is also exogenous, labor's "consumption wage," w^t/p_C^t, is entirely determined by period t variables. (Notice that even in the strong version, it could be that any or all firms are unconstrained by their initial ownership of

---

3. Forget (1992) emphasizes that even in his early writings J. S. Mill recognized that the wage fund was not fixed at a point in time.

capital: they could have access to capital markets that allow them to borrow some or all of the wage and other factor payments required at t.)

This formulation of the wage fund fails to mention, much less explain, the productivity of labor or the profitability of hiring labor; labor's real "product" wage can only be analyzed in reference to the output appearing at $t + 1$. Thus, although legions of commentators have insisted that a strong version of the wage fund is inconsistent with neoclassical factor price theory, it plainly is not. Specifically, firms can obey the relevant marginal productivity relation between wage payments at time t and the value of output that results at $t + 1$. Let $f(l')$ denote the output of some industry in period $t + 1$ as a differentiable function of labor input applied at t, p_f^{t+1} denote the price of this output in period $t + 1$, and r denote the interest rate between periods t and $t + 1$. (It could of course be that there is only one sector, in which case p_C^t and p_f^{t+1} are the prices of the same good at different points in time.) Given that wages are paid one period prior to the appearance of output, profit maximization requires that w^t equal the discounted marginal product of labor, that is,

$$w^t = \frac{1}{(1+r)} p_f^{t+1} \frac{df(l')}{dl^t}.$$

Suppose now that there is an exogenous productivity shock that increases

$$\frac{df(l')}{dl^t}$$

for all values of l'. Clearly there is no conceptual difficulty in simultaneously maintaining the wage fund claim that w^t/p_C^t is unchanged and the marginal productivity claim that

$$\frac{1}{(1+r)} \frac{df(l')}{dl^t}$$

rises (conditional, of course, on l' not falling). One need only assert that L^t, which is equal to the sum of the l' across sectors, and C^t remain unchanged. For the latter, the wage goods rigidity thesis will suffice.

The wage fund theory, since it has nothing to say about the prospective product wage, does not contradict later marginal productivity theories of factor demand. By the same token, the wage fund also cannot determine the product wage. In the absence of differentiable production functions, the wage goods rigidity thesis does not bar the indeterminacy of factor prices when calculated in terms of prospective output; it simply has no bearing on the matter.

Historically the wage fund theory came under attack in the late 1860s, in part triggered by practical controversies over the effect of trade unions on wages and employment. Several critical questions were posed. First, at a point in time, is the stock of consumption goods available to workers fixed in size, even approximately? If wage goods cannot be distinguished categorically from other consumption goods, wage increases might reduce capitalists' current consumption and augment the wage fund. Second, must workers be provided with a consumption advance at all? If wage payments are used to purchase consumption goods from the output currently being produced, any constancy of the preexisting stock of consumption goods is irrelevant.[4] These two criticisms challenge the wage goods rigidity thesis and thus address the wage fund as a theory of the consumption wage; in terms of the earlier model they challenge the exogeneity of C' and the requirement that equation 3.3.1 holds, respectively.

Finally, critics argued that employment decisions depend on the prospective profitability of the amount of labor hired, that is, a comparison between the cost of labor and the value of output produced. While the wage fund does not contradict this last point—one can defend the wage fund as a theory of the consumption wage while maintaining that prospective profitability governs hiring decisions[5]—the criticisms are linked historically. Advocates of the first two objections were obliged to provide at least some explanation of how wages are linked to the level of labor hired in equilibrium.

William Thornton, the most influential critic of classical wage theory, forcefully championed the prospective profitability view of factor demand. Thornton saw the demand for labor as technologically determined by the amount of "work," or production capacity, available. Employers will hire this amount of labor as long as the wage is less than the value of output produced per worker; variations in the wage below this level have no effect on labor demand. Since he also assumed that labor supply is inelastic, Thornton concluded that market forces alone cannot determine wage rates. In his words, "price may vary exceedingly without the slightest variation in the relations of supply and demand."[6]

The appearance of indeterminacy was due to the adoption of the prospective profitability view of labor demand; without marginal productivity, or some comparable mechanism, the profitability model is not analytically closed. As chapter 2 amply demonstrates, the requirement that firms make zero economic profits in equilibrium does not pin down factor

4. For samples of the first criticism, see Thornton (1869, pp. 84–85) and Jenkin (1868); for the latter, see Walker (1876, chap. 8) and Marshall and Marshall (1879, bk. 3, chap. 6, sec. 4). Longe (1866) seemed to make both arguments; it is less clear, however, whether he was trying to explain money wage payments or the real consumption wage.

5. See Walker (1876, chap. 8), who recognized that under some circumstances workers' current consumption might be fixed by past accumulation, but insisted that employment decisions nevertheless depend on prospective profitability.

6. Thornton (1867, p. 552). See also Thornton (1869, bk. 2, chap. 1). It is instead "competition," Thornton's term for negotiation based on the relative bargaining strength and patience of employers and workers, that determines wages. Jenkin (1868), though his reasoning was not as fully developed as Thornton's, came to similar conclusions when he argued that due to the presence of fixed capital, capitalists might not cut employment in the face of higher wages.

prices. In fact, Thornton's indeterminacy argument directly translates into the indeterminacy example discussed in sections 2.3 and 2.4. Labor and production capacity are the two factors; a comparison of the wage with the value produced by labor reproduces the break-even or zero profit requirement for the firm (i.e., for a single activity). Thornton, of course, did not present a formal model; but his writings grasped the basic economic logic of a rigorous indeterminacy conclusion.

In response to Thornton's attack, John Stuart Mill, never the most detailed expositor of the wage fund, conceded in 1869 that the theory must be abandoned, although primarily on the grounds that there is no fixed predetermined fund. Mill's concession and the decades of polemics it provoked undercut the classical school's claim to a comprehensive theory of factor pricing. To be sure, prior to the 1890s the growing neoclassical movement also could not offer a unified theory, and some of the early neoclassicals even held to aspects of the wage fund. But the wage fund debacle nevertheless wounded classical orthodoxy and, given the neoclassical challenge on the horizon, at an inopportune moment. Indeed, the economist and philosopher Henry Sidgwick, writing midway between the classical and neoclassical eras, credited the disarray of English economics to the combined influence of the wage fund controversy and Jevons's economics (1883, pp. 4–5).

Controversy over the wage fund persisted through the end of the nineteenth century. The wage fund, as a theory of the consumption wage, could not be definitively refuted; it could hobble on by relying on diluted forms of the wage goods rigidity thesis. Hence, no matter how many times critics insisted on the variability of the size of the fund, fundamentalists would always retort that the preexisting stock of wage goods still placed approximate short-term bounds on working class consumption.[7] Since the prospective profitability view of labor demand decisions did not address, let alone disprove, this empirical claim, wage fund advocates had no reason to back off.

3.4 J. S. Mill and elastic factor supply

The bankruptcy of classical theory is amply illustrated by John Stuart Mill's curious role in the wage fund episode. Why did Mill discard the wage fund when he had no substitute theory of short-run labor demand? Part of the answer is that Mill was willing to fall back on the Malthusian, long-run account of wage determination. In Mill's hands, the population principle was softened in some dimensions—emphasis was given to the potential for the zero population growth wage rate to be raised by improvements in the moral condition of the working class, the experience of economic

---

7. See Gordon (1973) on this point and for an overview of the waning years of the wage fund theory.

prosperity, and the emancipation of women—but its underlying logic remained unaltered.[8] When wages afford a standard of living above the "habitual standard" or "moral minimum," increases in population result and, all else being equal, lower wages. Indeed, Mill's primary modification was to accelerate the time frame in which the population mechanism operates. The change is strikingly evident in Mill's views of medium-term policy questions. For instance, Mill deviated from Ricardian orthodoxy by questioning the advantages of permitting unrestricted imports of grain: if the temporary increase in the real consumption wage stemming from lower grain prices does not make a "permanent impression" on the workers' habits and requirements, they will "soon slide back into their former state": due to population growth, wages will rapidly return to the preexisting zero population growth wage rate [Mill (1848, bk. 2, chap. 11, sec. 2, p. 348)]. To take another example, Mill held that the unionization of workers in one industry will not impose any permanent cost on workers in other industries. Even though the price of the output of the newly unionized industry will rise, the general wage rate in the economy as a whole will return in time to the standard determined by the "habitual requirements of the labouring people." Mill concluded that "wages never fall permanently below the standard of these requirements, and do not long remain above them" (1848, bk. 5, chap. 10, sec. 5, p. 935). Thus, although analysis using the wage fund also appeared in Mill's writings, he was not left stranded without it; indeed he was quick to point out that his rejection of the wage fund left the population principle unimpugned (1869, p. 645).

Mill's use of Malthusian theory was only one instance of his chronic and implausible use of long-run elastic supply to determine factor prices. Just as the population mechanism implies that labor is elastically supplied at the subsistence wage, Mill reasoned that the access of developed economies to foreign markets implies that capital for domestic purposes is elastically supplied at the (unique) critical interest rate at which capital flows abroad. Once the interest rate has reached this "practical minimum," any further accumulations of capital are exported; contractions in savings only diminish capital outflows, leaving the domestic interest rate unaffected.[9] Although minimum rates of profit were conjectured as theoretical possibilities by the other major classical economists, Mill was unusual in that he considered his minimum rate to be relevant for policy making. As in his analysis of wages, Mill drew distinctive and heterodox conclusions. Moderate government deficits do not crowd out domestic investment in developed economies but

8. For general principles, see Mill (1848, bk. 1, chap. 10, and bk. 2, chap. 11). The broader political motivations of Mill's recantation are discussed in Forget (1992).

9. Mill (1848, bk. 4, chap. 4, sec. 8). When economies have no access to foreign markets, Mill still clung to the elastic capital supply conclusion: the interest rate is then driven to a different, but still fixed, theoretical minimum rate at which the motive to save would come to an end. Indeed, an opulent economy such as England is within a "hand's breadth" of this theoretical minimum.

merely reduce the export of capital. At worst, a temporary increase in the profit rate will result; but within "a year or two" new domestic savings appear that drive the profit rate back to the minimum.[10]

The analytical mechanisms at work in Mill's population theory and his capital theory are functionally identical. If the price of some factor—labor or savings—is above its exogenously specified long-run value, boundless increases in supply result until the factor price returns to its natural rate.[11]

Of course, Mill's explanations were persuasive only to the extent that the underlying assumptions of elastic factor supply were credible and applicable to the time span under consideration. Particularly in the case of wages, Mill's medium-run applications of the population principle were unconvincing to all but the most fanatical Malthusians. Economics could not resort to an ultraclassical reliance on elastic factor supply; it had to face squarely the problem of how to price nonproduced factors of production.

3.5 Between the wage fund and marginal productivity

After the disintegration of the wage fund, what alternative accounts of wage determination were available? In the 1870s and 1880s, the prospective view of aggregate labor demand became increasingly widespread, especially in the wake of its exposition by the American economist Francis Walker. Walker, heavily influenced by Jevons, was perhaps the leading theorist of factor pricing during the interregnum between the wage fund and marginal productivity theory. He argued that employment decisions were driven by calculations of the profitability of labor; given the price of output, wages were therefore linked to the productivity of labor.

In the details of his equilibrium theory, Walker proceeded in highly aggregated terms. Following Jevons, he argued that wages are the residual share of output after profits, interest, and rent are deducted. Hence, if nonlabor shares are fixed, increases in productivity lead to increases in wages [see Walker (1875, pp. 102–104, 113), Walker (1876, chaps. 8–9), Jevons (1871, chap. 8)]. Here Walker used the fact that aggregate factor income adds up to the value of total output, a principle that had been a linchpin of economic theory since Ricardo, for whom the share of profits in output at a point in time was determined as the residual after deducting wages and rent, which in turn were determined by other mechanisms. The difference in the 1870s was that the wage fund and Malthusian population theory

---

10. Mill (1848, bk. 4, chap. 5, sec. 1). Using similar reasoning, Mill concludes that a tax on profits in a developed economy will not in the end lower the rate of profit. See Mill (1848, bk. 5, chap. 3, sec. 3).

11. The reader may wonder how it is that the profit and wage rates are consistent with one another, given that both are exogenously specified. Mill's answer was that land rents adjust to ensure that factor shares add up to the total product; the margin of cultivation will extend or contract up to the point that the exogenous wage and profit rates exhaust the total value produced on marginal land.

could not be used to pin down labor's share. Since the adding-up principle cannot determine both the wage and profit shares as residuals, theories such as Walker's needed to explain how all nonlabor shares are determined. Walker made some headway in this regard, but he was unclear at key junctures. In particular, while repeating the standard conclusion that interest rates are forced down by the accumulation of capital, he did not explain why [see Walker (1883, pt. 4)].

Other theorists also used the fact that factor shares add up to the total product, but were more specific about the mechanics linking wage and profit rates. The key additional postulate was that savings depend positively on the interest (or profit) rate. This principle had long been a staple of classical theory, though it appeared in dramatically different guises. In Mill's case, for instance, savings increase with the profit rate due to an intertemporal substitution of consumption, while for Marx, increases in the profit rate augment capital accumulation due to the fact that capitalists save and workers do not. But the functional dependence of capital investment on the profit rate is much the same in both accounts.[12] The sensitivity of investment to the profit rate helped to solve the wage determination puzzle because of the potential influence of changes in capital on the labor market. For instance, Cairnes argued that the wage rate is in equilibrium if the implied profit rate induces a volume of capital investment that fully employs the labor supply. An increase in the wage above this equilibrium value would lower the profit rate; invoking Mill's account of the incentive to save, Cairnes reasoned that investment in physical capital and wage advances must then diminish. After a period of time, unemployment would result.[13]

Only a few years after Cairnes, Alfred Marshall put forward a similar account in his early writings. An increase in wages and commensurate decline in profits will, due to capitalists' larger saving propensity, lower capital investment and hence future labor demand [Marshall and Marshall (1879, pp. 201–202)]. Strikingly, Marshall replicated Marx's understanding of how savings and profit rates are linked. Marx himself came close to advocating the entirety of the Cairnes-Marshall position, except that he argued that the wage adjustment process cycles: capital accumulation first bids up the wage rate, then retracts in the face of a falling profit rate, and then advances again once unemployment causes wages to fall [cf. Marx (1867,

---

12. There is one difference. Mill's reasoning applies to the profit rate earned on investment in future production; Marx's applies to the profit rate earned on already existing capital.

13. Cairnes (1874, pt. 2, chaps. 1 and 3). Cairnes only intended this explanation to apply unadorned to countries near Mill's theoretical minimum rate of profit (see footnote 9); in other situations, rising wages induce capital flight, thus leading to roughly the same outcome. Matters are also complicated by the fact that Cairnes cast his theory as a defense of the wage fund. But since neither total capital nor the wage fund remains fixed as wages change, Cairnes's defense was more terminological than substantive. Furthermore, the causal mechanism of Cairnes's theory can be stated, as I have above, with no reference to the wage fund. For a contrasting view, see Hollander (1985, chap. 6).

chap. 25, sec. 1)]. Marx's overall theory of wage determination contains other elements, such as technological change, that systematically displace the wage adjustment cycle, but the causal link between investment and the wage rate is the same mechanism that appeared in Cairnes and Marshall.

Cairnes and Marshall implicitly took the long-run view of equilibrium discussed in chapter 2. In both Cairnes-Marshall and the no-choice-of-technique model of section 2.7, neither factor demand or supply responds to contemporaneous changes in factor prices. But in the long-run, equilibrium requires that the (exogenous) factor supplies are fully utilized. If there is one basic factor—labor, in Cairnes-Marshall—and factor proportions are fixed, full employment determines the equilibrium level of capital investment. (See equations 2.7.8–2.7.10.) The interest rate and the wage are then determined by the dual requirements that agents save the equilibrium level of capital investment and that factor shares add up to total output. Since equilibria are steady state, the requirement on capital investment appears as the condition that there is no net savings (2.7.8 and 2.7.10); the adding-up principle appears as the zero profit condition 2.7.9.

The Cairnes-Marshall theory suffers from the standard drawback of long-run equilibria: changes in factor prices take time to induce disequilibrium. As Cairnes and Marshall were well aware, if firms have fixed capital equipment, increasing wage rates do not affect the current labor market; they only diminish labor demand indirectly by discouraging the accumulation of capital [see Cairnes (1874, pt. 2, chap. 3, sec. 3) and Marshall and Marshall (1879, p. 201)]. Furthermore, if the increase in the wage is known to be temporary, Cairnes's argument is altogether inapplicable; with the incentive to invest unaffected, there is no reason for capital investment to diminish.[14] I have already discussed the analytics of this point in chapter 2; if current factor prices can change independently of future factor prices (and no other mechanism, such as marginal productivity, is present), factor price indeterminacy can result.

The parallels between the factor price theory of the 1870s and 1880s and the Hicks-Robertson long-run theory should come as no surprise. After the collapse of the wage fund, both classical thinking and the emerging neoclassical theories had no short-run account of labor demand. Interwar neoclassicism found itself in the same position when it tried do without marginal productivity. For both eras, therefore, only arguments for long-run determinacy could be constructed.[15]

14. In Marshall's case, a temporary increase in the current wage does diminish aggregate investment (since the income distribution still changes), and hence future employment.

15. The highly aggregated Cairnes-Marshall theory is not as developed as the Hicks-Robertson theory. If the entire economy uses only one activity, the adding-up constraint—which in chapter 2 is a zero profit condition—can only determine one factor price as the residual. Even when there is no choice of technique, the Hicks-Robertson model is more flexible: by letting output be disaggregated, additional zero profit conditions are introduced, allowing for more than one scarce basic factor.

3.6 The emergence of marginal productivity

Marginal productivity resurrected the short-run theory of factor demand. The Thornton indeterminacy argument now had a response: changes in factor prices induce factor substitution, it was claimed, altering factor demand and disturbing equilibrium. The prospective profitability paradigm was thus made consistent with the determinacy of factor prices.

The invention of marginal productivity theory in the late 1880s had close ties to the developments of the previous 20 years. Walker's theory that the productivity of labor was the primary determinant of wages gained wide currency.[16] Given the new popularity of calculus and explicit models of maximization, marginal productivity was then a mathematically natural step. In fact, Walker himself, although he did not quite put forward a marginal productivity theory, extended the use of differential rent to other spheres and occasionally deployed marginalist reasoning.[17] At least on the American scene, the specific line of development from Walker is easy to discern. Henry George combined Walker's view linking wages to productivity with classical rent theory to conclude that wages were equal to the product of labor on marginal (no-rent) land; George's theory then provided the direct inspiration for J. B. Clark's marginal productivity theory [see George (1879, bk. 1, and bk. 3, chap. 6) and Clark (1899, p. viii)].

In the new approach, factor payments were treated, at least analytically, as simultaneous with a firm's sales, and as a consequence, the classical concern with providing workers with consumption goods to tide them over during production faded even further from view. The fact that some factor owners might still need or desire to consume prior to the appearance of the output they are currently producing could still be accommodated of course. If workers happen to want to use some fraction of their prospective wages prior to the completion of production, they can be paid early, in effect receiving interest-bearing loans; indeed, early payment need not be contracted with the employer.[18]

As time went on, however, most theoretical treatments put aside this minor wrinkle. Marshall took care in his earlier writings to note that if a factor paid in advance produces an identifiable output, then the factor can only be said to earn the discounted value of the output produced. By the mid-1890s, however, in the wake of fully articulated marginal productivity theories, Marshall stopped mentioning this refinement.[19] And Wicksteed's widely influential 1894 treatise on marginal productivity adopted the

16. On Walker's remarkable influence, see Taussig (1896, pp. 298–299).

17. See Walker (1876, p. 129), for example, where he writes that "so long as additional profits are to be made by the employment of additional labor . . . a sufficient reason for production exists."

18. For example, see Walker (1876, pp. 133–136). There are classical antecedents to this view, of course.

19. Compare Marshall and Marshall (1879, bk. 2, chap. 11, sec. 5) and Marshall (1895, bk. 6, chap. 1, sec. 7–8).

modern-day static point of view: there is no explicit accounting of the times at which factor payments and output sales occur. In fact, Wicksell, in order to emphasize the close connection between factor prices and physical productivity, not only provisionally assumed that factor payments were temporally simultaneous with the outcome of production but also were made with the actual physical output produced (1901, pp. 108–109). In all of these accounts, when factors are paid and the dates at which factor owners happen to spend their income were simply no longer part of the theory of distribution.[20]

3.7 Conclusion

The history of factor price theory in the nineteenth century is curiously similar to its development in the twentieth century. In both cases, a theory of short-run factor pricing—the wage fund or marginal productivity—originally argued for point-in-time factor price determinacy. Although internally consistent, both accounts ultimately faced external challenge: the wage fund due to the implausibility of the wage goods rigidity thesis and its neglect of the link between labor demand and profit maximization, and marginal productivity due to its factor substitution assumptions. In both eras, some theorists recognized the deficiencies of the orthodox account and admitted that point-in-time determinacy could not be achieved; as a substitute, they argued that at least sustained changes in factor prices were inconsistent with equilibrium.

Still, the pre–World War II chapters of factor price theory did not unwittingly replicate the flaws of preceding eras. Marginal productivity, after all, presented a new theory of short-run factor demand. And the interwar reformulation (and improvement) of long-run equilibria was a legitimate response to the difficulties of marginal productivity and did not downplay the lack of arguments for short-run determinacy. Postwar general equilibrium theory, on the other hand, unaware of the near-century-long effort to build a determinate theory of distribution, unknowingly knocks out all supports holding up the edifice.

20. Intertemporal equilibria, which dramatically extend the collapsing together of transactions taking place at different times, thus follow in the footsteps of a founding strategy of neoclassicism.

4

The Ordinal Revolution

4.1 Introduction

Contemporary ordinal preference theory rejects hedonism and cardinal utility as proper starting points for explaining economic behavior. The axioms of consumer theory, it is now said, should be imposed on choices, not on the psychology underlying choice. In the early neoclassical era, in contrast, hedonism provided rationales for assumptions on behavior. The completeness, transitivity, and convexity of preferences were thereby grounded by a substantive account of economic rationality.

Hedonism is a deeply flawed theory of economic motivation. Unfortunately, however, ordinalism has not only rejected the particular theory that agents are pleasure seekers, but the very project of explaining why neoclassical behavioral assumptions characterize agents' interests. Lacking psychological foundations, the axioms of preference theory in-stead persist as primitives, unexplained and unjustified. Ordinalism simply attaches the label "rationality" to the completeness and transitivity of preferences; and this equation, which makes it seem as if completeness and transitivity characterize consistent goal-seeking conduct, has hidden the challenges of justifying postulates of rational behavior.

Once the methodological rules of ordinalism are repealed, the richness and complexity of the concept of rationality emerges: transitivity can be justified at a high degree of generality; convexity has plausible if not iron-clad rationales; completeness, however, cannot be supported.

I begin the chapter with a few observations about the problems in classical theory that neoclassical demand analysis addressed and how early neoclassical utility theory furthered this program. Classical theory did not explain pricing in pure-exchange environments in any detail or offer foundations for demand. Neoclassical demand and equilibrium analysis helped fill this gap; and utility theory demonstrated why demand functions are reliably stable through time and lead to determinate equilibria.

The core of early utility theory was its account of deliberation: agents were assumed to weigh their options based on the amount of pleasure choices deliver. Along with supplementary hypotheses covering intertemporal decisions and choice under uncertainty, hedonism underlay early neoclassical predictions about preference and behavior. Theorists acknowledged that agents do not always act according to these dictates; but utility theory prescribed ideals of rationality and explained behavior in terms of how closely economic decisions conform to these ideals.

Due to its repudiation of formal explanations of the logic of assumptions on preferences, ordinalism has lumped together all psychological theory going beyond preference. This practice is too crude; we will need to distinguish between cardinality and other nonordinal properties of preferences. A plausible middle ground then takes shape between the ordinalist rejection of psychology and the cardinal view that agents can form judgments of preference intensity. Although they are nonordinal properties of utility, diminishing marginal utility and "psychological concavity" impose less exacting (and hence more plausible) requirements on what agents experience than does cardinality.

I then turn to ordinalism's key methodological claims. Preference theory since the mid-twentieth century has asserted that psychological assumptions going beyond preference are both unfalsifiable and superfluous for a science of behavior. In reality, nonordinal psychological assumptions have always been and continue to be indispensable to choice theory; even the validation of ordinal assumptions presupposes an introspective and psychological interpretation of what field of objects an agent's preferences are defined over. Moreover, assumptions of economic rationality are not direct generalizations from empirical data; they are attempts to axiomatize the link between choice and well-being and at most posit long-run predictions of behavior. Consequently behavioral axioms must be accompanied by explanations of why they characterize agents' interests. Neoclassical economics was built on the principle that consumer demand must be given foundations; for this project to succeed, a defense of the logic underlying ordinal postulates is just as important as explaining demand in terms of preferences.

The success of ordinalism therefore hinges on whether it can provide rationales for assumptions on preferences that are significantly more general than those offered by the early neoclassical psychology it claims to displace. Ordinal theory itself has not undertaken this investigation; we have to provide the missing pieces. No uniform answer emerges. I look first at the convexity of indifference curves. While psychological concavity is the natural successor to early neoclassical arguments for convexity—and is a strictly weaker assumption than earlier mixtures of cardinality and diminishing marginal utility—it is nevertheless a nonordinal property of utility. But other psychological explanations of the convexity assumption are also available. Hence, although no single rationale for convexity operates at the level of generality that ordinalism aims for, the multiplicity of rationales argues, in this case, in favor of the ordinalist practice of placing assumptions on preferences rather than on psychological attributes. Still, the theory of convexity that emerges is dramatically richer than the spare ordinal account omitting all psychological foundations.

It is easy to provide ordinal arguments for why transitivity is a basic axiom of rationality; completeness, on the other hand, is problematic. Without hedonism's rationale for why agents can form psychological preference judgments, contemporary preference theory has had to rely on the argument that agents can always be compelled to choose between any pair of options. These choices, which must be complete, are then interpreted as agents' preferences. By distinguishing between choice and preference, I argue that although transitivity is a reasonable requirement on preference orderings, choice behavior need not always be transitive. The ordinalist interpretation of choice as preference therefore breaks down, and undermines the rationales that can be provided for transitivity.

This failure is symptomatic of a deeper pattern: preference theory has repeatedly adopted simple postulates, such as hedonism, which imply that agents can globally order their choices. With time, the limitations of these postulates are exposed and their underlying principles are rejected. Although the rationale for completeness then disappears, economic theory has nevertheless usually retained completeness as an unargued-for primitive. I illustrate another example of this pattern in a brief appendix examining the theory of choice under uncertainty.

Some of the historical issues raised by cardinality and the rise of ordinalism are treated separately in chapter 5. The next two sections of this chapter are also largely historical. Since only a few of these remarks are referred to again, these sections can be skipped with little loss of continuity.

4.2 Demand analysis and neoclassical economics

Unlike the theory of factor pricing, where classical and neoclassical economists faced similar indeterminacy problems, the important changes in utility theory have been exclusively neoclassical developments. There were classical accounts of economic psychology—and they even cast choice in terms of utility and desire—but the theories remained unelaborated. To avoid examining the dependence of economic outcomes on agents' psychological valuations, classical economists would sometimes relabel offending topics as outside the domain of economic science. Ricardo (1817, p. 12) famously excluded the pricing of nonproduced consumption goods—"rare statues and pictures, scarce books and coins"—from his formal theory of value; John Stuart Mill (1844, p. 132) held that the "laws of . . . consumption" were not part of political economy but were noneconomic "laws of human enjoyment." When the link between market outcomes and the psychology of consumer choice was scrutinized, the theory that resulted seems shallow by contemporary standards. In his analysis of saving, for instance, Mill simply assumed that there is a cutoff rate of interest above which agents accumulate capital and below which they do not, thereby reducing the effect of intertemporal choice on the long-run rate of interest to the specification of a single number.[1] Looking back from the vantage point of 1890, Marshall (p. 148) judged that "until recently, economists said little on the subject [of demand and consumption], because they really had not much to say that was not the common property of all sensible people."

Although classical theorists recognized the role of demand in price determination, they did not integrate demand and preferences and lacked a precise system to account for the influence of demand on prices. For instance, when Mill used what amounted to a model of pure exchange to study the influence of demand on international relative prices, he could offer precise comparative statics only for two good numerical examples with unit elasticity import demand functions and inelastic export supply. Mill recognized how special his assumptions were, but without them he could only assert the amorphous principle that equilibrium prices depend on relative demand. Indeed, Mill acknowledged that multiple or even a continuum of international trade equilibria were possible, but had no way of integrating this fact into his theory.[2]

Mill had no theoretical apparatus capable of analyzing the potentially complex influence of demand on prices. The neoclassical movement did. Marshall, having developed demand and supply curves in the 1870s, represented import and export demand functions with offer curves, thus effortlessly and concisely reproducing Mill's theory of international trade [Marshall (1879)]. But where Mill had been precise only in the case of unit elastic demand curves, Marshall could analyze equilibrium price determination under any specification of demand. On the vexed indeterminacy question, Marshall established, once and for all, that multiple equilibria could not be excluded as pathological; he also identified a broad class of cases in which equilibrium is unique. Marshall did not dispute Mill on any point of economic substance; the importance of Marshall's contribution lay in the graphical apparatus itself and the new topics—stability, the dependence of comparative statics on demand elasticity, etc.—that could now be addressed.

The inadequacy of the classical vocabulary became manifest in the controversies surrounding William Thornton's late-1860s criticisms of market equilibrium theory. In chapter 2, we considered Thornton's argument that the forces of supply and demand can leave wage rates indeterminate. Accompanying his particular claims about the labor market, Thornton

---

1. See, among other places, Mill (1848, bk. 4, chap. 4., especially sec. 3).

2. Mill's analysis essentially took its final form in Mill (1852, bk. 3, chap. 18, particularly sec. 6–8). See Appleyard and Ingram (1979) and Chipman (1979) for rival interpretations. The fact that Mill has been understood in such different ways is further testimony to the unwieldiness of his analytical system.

issued more sweeping criticisms of supply and demand theory. Thornton's numerous lines of attack included two examples that communicated his most celebrated points and provoked wide commentary.[3] The first example uses the same logic that Thornton applied to factor markets: when quantities supplied and demanded coincide and do not vary as a function of price, the equilibrium price is indeterminate.[4] In the second example, firms have a reservation price $\bar{p}$ below which they are unwilling to offer output for sale and at which they offer some fixed, strictly positive quantity $q_s(\bar{p})$. If the demand at $\bar{p}$, $q_d(\bar{p})$, is less than $q_s(\bar{p})$, Thornton supposes that $q_d(\bar{p})$ units will be traded at price $\bar{p}$. Consequently, if $q_d(\bar{p})$ is strictly less than $q_s(\bar{p})$, supply will not equal demand (see figure 4.1). What is more, if new firms with the same reservation price $\bar{p}$ enter the market, $q_s(p)$ will increase to $q'_s(p)$ but the market price and quantity traded will remain unchanged, thus violating the classical precept that increases in supply lower price and raise quantity. Mill responded by conceding the practical importance of Thornton's case for the labor market. As a matter of general theory, however, Mill held that supply and demand analysis remained substantially unthreatened. Thornton's examples, Mill pointed out, hinge on either inelastic demand curves, which in large markets Mill believed to be "the next thing to impossible," or supply functions demonstrating an "extraordinary" jump [e.g., from 0 to $q_s(\bar{p})$ in fig. 4.1] [Mill (1869, pp. 637, 638)].

Mill's response was effective on its own terms, but the controversy was symptomatic of a lack of analytical detail in classical equilibrium theory. What conditions exactly were necessary for supply and demand equilibrium to exist, for equilibria to be determinate, and for comparative statics to have "normal" properties?

Thornton's criticisms of supply and demand theory, like Mill's theory of international price determination, were later reexamined graphically. In fact, Thornton's case was the subject of the first application of supply and demand curves, by Fleeming Jenkin in 1870. Jenkin redescribed Thornton's first example as arising from supply and demand curves that overlap over a range of prices. Like Mill, he did not deny that the example was theoret-

3. See Thornton (1869, bk. 2, chap. 1) for his analysis of supply and demand theory. As it happens, it was also Thornton who pointed out to Mill the potential indeterminacy of equilibrium prices in models of international trade (discussed above); see Mill (1865, bk. 3, chap. 18, sec. 6).

4. As Negishi (1986) has emphasized, the pertinent example of the second edition of *On Labour* [Thornton (1870)] has demand as a strictly decreasing function of price; and Thornton may have intended this to be the case in the first edition as well. Negishi (1986, 1989a) offers an interesting disequilibrium interpretation of Thornton's meaning [see also Ekelund and Thommesen (1989) for a rebuttal, and Negishi (1989b)]. Note though that Thornton's intentions have little bearing on the robustness of mainstream classical theory; even if Negishi is correct, subsequent discussion took demand in Thornton's first example to be completely inelastic. It may even be, as Negishi suggests, that Thornton's most interesting points—e.g., that most exchanges occur during the process of market equilibration and at nonequilibrium prices—are not addressed by his famous examples.

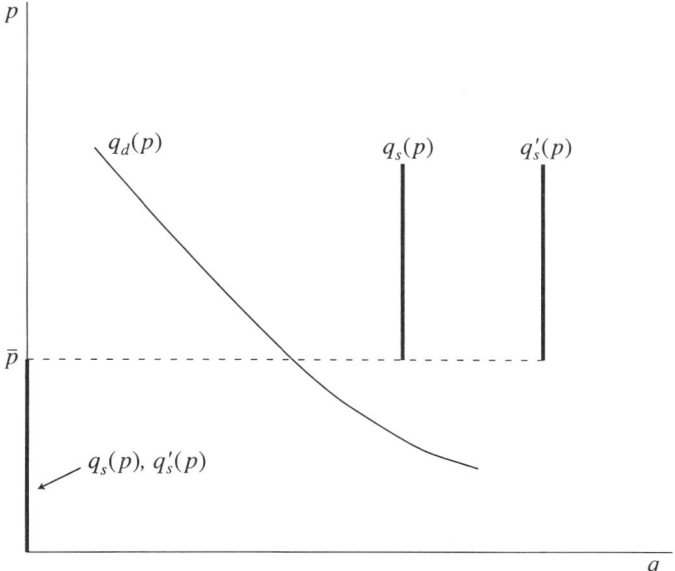

Figure 4.1 Thornton's attack on supply and demand theory

ically possible, but his graphs make the indeterminate case appear unusual [Jenkin (1870, p. 85)]. Jenkin also hinted at a more contemporary response to Thornton's second example. Thornton's and many other verbal treatments of supply and demand implicitly treated demand and supply as single-valued functions of price. It is this presumption, combined with the presence of a reservation price, that forces the discontinuity of supply at $\bar{p}$ in Thornton's example. Jenkin's graphs, on the other hand, depict producers as having perfectly elastic supply at $\bar{p}$, allowing $\bar{p}$ to be an equilibrium.[5] Whatever Thornton's view of this proposal might have been, perfectly elastic supply curves became an easy thought once supply and demand graphs were integrated into economic analysis. The mutual consistency of market clearing and the comparative statics conclusion that increases in supply need not lower prices could then be established. Again, it is not that the proto-neoclassical position differed substantially from Mill's; both acknowledged Thornton's examples as theoretical possibilities and minimized their practical likelihood. But the neoclassical innovations shed fresh light on Mill's position, and new ideas, such as perfectly elastic supply, became easier to conceive.

5. See Jenkin (1870, fig. 11 and its legend); see also p. 92 for a discussion of elastic supply curves. Thornton also drew a passing comment from Marshall, who argued that Thornton had not grasped that indeterminacy is a larger phenomenon that occurs whenever supply and demand curves overlap. See Whitaker (1975, vol. 1, p. 155).

4.3 Hedonism and its advantages

Even if a formal theory of supply and demand can be said to solve various problems in classical economics, when unaccompanied by a utility-based explanation of individual behavior, market equilibrium theory made little headway on its own. Jenkin remains an obscure footnote in the history of economic theory. It was Marshall's utility-based *Principles of Economics* that became the textbook of English economics, not his graphical *The Pure Theory of Domestic Values* or *The Pure Theory of Foreign Trade*, which contain little and no utility theory, respectively. And Walras, to take a last example, held off publishing his general equilibrium theory until he could incorporate a marginal utility derivation of demand functions.[6] Why could supply and demand theory not stand on its own?[7]

Before addressing this question, let's look briefly at hedonism's role in early neoclassical theory. Consumption and each increment in consumption were identified with an experience of pleasure or utility; agents in the theory aim to maximize the extent of this experience. Optimality requires the now-familiar condition that expenditures be allocated so that the marginal utility of each good consumed at a positive level is proportional to its price. In English versions of early utility theory, this condition was sometimes awkwardly expressed as the requirement that consumers equate the gain in utility from spending an additional unit of money on goods consumed in positive quantities to the "marginal utility of money," Marshall's term for the maximal gain in utility obtainable from an (infinitesimal) increase in money income.

The core assumption of early utility theory was the quasi-physiological rule that the marginal pleasure of each good falls with increases in the amount consumed. Along with the requirement—sometimes explicit, sometimes implicit—that utility is additively separable ("independent") across goods, diminishing marginal utility implies that indifference curves are strictly convex. Consumers facing fixed prices therefore have unique utility-maximizing consumption choices. Diminishing marginal utility and additive separability further imply that increases income are allocated to all goods consumed in positive quantities; consequently, increases in income must lower the marginal utility of money.

One of the appeals of early neoclassical utility theory and of diminishing marginal utility in particular was that earlier intuitions about consumer choice could be formalized and elaborated. Consider the desire for variety.

6. According to Jaffé (1976), Walras added marginal utility theory as an explanation for the demand functions that had already appeared in prototypes of his general equilibrium model. On the non-Jevonian character of Marshall's early writings, see Hicks (1976).

7. Various later attempts, such as Cassel's, to eliminate utility maximization and take demand functions as primitive gained few adherents. And in the contemporary era, Samuelson's (1938a) proposal to place assumptions directly on demand functions has not displaced preference-based accounts of demand.

A concentration of expenditure on a small number of goods is likely to be nonoptimal since the marginal utility per dollar of purchased goods would fall below the marginal utility per dollar of goods not purchased.[8] The ostensible fact that rising wealth leads to increases in consumption diversity could also be easily explained. Early theory supposed that the marginal utility of a good would eventually decline to a very low level, often to zero. Hence, if expenditures were artificially restricted to a fixed number of goods, the marginal utility of money would decline to zero as income increases. An optimizing agent should therefore progressively introduce new goods into his or her consumption portfolio, even though the marginal utility of the first units consumed is low relative to the marginal utility of the first units of goods already being consumed. In stories such as this, everyday phenomena found parallels in the formal language of utility theory, extending the theory's scope and adding to the confidence of its adherents.

Utility theory also offered philosophical appeal. The economic theory of utility maximization was, and remains, the model extension of philosophical utilitarianism into the social sciences; in England in particular, it therefore inherited an immediate authority. More generally, utility theory provided a mathematical link between unobstructed market activity and the satisfaction of individual welfare. Economists had long backed the liberal view that individuals were the best judges of their own interests, and that in the absence of countervailing considerations individuals should be granted wide latitude in decision making. Utility maximization was one, if not the only, way of providing a foundation for this position. In the theory, agents do not accept traditional or customary restrictions on what goals to pursue; they have specific individual interests and privileged knowledge of what those interests are. The case for agents being given authority over the allocation of resources gained immediate support.

The intuitive and philosophical dimensions of utility theory would have been attractive under any circumstances; but the greatly expanded formal role of demand in price determination made the need for a foundation for demand functions acute. Theoretically desirable features of demand and equilibrium had to be derived rather than simply posited; otherwise the conclusions of a demand-based theory would have seemed ad hoc. Classical theorists had earlier explained long-run prices through production costs, which in turn were rooted in the exogenous facts of technology. Changes in technology were assumed to be slow enough that prices would roughly track relative costs; in terms of the theory, therefore, prices were predictable and stable through time. Correspondingly, a theory emphasizing the long-

---

8. See Jevons (1871, p. 63) and Marshall (1890, p. 155). Jevons took care to credit the principle of preference for variety to Nassau Senior, thereby portraying utility theory as providing rigorous foundations for the conventional wisdom of earlier economists: "[diminishing marginal utility] is the real law which lies at the basis of Senior's so-called 'Law of Variety.'"

term role of consumer demand had to explain why demand is neither erratic nor unpredictable.

Tethering demand theory to a physiological account of the production of pleasure secured this goal. Jevons, the founder of English neoclassicism, argued that utility theory and the principle of diminishing marginal utility gave "a physical groundwork [to economics], showing its dependence on physiological laws."[9] When he considered labor supply, for example, Jevons detailed the natural "laws" governing the disutility of labor, noted various trade-offs—between discomfort and the physical weight a worker carries, between fatigue and the speed of work—and even conducted experiments to determine maximum labor efficiency (1871, pp. 191–197). Jevons took the fact that maxima could be objectively estimated, and that agents routinely make such calculations on their own, as illustrations of "the physical basis of political economy." Jevons could therefore claim a grounding in exogenous, natural facts and a temporal stability to economic phenomena comparable to what the classicals had achieved.[10]

Hedonism simultaneously opened the door to differential calculus, allowing economic behavior to be characterized mathematically as a system of equations. The neoclassical movement needed explicit arguments that its models were closed, and the simple mathematics of counting equations and unknowns provided an appealing solution. Seeing calculus as the native language of science, the new theory happily assumed that utility functions were differentiable. Consumer behavior could then be described by a set of first-order conditions in which the number of equations equals the number of endogenous variables. Although not a watertight argument for determinacy—an equality of equations and unknowns is neither necessary nor sufficient for determinacy—this reasoning at least provided a rudimentary case.

Consumption expenditure decisions were only the first application of this technique; setting out first-order conditions and comparing the number of equations and unknowns pervaded early neoclassical economics. Jevons's *Theory of Political Economy* alone contains a wealth of examples. In addition to his account of labor efficiency, Jevons modeled how a Robinson Crusoe figure should parcel out fixed stocks of resources among competing uses and how to calculate the optimal consumption plan for a ship with a limited food supply and a trip of uncertain duration (1871, pp. 68–71, 76–78). The appeal of the method to Jevons was clear. In reference to a typical maximization problem, Jevons remarked that "the theory of utility gives, theo-

---

9. Jevons (1871, p. 65). Prior to the dominance of Marshall's symmetric treatment of demand and supply, the need for an exogenous factor underlying consumer choice was particularly pressing. In Jevons's awkward sequential schema, cost affects price only indirectly, through changes in the level of production; "value depends solely on the final degree of utility" (1871, p. 160).

10. The achievement was short-lived however; see section 5.3.

retically speaking, a complete solution of the question" (1871, pp. 68–69); he went on to show that the appropriate system of first-order conditions provides a determinate algebraic answer.

Once consumption decisions were presented as maximization problems, it was easy to extend determinacy arguments to the interacting consumption decisions of multiple agents. In the foundational general equilibrium models of both Jevons and Walras, counting equations and unknowns again furnished the key reasoning; when added to consumers' equilibrium conditions, the requirement that markets clear provided enough equations to pin down relative prices. The two models differ somewhat in the details. Walras's reasoning, subsequently more influential, took the indirect route of first aggregating consumer decision making into market demand functions and then setting demand equal to supply. Jevons formally dealt with economies with only a small number of agents and analyzed equilibria by considering simultaneously the first-order conditions of all agents in the model; market clearing was imposed by defining utilities in terms of agents' net trades.[11]

The ability of early utility theory to provide foundations for demand can be seen in Jevons's replies to Thornton's criticisms of supply and demand theory. Given when he was writing, it was natural for Jevons to respond to Thornton's position; as it happened, Jevons's discussion of Thornton served as his first "illustration" of the determinacy of market exchange. Jevons ascribed the difficulties raised by Thornton's examples to the fact that the quantities of goods do not permit "continuous variation"; that is, Thornton's consumers purchase relatively large, discrete units of commodities.[12] When goods are indivisible, Jevons's calculus-based equilibrium conditions cannot be applied. Jevons conceded that in such cases a purely economic determination of the value of goods is not possible and he acknowledged Thornton's criticisms. But when goods are divisible, Jevons believed that his counting of equations argument provided a perfectly adequate demonstration of determinacy.

Jevons's rebuttal to Thornton had clear advantages over Jenkin's graphical treatment. Algebraic arguments for determinacy are generalizable to an arbitrary number of goods or individuals; graphical arguments are restricted to two or three dimensions. More fundamentally, by deriving demand functions from utility maximization, Jevons's theory offered arguments for the attributes of demand functions. Jenkin's and the early

11. See Walras (1874, pp. 153–172) and Jevons (1871, pp. 95–103, 113–117). The weakness of Jevons's framework was that he defined relative prices implicitly as ratios of net trades and not as separate variables, making extensions to arbitrary numbers of goods and agents difficult.

12. See Jevons (1871, p. 106); see also pp. 122–124. Jevons may also have been referring to the discontinuity in Thornton's second example.

Marshall's procedure of taking demand functions as primitive precluded this possibility.[13]

Edgeworth exemplified the early neoclassical confidence in the power of maximization and determinacy analysis to disentangle subjects that had been the preserve of what was now considered untutored folk wisdom. With characteristic assurance, Edgeworth set out an examination paper in one of the appendices to *Mathematical Psychics*, "Social problems to be solved without mathematics," consisting mostly of simple maximization problems. The moral, of course, was that without the neoclassical formalizations, precise, determinate solutions were unobtainable.[14] Marshall was at one with Edgeworth on this point, despite Marshall's occasional downplaying of formal mathematics. Marshall was hardly contemptuous of the literary style of earlier, classical writing; he was a master of the same genre. But Marshall's belittling of the common-sense observations of preneoclassical demand theory, mentioned earlier, meets with Edgeworth's attitude toward the mathematically illiterate. Marshall's verbal transcriptions of the utility calculus established the same theoretical closure as the algebraic originals.

4.4 Early neoclassical accounts of deliberation

From the ordinal point of view, early utility theory is distinctive in that it tried to explain how individuals make decisions and deliberate about their choices. A specific causal mechanism, the pursuit of pleasure, was said to underlie standard consumption choice and provide a criterion by which agents decide which actions best promote their well-being. This prescriptive dimension additionally accounts for why agents in the theory cannot be permanently stymied and complain that they do not know how to choose. If introspection does not directly reveal the technology of pleasure, experimentation will detect what goods deliver pleasure and in what amounts. The theory thus provided a rationale for what is now known as *completeness*, the assumption that an agent, when facing any two options, will weakly prefer at least one of the options to the other.[15]

Pleasure maximization also explained why agents choose in accordance with transitivity. The reduction to a single psychological dimension implies scaled and thus transitively ordered magnitudes (whether scaled cardinally or ordinally, I leave open for now). The convexity of indifference curves,

---

13. The determinacy of equilibrium may have been the high point of early neoclassical reasoning from first principles, but not all desirable properties of demand could be derived satisfactorily. Early neoclassical economists took it as obvious that the demand for a good should be decreasing in the good's price, even characterizing this property as a law. But the law could not be demonstrated from utility maximization alone; other devices, such as a constant marginal utility of money or additively separable utility functions, had to be added.

14. See Edgeworth (1881, appendix 2), "On the importance of hedonical calculus."

15. As is standard, I use expressions such as "*x* is weakly preferred to *y*" to mean that *x* is either strictly preferred or indifferent to *y*.

although not a characteristic of rationality narrowly construed, was also readily accounted for; it follows from additive separability and diminishing marginal utility.

Hedonism's account of deliberation can be seen in the way the term "utility" was used. At least in the first years of neoclassical economics, utility functions signified psychological processes and were not simply convenient tools for summarizing preferences. Jevons was well aware that, as a matter of definition, one could "call any motive which attracts us to a certain action pleasure, and that which deters pain." But the consequence would be that "it becomes impossible to deny that all actions are prompted by pleasure or by pain" [Jevons (1871, p. 31)]. Utility would then lose its power as a psychological hypothesis; it would not explain how choices come to be ranked. For example, Jevons recognized that "higher" pleasures, such as those that appeal to moral considerations, often trump material pleasures. But opting for the higher pleasures does not give agents more "utility" in Jevons's terminology, since such decisions are not made by comparing quantities of pleasure and pain. In fact, only within the realm of standard economic goods, which call upon the "lowest rank of feelings," is the hedonic calculus an accurate psychology.[16]

Curiously, the early neoclassical account of rational deliberation allowed for a rich description of irrational ("incorrect") behavior. In the case of static choice over consumption goods, the potential for irrationality remained circumscribed. If, perhaps due to having not yet sampled a good, an agent consumes a good at a level where its marginal utility per dollar is lower than the marginal utility of money, the consumption of such a good will be decreased; adjustment continues until the marginal utility per dollar is aligned with the marginal utility of money. Consumption experiences thus show individuals whether their consumption choices are utility maximizing and, if not, how to correct them.[17]

The more impressive account of irrationality came in the theory of intertemporal choice. Early utility theory held that under ideal circumstances individuals should not discount future pleasures since lifetime welfare is maximized only when current and future utility are given equal weight. But agents are not "constituted in this perfect way"; future utility is usually less influential than current pleasure [Jevons (1871, p. 76)]. Agents effectively multiply future utility by a discount factor less than 1; the extent of the difference between 1 and the discount factor measures an agent's irrationality. The degree of irrationality is not fixed or given, however; it varies according to an agent's self-control and willingness to consider the

16. Marshall also held that there were incommensurable classes of desires. "Much of the best work of the world has no price, and evades altogether the economic calculus" [Marshall (1890, p. 81)].

17. But see Cooter and Rapoport (1984) on Pigou's treatment of the consumption errors of the poor.

future and therefore fluctuates through time.[18] Indeed, the very fact that agents discount the future, that they are not perfectly constituted, is itself reason to suspect that behavior might subsequently change: reflection on an irrationality can lead to a revision of conduct.

The critical feature that allows behavior to be labeled as less than rational is the specification of decision-making criteria that are independent of agents' realized actions. Most economic theories of choice designate *some* patterns of behavior as irrational; it is the abundance of prescriptive rules that distinguishes early neoclassical from current-day utility theory.

To see a final example, consider the early neoclassical theory of choice under uncertainty. Following the Bernoullian tradition, Jevons and Marshall held that the utility of each prospective consumption good should be weighted by the (objective) probability that the good will be consumed. The first-order conditions characterizing rational choice therefore require that marginal utilities are also weighted by probabilities.[19] Since these marginal utilities are decreasing functions of quantity, it follows that gambling at fair odds is "an economic blunder."[20] Once again, the early neoclassical theory argued that there are correct and incorrect ways to make decisions.

4.5 Ordinal preference theory

The contrast between nineteenth century hedonism and the ordinal theory of the last 60 years is stark. Where Jevons and Edgeworth were committed to pleasure seeking as a theory of economic motivation, Hicks and Samuelson, and later Arrow and Debreu, rejected all but the sparsest psychological details. An agent's ordinal preference for option x over y simply indicates the relative ordering of the options and not that x delivers some specified multiple of y's pleasure or even that pleasure is the motivating factor. Indeed, contemporary economics relinquishes any attempt to specify the motives underlying choice. Preference itself is now the primitive element of consumer theory; there is no need to peer into agents' psyches. Utility functions consequently assume a more limited role. Instead of denoting the psychological state corresponding to a consumption choice, a utility function is now simply an index of preference. Utility "does not *measure*

18. Marshall's position, which began near Jevons's [see Marshall (1890, p. 153)], changed somewhat through time. By the final edition of the *Principles*, discounting was nearer to being a trait than a flaw; but an agent's discount rate could still vary over time [Marshall (1920, p. 120)]. As we will see in chapter 7, conflicting positions on the irrationality of discounting persisted in later decades. The portrayal of discounting as irrational, and therefore not fixed through time, reaches back to Smith's view that the sacrifice of a future pleasure for a lesser amount of present pleasure is a failure of prudence and self-command. See Smith (1759, pp. 189, 215).

19. See Jevons (1871, pp. 75–78), who simply begins with first-order conditions, and Marshall (1890, pp. 153–154).

20. Marshall (1890, p. 741). Marshall allowed that the intrinsic pleasure of gambling might outweigh what would otherwise be a loss in expected utility.

but merely *indicates*" preference [Allen (1933, p. 111)]; its continuing use is due only to its concision as a mathematical object.

What meaning does ordinalism ascribe to preference? In some formulations, preference is understood solely as choice. To say that an agent strictly prefers x to y is equivalent to saying that x is systematically chosen over y. In Arrow's words, the basis of ordinal theory "is the strict link that is established between preferences and choices under certain hypothetical conditions. Thus, the phrase 'x is preferred to y' means 'if x and y were offered, x would be chosen'" (1952, p. 47).

Most versions of ordinalism attach at least a minimal psychological content to the interpretation of preference. Aware that depriving preference of all connection to an agent's well-being would endanger even the simplest welfare conclusions, an agent's preference of x over y is usually taken to imply that the agent believes his or her goals are better served by x than by y.

Indeed, contemporary theory usually goes further and supposes that an agent's choices reveal the best way, given the information available, to serve the agent's welfare. A single psychological direction running from "worse off" to "better off" is thus attributed to preference. But any broader theory of how an agent comes to order and prioritize goals remains off limits. The prescriptive content of preference theory is thus sharply restricted; since only the observation of choice can show what promotes an agent's welfare, preference theory itself cannot resolve any decision-making dilemmas.

At the same time, the new psychological agnosticism has freed economics from hedonism's narrow view of economic behavior. Although Jevons, Marshall, and Edgeworth had allowed that agents can be motivated by altruism and other "higher" principles, they placed such behavior outside the domain of economic analysis. In contrast, the agents of contemporary preference theory can, in Gary Becker's words, be "selfish, altruistic, loyal, spiteful, or masochistic" and can be influenced by "moral and ethical considerations" (1993, pp. 386, 390). Economic analysis has ingeniously pursued the strategies that rational agents can employ to serve this expanded menu of ends; Becker's own analyses of the economics of the family exhibit many notable examples. It is true that expansions such as Becker's are more the exception than the rule. The principal theories of market behavior continue to characterize behavior as narrowly self-interested, possibly due to a conviction that narrow self-interest, in fact, preponderates. But here too, ordinalism has admitted new interpretations of behavior. Early utility theory imagined that agents make consumption decisions by comparing the pleasure delivered by alternative consumption choices. In the new view, self-interested choice is still thought of as optimizing—in the sense that an agent chooses only options that are (weakly) preferred to all others—but the rationale underlying choice is left as a black box. Preferences over foodstuffs, to take a simple example, can be based as legitimately on an agent's allegiance to religious dietary law as on considerations of sensory pleasure. Thus, although the rejection of hedonism would introduce new problems, preference theory became manifestly more realistic. And the assumption that individuals choose rationally, without the contrivance of hedonistic comparisons, has its own philosophical appeal, drawing on long-standing liberal descriptions of individuals as deliberating self-seekers, and, going further back, to the idea that reason can settle all questions of value. Hedonism in comparison was a narrow and confining psychology.

Compared to the effortless tractability of utility functions, the first mathematical characterizations of ordinal preferences were clumsy. Hicks and Allen, in their foundational papers of 1934, represented preferences with indifference curves or surfaces. Hicks used two-dimensional graphs, and such an approach obviously cannot go beyond three dimensions. Allen's use of the slopes of the tangent planes supporting indifference curves could at least be generalized to an arbitrary number of dimensions. But Allen's technique is algebraically unwieldy; indeed, Allen's original paper only provided an explicit treatment for two and three dimensions. It is also mathematically awkward, when there are three or more goods, to impose restrictions (integrability conditions) on the slope functions that guarantee that preferences are transitive. And by supposing that a unique hyperplane supports each point on an indifference surface, Allen's method could only describe differentiable preferences.

Utility functions were simply too mathematically useful to be sacrificed. They therefore continued to be used, but now with the proviso that only properties preserved under monotonically increasing transformations of utility functions should be imposed as assumptions. Since monotonic transformations maintain the ordinal ranking of any set of options, these attributes are sometimes called the *ordinal properties* of a utility function. The prime case of a *non*ordinal property is diminishing marginal utility, the property of a utility function u that $\partial^2 u(x)/\partial x_i^2 \leq 0$ for all x and all goods i. To confirm that diminishing marginal utility is nonordinal, apply the monotonic, twice-differentiable transformation F to u. Differentiating twice, we have

$$\frac{\partial^2 F(u(x))}{\partial x_i^2} = F''(u(x))\left(\frac{\partial u(x)}{\partial x_i}\right)^2 + F'(u(x))\frac{\partial^2 u(x)}{\partial x_i^2}. \qquad (4.5.1)$$

Hence, if $F''(u(x))$ is positive and of sufficiently large magnitude (and since $F'(u(x))$ is nonnegative), the sign of $\partial^2 u(x)/\partial x_i^2$ and (4.5.1) can differ. The assumption of diminishing marginal utility therefore became a prime target of the ordinalists.

In terms of generality, beginning with utility functions reverses the advantages and liabilities of the indifference curve approach. Preferences need not be differentiable, but since a utility function assigns a real number to each consumption bundle, and numbers are transitively ordered, the assumption of transitivity is preordained. More embarrassingly, taking utility functions as primitive, even if the entire set of ordinal representations rather than a single function is posited, ill suits a theory supposedly eschewing utility as a foundational entity. (In fact, ordinalists of the 1930s and 1940s rarely employed the entire set of ordinal utilities; they only considered the utilities generated by differentiable transformations F, thus illicitly importing at least some nonordinal properties, e.g., continuity, into their analysis.)

Binary relations masterfully solved these difficulties. Taking the binary relation of weak preference, which I denote by $\geq$, as primitive allows all of the attributes of preferences—completeness, transitivity, convexity, even differentiability—to be stated as independent assumptions; they are not an automatic by-product of the mode of analysis. For an arbitrary pair of objects a and b, the relation $\geq$ allows a to be strictly preferred to b, denoted $a \succ b$, when $a \geq b$ and not $b \geq a$; b to be strictly preferred to a, defined analogously; a and b to be indifferent, $a \sim b$, when $a \geq b$ and $b \geq a$; and a and b to be unranked when not $a \geq b$ and not $b \geq a$. Since weak preference relations express (at most) the relative ranking of options, they are a natural match with ordinal theory.

Some of the first ordinalist writings in the 1930s took the relative ranking of pairs of options as their starting point, but it was not until axiomatizations of choice under uncertainty in the 1940s and early 1950s that it became common to place assumptions directly on binary preference relations. The chapter on consumer theory in Debreu's *Theory of Value* (1959) sums up this line of development. All restrictions on preferences are placed on the binary relation and treated as separate conditions, resulting in a theory of great simplicity and generality. A direct assumption of transitivity replaced the messy integrability conditions of the indifference curve approach. The assumption of diminishing marginal rates of substitution in the Hicks-Allen approach or the assumption that utilities are quasi-concave (expressed in the 1930s and 1940s with a maze of determinants) was replaced with the concise condition that the set of consumption vectors preferred to any fixed vector is convex.[21] The differentiability assumption, imposed in most prewar utility theory, could easily be omitted (and in fact was shown to be unnecessary for the existence of equilibrium).[22]

Most significantly, Debreu provided intuitive sufficient conditions for preferences to be representable by utility functions. The very existence of

21. In referring to convex indifference curves as showing diminishing rather than increasing marginal rates of substitution, I am using the terminology of Hicks (1939b) rather than Hicks and Allen (1934). Hicks, it should be noted, ultimately signed on to the binary relation approach; see Hicks (1956).

22. The differentiability assumption in preference theory has rarely been the object of internal challenge; thus, there is an asymmetry relative to the historical debates over marginal productivity, discussed in chapter 2. The question therefore arises: can the nondifferentiability of utility functions, like the nondifferentiability of production functions, lead to an indeterminacy of equilibrium? It can, but in an exchange economy, indeterminacy requires the presence of unlikely (i.e., measure-zero) endowments. And in contrast to models of production, exchange economies do not change their endowments through time; hence, the improbability of such endowments is a convincing reason to dismiss the phenomenon.

a utility function thus became an attribute of preferences rather than a mathematical or psychological presupposition. In the wake of this result, utility functions have gained a renewed respectability. A genuinely ordinalist foundation for utility functions is available on demand; hence utility need not signify anything above and beyond its recapitulation of preference information.

Indeed, the primacy of preference over utility has become so firmly ingrained in the economist's mind that curious reversals of terminology have entered the current-day vocabulary. For example, the expression "agents are utility maximizers" may betray a lingering allegiance to early neoclassical dogma; but officially at least it is understood as an abbreviation for the assumption that agents have complete, transitive, and continuous preferences, not as a reaffirmation of nineteenth-century hedonism.

4.6 Ordinalism versus cardinalism

The ordinal revolution rebuilt the foundations of preference theory, not its applications. Indeed, since ordinalism holds that it is perfectly legitimate to use utility functions to summarize preferences, consumer behavior could be described by the same maximization problems studied prior to the 1930s. The mathematical derivation of demand functions therefore remained unchanged, and demand-based analysis could proceed as before. For example, study of the determinacy of equilibrium, though inherently demand theoretic, continued to employ the same method of counting equations and unknowns. (This technique has been refined extensively since the 1930s, but the new developments are unrelated to the changes brought by ordinalism.) Even the innovations in positive consumer theory historically associated with ordinalism have nothing intrinsically ordinalist about them. One can derive the Slutsky restrictions on demand functions, for example, independently of whether or not one imputes to utility functions any psychological content beyond their ordinal properties.[23]

What then was wrong with early utility theory? The ordinalists directed their fire both to what they saw as unnecessary psychological theorizing and to the psychological conclusions that early neoclassical economists seemed to infer from choice behavior.

The main psychological doctrines at issue were hedonism, which I have already discussed, and cardinality. A cardinal comparison is a gauge of the intensity of preference measuring one gain or loss in well-being relative to another, for example, a judgment that a 5% increase in income yields, say, two-thirds of the psychic gain of a 10% increase in income.

Formally, let (x^1, x^2, x^3, x^4) denote four consumption vectors such that x^3 and x^4 are not indifferent, and let $c(x^1, x^2, x^3, x^4)$ be the ratio of the change

---

23. See, for example, Samuelson's derivation of the Slutsky equation (1947, pp. 100–107), where the remark that the Slutsky restrictions are not dependent on the choice of utility index (p. 104) is logically distinct from the substance of the proof.

in an agent's well-being due to a move from x^1 to x^2 relative to the change in well-being due a move from x^3 to x^4. The quantity $c(x^1, x^2, x^3, x^4)$ is the *cardinal comparison* corresponding to (x^1, x^2, x^3, x^4); it is easiest to think of $c(x^1, x^2, x^3, x^4)$ as the comparative judgment an agent makes when reflecting on two different changes in consumption. Any utility representation u of an agent's preferences implicitly defines a system of cardinal comparisons: for each (x^1, x^2, x^3, x^4), simply interpret

$$\frac{u(x^1) - u(x^2)}{u(x^3) - u(x^4)}$$

as the ratio $c(x^1, x^2, x^3, x^4)$. I therefore say that a function u *represents* an agent's cardinal comparisons if, for all (x^1, x^2, x^3, x^4) with x^3 and x^4 not indifferent,

$$\frac{u(x^1) - u(x^2)}{u(x^3) - u(x^4)} = c(x^1, x^2, x^3, x^4).$$

It is easy to show that two utility functions u and v representing the same ordinal preferences also represent the same cardinal comparisons if and only if there is some positive constant a and some constant b such that $u(x) = av(x) + b$ for all x. Following a common tradition, I call transformations from v to u of this form positive *linear* rather than positive *affine* transformations.

Nonlinear transformations of utility therefore change the implied ratios of utility differences: if u and v differ by a nonlinear monotonic transformation, the $c(x^1, x^2, x^3, x^4)$ functions implied by u and v will not be the same. Hence, two agents with identical ordinal preferences can diverge in their cardinality judgments.

Since cardinal comparisons are preserved only under linear transformations, cardinality is a nonordinal property of utility. But cardinality is just one form of nonordinality; the ordinalists claimed that *any* assumption of a nonordinal property of utility is illegitimate. Thus, in addition to hedonism and cardinality, ordinalism implicitly addressed a third psychological proposition—that agents experience at least some psychological sensations that go beyond ordinal preference.

Ordinalism has no direct stake in disputing the truth of any of these three psychological theories. One can believe that agents are hedonists and cardinalists, without also asserting (falsely) that cardinal comparisons of pleasure are required for economic decision making or that intensities of preference can be deduced from choice behavior. Indeed, denying the third psychological doctrine would be foolhardy. In the intellectual fervor of the 1930s, some may have been near to such extreme psychological skepticism, but ordinalism need not embrace such a position.

It is the link between these psychological positions and economic behavior that ordinalism takes issue with. Two objections were made: an indisputably correct claim that cardinal and other nonordinal properties of utility functions cannot be deduced from preferences, and a more contro-versial assertion that consumer theory should not use cardinality or other nonordinal properties as theoretical primitives. The strongest defense of the latter position argues that psychological theorizing going behind preference is an unnecessary excursion outside the domain of economic analysis. Hicks, in *Value and Capital* (1939), provided the classic statement. After demon-strating that cardinal judgments cannot be inferred from preferences, Hicks conceded that there could well be other grounds "for supposing that there exists some suitable quantitative measure of utility, or satisfaction, or desiredness . . . If one is a utilitarian in philosophy, one has a perfect right to be a utilitarian in one's economics. But if one is not (and few people are utilitarians nowadays), one also has the right to an economics free of utili-tarian assumptions" (1939b, p. 18). Hicks located the advantage of ordinal preference theory in its generality, in the fact that ordinalism is not tied to utilitarian psychology or to any other detailed model of decision making. If economists care only about preferences, why make assumptions on any-thing deeper? To do so only risks stepping into the quagmire of psycho-logical controversy. I take up Hicks's pivotal defense of ordinalism in detail in section 4.8.

Once the primacy of preferences is accepted, the prohibition of assump-tions on nonordinal properties of utility follows as an explicit result. According to the ordinalists, nonordinal properties of utility—most promi-nently, judgments of cardinality—are banned because they are unnecessary to a characterization of choice behavior. By extension, ordinalism also rules out any concrete theory of economic motivation.

The impugning of assumptions placed on anything other than choice behavior has led ordinal theory to group together all nonordinal charac-teristics of preferences. In reality, the three psychological doctrines above, though often considered interchangeable, plainly are not. Consider first hedonism and cardinalism. Cardinalism allows assertions such as "a move to x^1 is twice as preferred as a move to x^2," "a move to x^1 is twice as good as a move to x^2," or "a move to x^1 provides twice as much welfare as a move to x^2." None of these statements imply that pleasure is the basis of the com-parison. Similarly, a hedonist who is not a cardinalist can say "a move from x^1 to x^2 gives more pleasure than a move from x^3 to x^4," while remaining agnostic about the exact ratio of the two pleasure differences. Of course, hedonism provides the most common psychological justification for cardi-nality; and in order to be plausible, cardinality requires some account of how agents make judgments of preference intensity. Psychologically, there-fore, cardinality and hedonism are natural partners.

But the claim that agents have some more-than-ordinal reactions to choice is far weaker, and more credible, than the specific assumption of car-dinality: a person can be incapable of making precise cardinal comparisons, but still experience some sensations that, when represented in utility func-tions, are not invariant to monotonic transformations.

4.7 Diminishing marginal utility and psychological concavity

The distinction between cardinality and the broader possibility of extra-ordinal psychological judgment is no arbitrary construct. The core hypothesis of early neoclassical psychology—diminishing marginal utility—fits precisely into this space. Diminishing marginal utility is a weaker assumption than cardinality since an agent who experiences diminishing marginal utility need not also have the (cardinal) capacity of knowing the precise rate at which marginal utility declines. But diminishing marginal utility, since it is not preserved by monotonic transformations of utility functions (see section 4.5), is nevertheless a more psychologically demanding assumption than what is permitted by full-strength ordinalism.[24] Moreover, diminishing marginal utility becomes much more believable when any supposed links to cardinality are eliminated. The idea that further increments of a good are progressively less satisfying draws immediate introspective recognition. But who can claim to always know, what percentage of the utility of the nth unit of a good is delivered by the n-plus-first unit?

A formal treatment of the comparative strength of nonordinal properties of utility functions allows more precision. Earlier I pointed out that an agent's cardinal comparisons—a function $c(x^1, x^2, x^3, x^4)$—single out the set of positive linear transformations of a utility function u representing $c(x^1, x^2, x^3, x^4)$. Any linear transformation of u represents $c(x^1, x^2, x^3, x^4)$ and, conversely, any utility v representing $c(x^1, x^2, x^3, x^4)$ is a positive linear transformation of u. One advantage of using a set of utility functions to represent an agent's cardinal comparisons is that the properties held by all utility functions in this set are precisely the properties that a particular $c(x^1, x^2, x^3, x^4)$ entails, and the common properties of a set of utility functions can be slightly more convenient to analyze than the function $c(x^1, x^2, x^3, x^4)$ itself. For example, a linear transformation will multiply all first derivatives of a function by the same constant. Hence, for any x^1 and x^2 and any pair of functions u and v differing by a linear transformation,

$$\frac{\partial u(x^1)/\partial x_i}{\partial u(x^2)/\partial x_j} = \frac{\partial v(x^1)/\partial x_i}{\partial v(x^2)/\partial x_j},$$

where subscripts denote goods and superscripts continue to distinguish among consumption vectors. Cardinality therefore implies that, for any x^1

24. It is therefore unsurprising that although cardinality assumptions were challenged sporadically prior to the 1930s, diminishing marginal utility was the last tenet of early utility theory to be discarded officially. For this reason, no doubt, Hicks (1939b, pp. 20–22) placed diminishing marginal utility high on the list of features of early utility theory that had to be excised. According to High and Bloch (1982), Austrian economists of the early twentieth century also adopted the common pre-Hicksian mixture: they held to diminishing marginal utility but claimed that cardinality was inessential. See also Robbins (1932) on the ordinalist inclinations of the Austrian tradition.

and x^2, an agent experiences a unique ratio of the marginal utilities of any two goods.

More importantly, sets of utility representations provide a straightforward way to compare the strength of assumptions on the psychological sensations accompanying preference: one assumption is stronger than another (i.e., it requires utility representations to obey more properties) if the set of utility functions preserving the assumption is smaller. The strongest assumption on an agent's sensations is therefore that the set of psychologically accurate utility representations consists of only one function. In this (wholly implausible) psychology, only one utility number corresponds to each possible consumption experience. The weakest assumption for the type of agents we are considering (those with utility representations) is the ordinalist supposition that the set of acceptable utility representations consists of all monotonic transformations of some utility function for the agent. Cardinality lies between these extremes. Note that using sets of utility representations compares the strength of psychological assumptions relative to a fixed preference relation. It does not compare assumptions *on* preferences; it compares assumptions about what extra-ordinal sensations an agent has *given* his or her preferences.[25]

Now consider a preference relation that is representable by a utility function u with diminishing marginal utility, that is, with $\partial^2 u(x)/\partial x_i^2 \leq 0$ for all x and i. A glance at equation 4.5.1 reveals that any concave, strictly increasing, differentiable transformation F of u preserves this property. Hence, since any linear transformation is concave, the set of utility representations with diminishing marginal utility is larger (in fact, strictly larger) than the set of increasing linear transformations of any fixed u with diminishing marginal utility. On the other hand, for any utility with diminishing marginal utility, there are some monotonic transformations that will eliminate diminishing marginal utility. Hence, the assumption that agents experience diminishing marginal utility stands as a psychological compromise between cardinality and complete skepticism about nonordinal properties.[26]

Next, consider the assumption that utility is concave. Concavity extends the early neoclassical idea of diminishing marginal utility to all proportional changes in consumption, not just changes in the consumption of each good taken singly. Beginning at some consumption vector x, concavity requires that the increases in utility that come from adding proportions of any arbitrary vector y to x progressively decrease in size (and decreases in utility progressively increase in size). In early neoclassical theory's context of addi-

---

25. Although I am considering the strength of psychological assumptions, and not the question of interpersonal comparability, I am following the general approach put forward in Sen (1970, chap. 7 and 7*).

26. It is not, of course, the case that diminishing marginal utility, seen as an assumption on preference relations, is a weaker assumption than cardinality; but the ability to report diminishing marginal utility (when an agent's preferences can be represented by a u with $\partial^2 u(x)/\partial x_i^2 \leq 0$ for all x and i) is a weaker psychological requirement than cardinality.

tively separable utility functions, concavity is equivalent to diminishing marginal utility. But when utilities of goods are interdependent, diminishing marginal utility is a weaker assumption than concavity, that is, there are utility functions with negative own-second derivatives that are not concave. With two goods, for example, if increases in the consumption of one good increase the marginal utility of the other good by a sufficiently large amount, then progressive increases in the consumption of both goods (fixing the ratio of the two goods) can lead to larger and larger gains in utility even when the marginal utility of each good treated separately diminishes. Additive separability became steadily less popular with time, but theorists continued to assume diminishing marginal utility rather than concavity. This omission is only a technical oversight; both formally and intuitively, concavity generalizes diminishing marginal utility to the broader class of functions.

I will use the term *psychological concavity* to indicate that, at any point x, the set of psychologically accurate utility representations of preferences on any line intersecting x is nonempty and consists of all of the concave utility representations of the agent's preferences on that line. In other words, agents experience diminishing marginal utility in all directions but no further nonordinal psychological reactions: on any line, any concave function representing the agent's preferences is psychologically accurate. Psychological concavity takes an agent's psychological responses to consumption on lines as primitive; but it follows that the set of psychologically accurate utility functions (defined on the entire consumption set) is precisely the set of all concave utility representations. Just as in the case of diminishing marginal utility, this set of utility representations is smaller than the set of all ordinal utilities but larger than the set of linear transformations of some particular concave utility representation. (This follows from the fact that any increasing concave transformation of a concave function, and hence any increasing linear transformation, is concave.) Psychological concavity is therefore another example of a psychological compromise between cardinality and ordinality.

4.8 Should assumptions be placed only on preferences?

The ordinalist demonstration that the propositions of consumer theory depend only on properties of preferences has sometimes swelled into a claim that preferences are, in Samuelson's (1947, p. 91) words, "defined only by behavior." Rhetoric such as this was common in the 1930s and 1940s; it is difficult to know what to make of it. Conceivably the behavioral basis of ordinalism was intended as a claim that consumer theory could be reduced to observed facts themselves. Given the spotty empirical record of axiomatic consumer theory, such a move would leave ordinal theory on weak ground [see Sen (1973)]. And ordinalists (including Samuelson) have themselves emphasized the idealized, hypothetical quality of rational, preference-based choice. Hicks was particularly clear on this point.

Preference theory "proceeds by postulating an *ideal consumer*, who by definition is only affected by current market conditions, and asks how we should expect such a consumer to behave ... Actual consumers will be affected by other things than by current prices, and their behaviour need not therefore always satisfy the tests of consistency."[27]

The idealized nature of consumer theory is one reason why evidence of deviations from rationality has not yet overturned standard ordinalist theories. Ordinalism, like early utility theory, can accept the irrationality of momentary behavior as long as irrationalities are revised in situations of sufficient importance and given enough time. Empirical exceptions to rationality must be systematic, persistent, and of sufficient scale before they can corrode theoretical consensus. Hicks, it should be noted, did not believe that preference theory should avoid all contact with reality: ultimately an account of how and why the behavior of an ideal consumer differs from his or her empirical counterpart's would have to be provided. But even if such an explanation were at hand, consumer theory would still be an abstraction, not an accumulation of uninterpreted facts: observations of choice by themselves cannot capture the dependence of rational behavior on the external prerequisites of deliberation (e.g., on the "weightiness" of a decision or on having "time to think").

It is more likely that talk of basing consumer theory on behavior was simply shorthand for the familiar ordinalist principle that assumptions in consumer theory should be applied to preferences rather than deeper-level psychological phenomena. Is this principle justified? One defense draws on the informal behaviorism that has been commonplace in economics since Jevons; psychological assumptions going beyond choice, it is said, have the defect of having to rely on introspection for justification. Unlike choice behavior, which can be verified objectively, the testimony of introspection is inherently undependable. Unfortunately, ordinalism is subject to a similar charge. Rationality assumptions on ordinal preferences do not rest on empirical confirmation; they stand or fall on their plausibility and their congruence with psychological understandings of the ideal of consistently ordered choice.

The behaviorist will counter that although the assumptions of ordinal theory have not in fact been confirmed empirically, they are at least subject to empirical confirmation; cardinality and diminishing marginal utility, in contrast, must rely on introspection, which renders them unfalsifiable. But even granting that introspection does not provide evidence as trustworthy as choice behavior, it cannot be ruled out of scientific court. One person's introspection appears to others (including scientists) in facial expressions,

---

27. Hicks (1956, pp. 17, 18). As time went on, Hicks became firmer on this point. "The consumers who figure in econometric demand theory are not real people, though they may often look like real people. They are idealisations. It is therefore quite in order to assume they have fully formed scales of preference, or [ordinal] utility functions. One can do this, without implying that real people have anything of the sort." Hicks (1981, p. xiii).

heart rates, narrative accounts, and in direct affirmations of subjective feelings. Even if introspection itself is subject to behaviorist challenge, its observable manifestations cannot be. Psychology has its own perfectly respectable raw material, and inferences about the psychological states lying behind choice therefore cannot be rejected a priori on methodological grounds.

In fact, nonchoice information, far from being opposed to ordinalism, is essential to its intelligibility. Lionel Robbins, the forefather of ordinalism in England, held that it was crucial to preference theory that "we do in fact *understand* terms such as choice, indifference, preference, and the like in terms of inner experience." That agents pursue ends is fundamental to economic behavior; yet "the idea of an end . . . is not possible to define in terms of external behaviour only" [Robbins (1935, pp. 87–88)]. Robbins took agents' expectations of the future as the central instance of a nonbehavioral attribute that is indispensable to understanding behavior as rational. But since later theories of state-contingent choice have raised the possibility that expectations can be inferred from choice, Robbins's position needs to be developed further.

Understanding agents as goal seeking or rational lies in the meaning imputed to behavior. Hidden characteristics of decisions allow for multiple explanations of behavior, however; without limits on interpretation, any observed decision can be construed as rational. Faced with evidence of preference reversal for example—an agent strictly preferring a to b at one time and then b to a later—economists have a variety of explanatory options at their disposal. The agent could have received new information, or have preferences that depend on the date of consumption, or have preferences defined over intertemporal consumption vectors—the last case allowing preferences over future consumption to be affected ("reversed") by interim consumption, as when agents prefer variety.

Having *some* leeway to pick among interpretive frames of reference is crucial. Consider, for instance, an agent who at first chooses to retain $20 rather than purchase an umbrella to be delivered in a week's time but then, on the next day, reverses his preference and orders the umbrella. Consumption in the intervening 24 hours had proceeded as previously contracted and no new information about the likelihood of rain was received. After observing this behavior, a decision theorist accuses the agent of temporal inconsistency. The agent retorts that although he had no new information about the chance of rain, he discovered that bright sunshine is now considerably more likely, and the umbrella, he declares, can serve as a delightful parasol. He informs the decision theorist, who had taken pains to distinguish the umbrella next week when raining from the umbrella next week when dry, that the theorist's model employs an insufficiently refined state space, conflating sunny and cloudy-but-dry skies. His behavior is therefore rational. The credibility of this story hinges on interpreting the agent as pursuing a goal—being shielded from the sun—that someone might in fact seek. The necessity of distinguishing the plausible frames of references and goals from the implausible thus eliminates uninterpreted choice as a stand-alone test of rationality.

The determined opponent of nonchoice information may object that in standard economic environments there is a universal frame of reference against which rational choice postulates can be tested directly: each good should be distinguished by the date and completely specified state of nature at which it appears. Under this approach, a hallmark of general equilibrium theorizing, a vector of consumption goods is a plan indicating what good is consumed at every future date and under every possible resolution of all uncertainty. Even if agents only have partial information about which state will occur, they nevertheless have well-defined preferences over the set of all state-contingent consumption vectors; it will then be impossible to argue that we have omitted any relevant attribute of the objects of choice. This suggestion founders on the impossibility of constructing a complete description of a state of the world. There will always be some informational noise not yet incorporated into the description of states—from sunspots, say—that is rich enough to distinguish spuriously between any pair of observations of choice. By repeatedly refining an agent's choice set with respect to such states of nature, any pattern of behavior can be rationalized as consistent.[28] This pointless procedure would rob preference theory of any empirical content; avoiding vacuity therefore requires restrictions on the definition of the objects among which agents choose. But how can a spurious distinction among commodities be separated from legitimate distinctions? Only introspection or other nonchoice information can insist that the umbrella when there are sunspots is really the same commodity as the umbrella when there are no sunspots, while still permitting discrimination between rain and lack of rain and between sun and clouds. Choice alone is mute.[29]

Ordinalism cannot therefore fault early utility theory on the grounds that all nonbehavioral components of preference theory are inherently illegitimate. Outside of the Alice in Wonderland absurdity of completely specified states of nature, even tests of ordinal preference theory presuppose interpretive rules.

In addition to avoiding empirical vacuity, the interpretation of behavior, and not the mere statement of axioms on behavior, explains why some

28. That is, if we elicit an agent's preference between state-contingent options with respect to some description of a state space and later observe an apparently contradictory preference, we can construct a new, more elaborate state space that can distinguish the initial from the latter observation by some interim event (a sunspot).

29. For different arguments to similar ends, see Anand (1993) and Sen (1973, 1993). Anand argues that latitude to choose a frame of reference guts transitivity axioms of any content. But agents who obey transitivity (under some fixed interpretation of the objects of choice) are immune to the extractions of wealth that can accompany intransitivity (see section 4.10); thus, as long as theorists are prohibited from repeatedly changing the frame of reference, transitivity does place restrictions on choice. Sen argues that menu-dependent choice—e.g., someone who, out of politeness, always chooses the second-largest slice of pie—need not be irrational under the appropriate interpretive frame of reference, despite violating internal consistency on the standard interpretation of what constitute the objects of choice.

actions should be considered beneficial to an agent's well-being and others harmful. Real-world behavior, even if it were always rational, cannot identify the logic of agents' interests. Since preference theory rests on the normative and positive appeal of the goal-pursuing agent, arguments for why standard assumptions on preferences characterize rationality must be articulated. As we will see when we turn to the justification of specific assumptions, interpretations that go beyond the mere statement of patterns of behavior appear repeatedly.

The behaviorist justification of ordinalism can therefore be dismissed. But what of the more promising defense of ordinalism, the claim that psychological theorizing only decreases the generality of preference theory, discussed briefly in section 4.6?

The dividing line between economics and psychology is inevitably somewhat arbitrary; and little is gained from disputing exact contours. The perimeters of preference theory are in any case now well established internally; even if economics once took the psychological mechanics and intensity of preference to be worth explaining in their own right, it no longer does so.[30] For the sake of argument, let us agree that consumer theory should not attempt to explain or predict psychological phenomena that are unrelated to preference. It follows that psychological theory superfluous to the logic of an assumption on preferences should be avoided. If, to take the leading example, the capacity of agents to make cardinal comparisons does not help justify any important feature of preferences, then consumer theory has no reason to retain it, even if there is evidence to support it. But when a psychological explanation contributes to the rationale underlying an assumption, omitting the explanation undermines the broader theory. Indeed, disavowing all psychological theory is tantamount to leaving assumptions without any justification whatsoever; given how frequently the "realism" of neoclassical preference theory has been subject to both internal and external challenge, such a methodology is particularly imprudent.

Contemporary preference theory occasionally constructs arguments in favor of assumptions, but the process has remained piecemeal and casual. Often, justifications simply amount to informal assertions that an assumption embodies the ideal of rationality; loose appeals to the aesthetics of axioms are also common.[31] Rationality is undoubtedly at the heart of contemporary ordinalism; but since its possible component parts differ in how easy they are to justify, the definition of rationality is open to dispute. Some features are inseparable from action that is welfare enhancing, some not. Detailed and explicit defense of particular assumptions on preferences

30. In the 1930s and 1940s even ordinalists disagreed about the proper scope of consumer theory. Samuelson's revealed preference theory (1938a) began with rationality postulates on individual demand functions rather than preference relations.

31. See, for example, Kreps (1988, p. 3): "What constitutes a 'good' set of axioms? . . . axioms should be basic, primitive, intuitive, qualitative, etc."

is therefore necessary.[32] Explanation of the logic underlying a rationality assumption should not be confused with the empirical accuracy of that assumption. Debates over the latter have certainly been extensive; but, as I have stressed, a full defense of a theory of rational action must marshall arguments for why, given enough time and decisions of sufficient importance, agents should accept some courses of action and reject others.

The significance of formal arguments in favor of assumptions parallels the rationale for basing economics on a theory of preference. The theory of market behavior as a whole loses generality by explaining consumer behavior as preference driven. There are always other routes, in addition to preference, that could lead individual or market demand to have any specified set of attributes. For instance, as discussed in section 4.3, demand functions could be taken as primitive and simply assumed to generate determinate equilibria. The power of neoclassicism lies in the fact that it argues for demand having certain characteristics rather than simply presupposing those characteristics. If a preference-based approach to demand theory is justified, then preference theory itself can employ psychological assumptions that narrow the theory's scope: benefits in plausibility and explanatory power can outweigh small losses in generality.

Ordinalist methodology can be partially vindicated in cases where there are multiple psychological paths to an assumption on preferences. As we will see in the case of convexity, there is then no need to commit to one particular psychological mechanism. Rationales for attributes of preferences thus have a different logical character than the attributes themselves. Moreover, even when there is only one available rationale for an assumption, theoretical acceptance of that rationale can be tentative; further explanations may be forthcoming. These considerations do not lessen the need to provide *some* rationale, nor do arguments in favor of assumptions therefore have diminished status. The credibility of an assumption in all cases hinges on the union of the coherent arguments that can be amassed in its favor.

The methodological considerations discussed here hardly establish that early neoclassical psychology is indispensable to consumer theory. The ordinalist rejection of early neoclassicism can still be defended if it can be shown that the specific psychological assumptions employed in earlier theory were somehow unnecessary or ill advised. But discrediting early neoclassical psychology is not enough. Completing the ordinalist program requires showing that the early neoclassical rationales for the assumptions of consumer theory can be replaced with rationales of greater generality. A verdict on the success of this program cannot be rendered in the abstract. I turn now to a detailed look at specific assumptions, first convexity and then transitivity and completeness.

32. One decision-theoretic assumption, the independence assumption of expected utility theory, has been defended and criticized in detail. For samples, see Green (1987) and Raiffa (1968, chap. 4, sec. 9).

4.9 Convexity versus diminishing marginal utility

The most penetrating rearguard challenge to the ordinal revolution charged the new theory with failing to provide a convincing rationale for the convexity of indifference curves. Frank Knight was the key proponent of this view; but D. H. Robertson, who had the advantage of hearing the criticisms Knight provoked, argued the case more carefully. Robertson was well aware that demand functions could be derived from indifference curves and wisely gave ground to the ordinalist demonstration that cardinal comparisons cannot be deduced from consumption decisions. But diminishing marginal utility was a different matter:

> It seems much more in accordance with what we know of our own minds to suppose that the consumer has direct experience of the diminishing utility of particular things, and proceeds from this basis to work out when necessary his marginal rates of substitution, than to suppose that his primary experience is of a complicated network of ratios.[33]

Following Knight, Robertson also examined a specific example of how diminishing marginal utility had been used in earlier theory: the explanation of why increases in income, by diminishing the marginal utility of goods already consumed, expand the variety of goods purchased (see section 4.3).

> If, when my income increases, I decide to add champagne to my diet, the cause of my action is surely inadequately, even though not incorrectly, described by saying that there has been a [shift to a point on a higher indifference curve with a different] marginal rate of substitution between champagne and other things. For in the straightforward case nothing has happened on the side of the champagne, hitherto a stranger to my home, to account for the change. The cause of change must lie on the side of the other things, i.e. in the diminution of their marginal utility. Why not say so?[34]

Robertson distorted the ordinal position somewhat. Contrary to the first quotation, agents in ordinal theory do not need to have a primary experience of their marginal rates of substitution; indifference curves denote preferences, not psychological processes. But this is a quibble. Robertson's main message, that the psychological accuracy of diminishing marginal utility can justify its status as a postulate of consumer theory, is unaffected. More damaging to Robertson's cause was his belief that diminishing marginal utility necessitated the use of cardinal utility functions (1951, p. 18). Convinced by the ordinalist claim that one had to be either a cardinalist or an ordinalist, Robertson felt compelled to argue that cardinality was central to the plausibility of Marshallian thinking. "I do not deny that a reasonable account

---

33. Robertson (1951, p. 26). Knight (1944) is marred by misunderstandings, for example, the claim (p. 297) "if absolute marginal utility did not decrease, no determinate apportionment of income would be made." Perhaps because of Bishop (1946), Robertson avoided these lapses [as did Knight (1946)].

34. Robertson (1951, p. 27). The "straightforward case" refers to situations where the utility of each good is independent of the consumption levels of other goods.

of the behavior of the individual consumer can be built up without [cardinality utility's] aid; though I think that even in this field an analysis which makes use of it gives a more persuasive account of what really happens than one which does not" [Robertson (1957, p. 87)]. Taken at face value, Robertson's claim is dubious. Far from justifying the convexity of indifference curves or any other assumption in the positive theory of riskless choice, cardinality only burdens preference theory with an extraneous claim that agents can scale the intensity of their feelings. (On the other hand, cardinality can serve a substantive purpose in the theory of risky choice; see section 5.1.)[35]

Robertson's position would therefore be strengthened by discarding cardinality and insisting only on diminishing marginal utility—or, better, psychological concavity. Psychological concavity trivially implies that indifference curves are convex. Moreover, psychological concavity captures the entirety of the intuition behind diminishing marginal utility while eliminating all superfluous psychological structure. Still, a concavity explanation of indifference-curve convexity is not of maximum generality. As Robertson understood, there can be agents who do not experience diminishing marginal utility, whether generalized to psychological concavity or not, but whose indifference curves are convex. This follows from the fact that a convex agent's preferences can be represented by a nonconcave utility function; it could be that the set of psychologically accurate utility representations contains some of these nonconcave functions.[36] These possibilities did not trouble Robertson; he felt that theory could ignore the abstractly conceivable but practically remote cases.

Diminishing marginal utility is informally validated every time a student opens an economics textbook. Even though official theory does not provide rationales for convexity, introductions to economics cannot afford to be so cavalier. Textbooks typically resort to a defense that combines diminishing marginal utility (despite its purported link to cardinality) and an implicit assertion that the utility of goods is additively separable [see e.g., Samuelson (1976, chap. 22, including appendix)]. Psychological concavity, without abandoning the intuition behind diminishing marginal utility, obviates the need for such an analytically painful return to the past.

35. Knight (1944) also defended the early neoclassical status quo on the grounds that cardinal utility functions make interpersonal comparisons of welfare possible. See also Cooter and Rapoport (1984). As we will see in chapter 6, however, cardinality's empirical inaccessibility meant that it was of limited use in normative economics as well. But even if cardinality had provided foundations for welfare economics, the behavioral and welfare aspects of preference theory remain analytically distinct. Psychology is relevant to consumer theory only as motivation for behavioral predictions, not for its welfare implications.

36. There are also continuous, convex preference relations that cannot be represented by concave utility functions. Psychological concavity thus restricts the set of permissible convex preferences. The excluded preferences are somewhat exotic, however. Smooth, strictly convex preferences defined on compact sets always have concave representations. See Mas-Colell (1985, chap. 2) for further discussion.

Even pared of the link to cardinality, the case for psychological concavity as an *axiom* of consumer theory falls short. Psychological concavity is only one plausible argument for the convexity of indifference curves. There are other rationales that make no direct assumption that the intensity of satisfaction diminishes. Consider the following explanation, which I base on a brief remark of Kenneth Arrow, and which Arrow credits to Tjalling Koopmans.[37] Suppose that consumption purchases are held for some short period of time, say from time 0 to time T, and that an agent's welfare can be represented as the sum (integral) of the utility achieved at each moment from 0 to T. An agent holding a consumption vector z chooses the within-period temporal path of how z is consumed so as to maximize this sum. Observe that an agent with the commodity vector $\lambda x + (1 - \lambda)y, 0 \le \lambda \le 1$, could consume λx in λT of the time units and $(1 - \lambda)y$ in the remaining $(1 - \lambda)T$ time units. Hence, $\lambda x + (1 - \lambda)y$ can be consumed in temporally compressed replicas of how x and y would be consumed if only x or y were held. If x and y are indifferent, and the agent's utility at each instant from 0 to T is independent of the consumption at other instants, $\lambda x + (1 - \lambda)y$ will leave the agent at least as well off as x or y, that is, indifference curves are weakly convex. Furthermore, if there are superior ways of breaking down $\lambda x + (1 - \lambda)y$ into elementary consumption activities or of rearranging the timing of consumption, indifference curves will be strictly convex.

This reasoning is hardly ironclad; it supposes that preferences obey additivity and independence conditions.[38] But given the seemingly indisputable counterexamples to convex preferences—for example, the agent who is indifferent between red and white wine but strictly prefers either to a convex combination of the two—no amount of theoretical casuistry can conjure an a priori proof of convexity. After pronouncing the general rule, the early neoclassicals themselves would readily acknowledge the exceptions to diminishing marginal utility. For present purposes, however, the truth of indifference curve convexity is irrelevant. To validate the ordinalist claim to greater generality, it suffices to identify a credible scenario in which convexity does not rely on a justification rooted in diminishing marginal utility.[39]

37. Arrow (1951a). See Grodal (1974) for a formal treatment.

38. Also, the assumption that an agent's overall welfare can be represented as the integral of a momentary utility function can be understood as a move to cardinality. If only utilities with the integral form are psychologically accurate, then the set of psychologically accurate utility functions is unique up to a positive linear transformation. Of course, agents need not think out the implied cardinal comparisons. The assumption that the utility of individual commodities is additively separable is analogous; see the discussion of Fisher in section 5.4.

39. There are other, less convincing rationales for convexity. Hicks (1939b, p. 23) argued that a lack of convexity implies that there are some consumption bundles that an agent will not purchase at any price vector. Why this consequence is so unintuitive remained unexplained in Hicks's account.

The present position is nevertheless different from the standard ordinal view. Contemporary theory, when it argues for convexity, usually just rephrases the assumption, as in statements that agents prefer average over extreme bundles. Here, I have elaborated explicit rationales. Each of these rationales has the drawback of restricting the psychological mechanics behind preference; but if all such restrictions were rejected, we would be left without any articulated arguments for the convexity assumption.

Although Robertson's rationale for convexity cannot claim privileged status, the early neoclassical explanation of the introduction of new consumption goods fares somewhat better. Ordinalism's direct assumption of convexity does not, at least by itself, address the diversity issue. Agents with Cobb-Douglas preferences, for example, consume all goods at all income levels, and it is easy to construct convex agents who consume fewer rather than more types of goods as their income increases.[40] An ordinalist can, of course, just assume that preference relations happen to generate the income diversity correlation; but a bare assumption would not explain the relationship. On the other hand, the Robertson–early neoclassical argument implicitly supposes that agents consider the utility of goods not yet consumed to be independent of current consumption; and independence assumptions do not enjoy the plausibility they once had. More importantly, the issue of consumption diversity no longer seems so momentous; the absence of a contemporary account therefore amounts to only a minor failing.

4.10 Transitivity and completeness

Hedonism, by identifying preference with an ordered psychological scale, provided an easy rationale for why choice is transitive.[41] Given its anti-hedonist origins, ordinalism could not invoke this argument; but other explanations, at least as convincing and untainted by ties to any model of preference generation, can substitute. Suppose that an agent *substantively* violates transitivity: that is, suppose there are three options, x, y, and z, such that x is weakly preferred to y and y is weakly preferred to z, but where z is strictly preferred to x. Using the notation introduced in section 4.5: $x \succeq y, y \succeq z$, and $z \succ x$.[42] If, in addition, $x \succ y$ and $y \succ z$, the agent faces an immediate difficulty when choosing from the set $\{x, y, z\}$. Since each of the three

40. Convexity does provide a partial explanation of consumption diversity at a given income level: if a strictly convex agent can exactly afford two indifferent bundles, each including positive amounts of some good not included in the other bundle, there will always be a strictly preferred and affordable bundle containing positive amounts of all of the goods in both bundles.

41. The material in this section is analyzed more formally in Mandler (1998).

42. A slightly more general definition of a violation of transitivity is that the following conditions hold: $x \succeq y, y \succeq z$, and not $x \succeq z$. Of course, given completeness, the two definitions coincide.

choices is dominated by another option, preference maximization does not provide clear decision-making guidance.

The combination of $x > y$, $y > z$, and $z > x$ is an example of a strict preference cycle; more generally, a preference cycle occurs whenever there is a finite chain of options, $x^1, \ldots, x^n$, with elements 1 through $n - 1$ each strictly preferred to the next element in the chain and with the nth element strictly preferred to the first. Clearly, strict preference cycles preclude there being an undominated element in the set $\{x^1, \ldots, x^n\}$; in fact, for choice from finite sets, an absence of strict preference cycles (known as *acyclicity*) ensures that undominated elements exist.

Violations of transitivity need not lead to strict preference cycles; and therefore it is possible that an agent with intransitive preferences will have recourse to an undominated option. But under mild conditions, substantive intransitivities will lead to a second, more dramatic difficulty. In addition to the pure choices x, y, and z, suppose that the agent is also choosing among quantities of money (or some other good for which more is always strictly preferred to less). A completely described option then has the form $(w, \$_w)$, where $\$_w$ is a quantity of money. Assume that a mild form of continuity holds: if $(w, \$_w) > (v, \$_v)$, then for all $\$_\varepsilon > 0$ sufficiently small, $(w, \$_w - \$_\varepsilon)$ $> (v, \$_v)$. Suppose that the agent is again asked to choose from a set of three options $\{(x, \$_x), (y, \$_y), (z, \$_z)\}$ for which a substantive intransitivity holds; specifically, let $(x, \$_x) \geq (y, \$_y)$, $(y, \$_y) \geq (z, \$_z)$, and $(z, \$_z) > (x, \$_x)$. Imagine that the agent chooses one of the three options—for example, $(y, \$_y)$— either as an attempt to resolve the impasse that occurs with strict preference cycles or because $(x, \$_x) \sim (y, \$_y)$ and $(y, \$_y)$ is therefore undominated. If offered the option of switching to $(x, \$_x)$, the agent, weakly preferring $(x, \$_x)$ to $(y, \$_y)$, will not object. Since $(z, \$_z)$ is strictly preferred to $(x, \$_x)$, there is some positive quantity of money, say $\$_\varepsilon$, such that $(z, \$_z - \$_\varepsilon)$ is still preferred to $(x, \$_x)$. Choice in accord with intransitive preference can thus lead to an outcome unambiguously worse than one of the options originally available.[43]

An agent's loss of wealth can sometimes take a striking form, known as the *money pump*. Suppose that the agent's substantively intransitive preferences over x, y, and z are independent of the amount of wealth held. That is, for all values of $\$_w$, assume that $(x, \$_w) \geq (y, \$_w)$, $(y, \$_w) \geq (z, \$_w)$, and $(z, \$_w) > (x, \$_w)$. Assume also that the continuity condition continues to hold. If the agent begins with an arbitrary status quo choice, say $(z, \$_{\bar{w}})$, and uses his or her preferences to guide choice, the agent will willingly switch to $(y, \$_{\bar{w}})$, then to $(x, \$_{\bar{w}})$, and then to $(z, \$_{\bar{w}} - \$_\varepsilon)$ for some $\$_\varepsilon > 0$. Because of our independence assumption, this sequence of exchanges can be iterated, and

---

43. Similar drawbacks occur when the agent initially chooses $(x, \$_x)$ or $(z, \$_z)$. Also, under slightly strengthened assumptions, the agent's difficulty does not disappear if he or she refuses to switch between options that are indifferent. Beginning from $(y, \$_y)$, the agent can be offered $(x, \$_x + \$_{\varepsilon'})$, with $\$_{\varepsilon'} > 0$ small enough that there exists a $\$_\varepsilon > 0$ such that $(z, \$_z - \$_\varepsilon) > (x, \$_x + \$_{\varepsilon'})$.

more and more wealth extracted from the agent. (The maximal amount that can be extracted may be bounded, however.)

The root difficulty with intransitivity is that it prevents the ordering of even a finite number of options from best to worst. Sequentially, therefore, an agent's willingness to use binary preferences as a basis for choice can be turned against the agent and he or she can be manipulated into losing wealth. Faced with this pitfall, intransitive agents have excellent grounds for concluding that their behavior is irrational and should be revised. Preference itself may be scrutinized, or the connection between preference and choice broken. The conclusion of irrationality requires an interpretation going beyond choice; it rests on an understanding of agents as preference pursuing and wealth seeking. Note though that unlike the hedonistic rationale for transitivity, the present arguments only identify defects of intransitive preference; they do not explain how to arrive at a consistent ranking.

Completeness is more delicate. The original Jevonian theory guaranteed that an agent could (weakly) order any pair of choices. Even economic goods that at first appear qualitatively dissimilar will reveal themselves, after experimental sampling, as homogeneous agglomerations of pleasure. Predicaments of choice therefore do not arise. The rejection of hedonism eliminated the reduction of economic goals to pleasure; agents could now be motivated by any welfare-enhancing goal. But despite allowing a multiplicity of ends, ordinalism does not say how agents weigh conflicting goals. It does not prescribe an optimality criterion—or a method for resolving decision-making dilemmas—and therefore does not explain choice. Instead, ordinalism simply assumes that agents are endowed with some way of identifying which options are most preferred.

There is certainly a broad range of ways in which agents do rank choices. Individuals often make consumption decisions in order to further images of themselves that they find appealing. Decision making can then be conducted according to the preestablished associations of goods; when choosing a drink, for example, these connotations can make it easy to decide among mineral water, cola, or papaya juice. Some economic decisions are made according to abstract principles, for example, someone who judges that unrestrained materialism is disallowed and that, following religious law, one must give 10% of income to charity. And some decisions, of course, are made on the basis of physical gratification alone—that chocolate, say, is preferred to vanilla because it delivers more sensory pleasure. In all these cases, agents invoke some consideration—cultural, spiritual, or hedonistic—that specifies which end should be pursued; the optimal decision can then be determined.

When individuals are torn between rival criteria, however, they can face intractable decision problems. Economic examples range from the trivial to the serious. Should I go to an action movie or buy an edifying but dull book? Should I retire to an urban townhouse or a tranquil country home? Should I spend more on myself or contribute money to protect the environment? Such choices set one aim against another, and even after thorough examination, an agent may not be able to find a higher-order criterion that settles the conflict. Certain choices, the ones that do not require any ranking of incommensurable criteria, may be clear: in the case of choosing houses, for example, perhaps the spacious homes are preferred to the cramped, whether in the country or the city, and perhaps one architectural design is preferred to another. But how should the hard decision pitting urban life against rural tranquility be made? Out of necessity, an agent may have to choose. But since there is no reason why necessity or compulsion should generate a preference ordering, agents may have to turn to other decision mechanisms. One strategy is to hold to the status quo until an unambiguously better choice—one that is ranked relative to the status quo—becomes available; when it is feasible, this procedure has the attraction of avoiding changes that an agent might later regret. Randomizing among unranked options is another strategy. Decision making will then be unstable through time; agents can make and then reverse decisions, perhaps repeatedly, without receiving in the interim any relevant new information.

These examples treat disparate criteria as entirely noncomparable. Incompleteness need not take so extreme a form. Suppose an agent always values more of each of two goods, x_1 and x_2. Furthermore, at a certain consumption level of the two items, say x, suppose the agent prefers additional units of x_1 if no more than $g_x^- > 0$ of x_2 (per unit of x_1) are offered in exchange, and prefers a loss of a unit of x_1 when receiving at least $g_x^+ > 0$ of x_2 in exchange. Assume $g_x^+ > g_x^-$. The set of strictly preferred bundles is pictured as the lightly shaded area, P_x, in figure 4.2. (This set could have a smooth boundary, but the kink will simplify an interpretation provided later.) The agent has at least some preference judgments trading off one good against the other. The agent's incompleteness lies in the fact that the set of bundles that the agent regards as weakly inferior to x does not equal the complement of the set of strictly preferred bundles. Some bundles, such as y, remain unranked relative to x: these points are indicated as the darkly shaded areas of the figure.

The standard ordinalist rebuttal to apparent instances of incompleteness is to interpret agents' choices as their preferences. An agent who sticks to a status quo choice is revealing a preference for the status quo, and an agent who alternates between choosing x over y and y over x, or who randomizes between x and y, is revealing indifference between the options. Indeed, ordinalists argue that even when an agent claims to be unable to rank two options, a preference exists and can be elicited. To find the ranking of x relative to y, give the agent the option of choosing between the two; if neither is chosen, the agent is assigned a third option v ranked lower than either x or y (see fig. 4.2). The admitted preference of x or y over v can thus be used to force a choice between x and y. If x is repeatedly chosen over y, we infer that $x \succ y$; if, after many trials, x and y are each chosen on some occasions, we conclude that $x \sim y$.

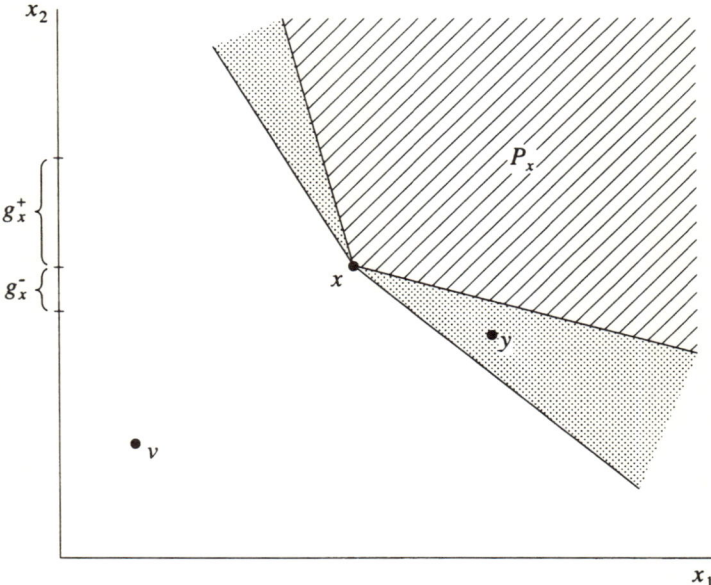

Figure 4.2 Partially incomplete preferences

The difficulty comes in interpreting such choices as indicating preference or indifference. Suppose that we repeatedly induce our agent to choose between pairs of consumption bundles, using v, if necessary, as a threat. The agent may want to hold to the status quo when not offered a preferred alternative, but suppose we prevent this behavior by not including the bundle just chosen in the pair next offered. (Let actual consumption occur after the entire sequence of observed choices; to ensure that each decision is taken seriously, suppose the agent is unaware of which choice will determine his or her final consumption.) We observe that x is chosen over y on some occasions, and y over x on other occasions. Under a completeness interpretation, the agent is indifferent between x and y. Now consider another consumption bundle, z, strictly preferred to x, but unranked relative to y [see fig. 4.3 (where, for simplicity, I have set $g_y^+ = g_x^+$ and $g_y^- = g_x^-$)]. The agent dependably chooses z over x, but displays the same vacillation between y and z as between y and x. Again interpreting vacillation as indifference, an intransitivity appears: $x \succeq y$, $y \succeq z$, but $z \succ x$.

The potential for incompleteness to appear as intransitive choice occurs systematically.[44] If a and b are two psychologically unranked choices, it is plausible that a and some sufficiently small amount of money will also be

---

44. Raz (1986, chap. 13) argues that the primary test of incompleteness is the appearance of intransitivity. See also Luce and Raiffa (1957, p. 25) and Anderson (1993, chap. 3).

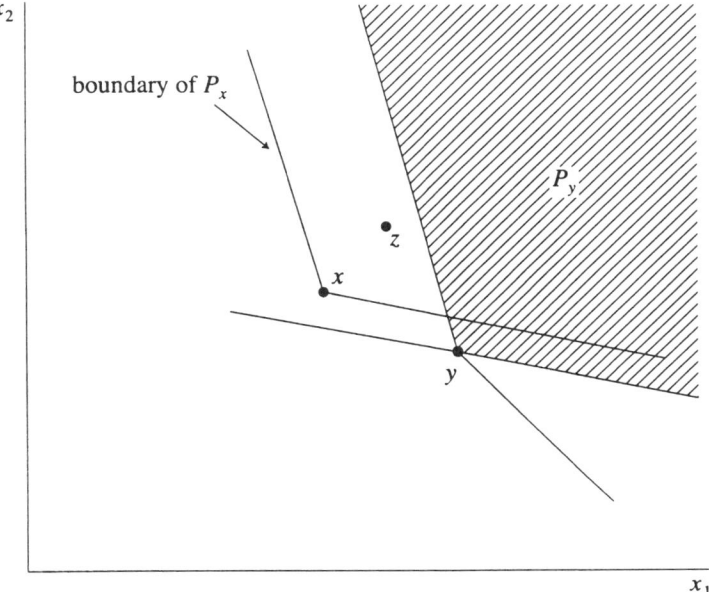

Figure 4.3 Preference incompleteness generating intransitive choices

unranked relative to b. Calling the new option $a \cup \$$, we appear to have $a \succeq b, b \succeq a \cup \$$, but $a \cup \$ \succ a$.

The committed advocate of the choice-reveals-preference view will insist that the appearance of intransitivity is simply an instance of irrationality. Furthermore, as with other cases of intransitivity, most agents after reflection will revise their behavior. But is it legitimate to apply arguments against intransitivity to the current case? Our earlier analysis of transitivity rested in part on showing that an agent with intransitive preferences can willingly be led, through a sequence of binary decisions, to options unequivocally worse than other options that had earlier been available. Interpreting unranked options as indifferent, an analogous series of decisions in the present example would lead an agent beginning with z first to y and then to x. But since the agent does not have a defined preference between z and y or between x and y, he or she need not agree to this sequence. Specifically, the agent, while remaining faithful to his or her preference ordering, can refuse to shift from y to x. (We must of course allow the agent to maintain the status quo if he or she desires; otherwise, if we forced the agent to switch options, there would be no paradox in ending up at an inferior option.) Note that the same agent might have earlier (prior to having the option of consuming z) been willing to switch from y to x; but since this pair of options is not ordered by preference, the agent need not make the same binary choice at all points in time. By making decisions that vary as a function of the options previously available, an agent can both choose intransitively and avoid being led sequentially to inferior outcomes.[45]

The strategic advantage of maintaining the status quo until offered a superior option is now clear: it provides a simple way of escaping the manipulations that can accompany intransitive choice. There is, furthermore, no irrationality in adopting status quo maintenance only in response to such manipulations. From the standpoint that choice reveals preference, however, our agent would be committing a second error. The agent's preferences now seem to vary with the context in which decisions are made. In the presence of manipulation and with y as the status quo choice, y appears to be strictly preferred to x. (The evidence for strictness could either be a repeated refusal to exchange y for x or, additionally, a rejection of arbitrarily small financial inducements to accept x over y.) With manipulation absent or if not allowed to hold to the status quo, the agent might vacillate between x and y. A dogged allegiance to interpreting agents as obeying the completeness assumption thus comes at the cost of having to admit the presence of multiple irrationalities.

A more detailed story illustrates the implausibility of definitionally insisting on completeness. In contingent valuation studies of environmental goods, agents consistently report that the amount of money they are willing to pay for a unit increment of environmental cleanliness—to clean an additional lake, say—is significantly less than the amount they will accept to permit a one-unit reduction in environmental quality.[46] There has been some controversy about the rationality of these survey responses (even supposing that agents regard unpolluted and reclaimed lakes as interchangeable). At a given level of wealth and environmental cleanliness, these valuations betray no internal inconsistency, even according to the most orthodox preference theory.[47] Referring again to figure 4.2, interpret x_1 as the quantity of clean lakes and x_2 as the agent's wealth level (used to purchase private consumption). An incomplete agent who maintains the status quo or an agent with complete preferences (who strictly prefers any element in P_x to x) will each announce a willingness to pay g_x^- for an additional clean lake and a willingness to accept g_x^+ in compensation for an additional polluted lake. The possible irrationality occurs if, at certain other wealth and lake combinations (such as y in fig. 4.3), similar willingness-to-pay and willingness-to-accept responses are elicited. Under a completeness interpretation—that is, if the points not in P_x and not in P_y are weakly inferior to x and y, respectively—the nonempty intersection of P_x and P_y implies

45. Putnam (1986), in contrast, argues that were it not for the value that agents place on making their own decisions, a rational agent lacking a complete preference ordering would have to choose transitively.

46. See Cummings, Brookshire, and Schulze (1986), for instance. Similar disparities occur with more prosaic choices; see, for example, Kahneman, Knetsch, and Thaler (1990). The environmental example is more evocative, however.

47. On this point, see Hanemann (1991).

that the agent has intransitive preferences. Under an incompleteness interpretation, the agent simply has not decided on a complete system of evaluations of private consumption and environmental quality. In the interim,
while weighing the matter, the agent decides not to move from the status
quo to an unranked choice; no intransitivity of preference is implied. Which
interpretation is more convincing?[48]

Agents with incomplete preferences can still be categorized as having
complete preferences that are context dependent or intransitive. As a pure
matter of labeling, there is little harm in these moves, though such accounts
may be at odds with agents' own descriptions of their decision making.[49]
What is important is that what I am here calling incompleteness does not
expose an agent to the unambiguous losses that agents with intransitive
preferences are subject to. Nor does incompleteness imply that agents assert
preference at one time and subsequently contradict themselves; wavering
agents can be well aware of their own incompleteness and need not claim
at any point that their choices reveal their preferences. Completeness is
therefore neither a consequence of rational self-interest nor of reasoned
reflection about choice.

Nevertheless, perhaps due to an association between incompleteness and
behavior that can be interpreted as irrational, completeness has long been
considered an axiom of rationality. The association is misleading: having
inconsistent preferences differs fundamentally from not having consistent
preferences. Choice guided by intransitive psychological preference cannot
credibly be interpreted as internally consistent. Incompleteness, on the
other hand, does not obligate an agent to choose inconsistently; incomplete
agents can even elect to choose as if they possessed complete, transitive
preference orderings. Indeed, this flexibility can help incomplete agents to
avoid certain transitivity manipulations [see Mandler (1998)].

Finally, notice the interdependence of justifications of transitivity and
completeness. As we have seen, an agent's choices (if they can vary as a
function of previously available options) can be intransitive without causing
the agent to end up with an outcome that is worse than a previously available option. Consequently, if preference is defined as choice, the completeness axiom is justified but the rationale for transitivity is undermined. On
the other hand, if preference is defined psychologically as an agent's judgment of his or her well-being, transitivity can be argued for convincingly,

48. Another possibility is to let preference relations change as a function of the agent's
status quo option. See, e.g., Tversky and Kahneman (1990). Such theories can allow each time
period's preferences to be both complete and transitive: for each status quo point x, simply
assume that any point not chosen over x is weakly inferior to x. Although this perspective
shares some ground with the incompleteness view, it obscures the temporal coherence and
consistency of those preference judgments that agents are capable of forming. Also, it provides
no direct evidence for interpreting unchosen points as inferior to the status quo, and cannot
empirically verify any preference judgments that do not involve the status quo.

49. Note that we cannot discriminate between the incompleteness and the context-
dependence/intransitivity interpretations on the basis of choice information alone.

but completeness cannot be justified. Under either framework, therefore, ordinalism cannot provide an adequate foundation for the entirety of its account of rational action.

4.11 Conclusions

Once the ordinalist presumption against foundations for preferences is overturned, the merits of early utility theory and ordinalism can be weighed. Ordinalism can provide compelling arguments in favor of transitivity and weaker considerations in support of convexity. Cardinality plays little or no role in these constructions, justifying one of ordinalism's claims to greater generality. Surprisingly, even diminishing marginal utility can be rid of its connection to cardinality and still preserve its power as a rationale for convexity. Agents may well make cardinal comparisons—as we will see in chapter 5, plausible independence conditions entail implicit cardinality judgments—but no argument for any primary assumption of ordinal theory is thereby bolstered.[50] But ordinalism's well-founded suspicions about the usefulness of cardinality have expanded into an unjustifiable discrediting of all theorizing that goes beyond the assertion of assumptions on preferences. The result has been to mask the substantial difficulties of replacing the rationale that hedonism once provided for the completeness assumption.

Is the difficulty of justifying completeness a problem for ordinalism per se? On the eve of Hicks and Allen's work in the 1930s, consumer theory's commitment to hedonism had largely vanished (see section 5.3). The features of early neoclassical consumer theory that still survived, cardinality and diminishing marginal utility, do not strengthen the case for completeness. It is therefore not surprising that Robertson, Knight, and other defenders of early neoclassical orthodoxy failed to draw attention to ordinalism's difficulty on this point. But to concentrate on the narrow change from, say, 1925 to 1950, is to miss the broader transformation of preference theory. Hedonism once provided economics with a comprehensive account of how agents order choices. By mid-twentieth century, this account had been rejected categorically; preference theory now simply assumed what had previously been argued for. And though the generation prior to Hicks took the first steps against hedonism, it was the 1930s ordinalists who affirmed an explicit methodology of disregarding psychological foundations; it is this methodology that has hidden the lack of a rationale for completeness.

The difficulty of justifying completeness obviously does not warrant a return to hedonism. Ordinalism can always rely opportunistically on hedonism, or for that matter on any ordering principle, without upholding the doctrine as a universal theory of motivation. That agents sometimes rank choices on the basis of pleasure can be used, whenever applicable, as a ratio-

50. The Arrow-Koopmans argument for convexity constitutes a partial exception. See footnote 38.

nale for believing that preference judgments exist. But this formal generality does not patch the substantive hole. Indeed, the long-standing absence
of a global rationale for completeness strongly suggests the frequency with
which choice is not governed by preference.

The dilemmas exposed by the rejection of hedonism pinpoint the weaknesses of preference theory. Neoclassical economics has long been criticized
for relying on narrow, implausible accounts of human motivation. Hedonism was the first object of this line of attack, and the criticisms of outsiders
in fact spurred the initial rejections of pleasure-based psychologies.[51] But
after a century of distancing itself from hedonism, preference theory can
no longer credibly be indicted on this score. It is now routine for the agents
of economic theory to desire entirely nonmaterial ends; even in cost-benefit
analysis, agents are allowed to pursue passive use values (e.g., simply
knowing the environment is unspoiled) in addition to private consumption.
More recently, preference theory has been analogously criticized for its allegiance to the idea that agents are self-interested. Perhaps as a response,
theories of altruism, consumption externalities, and, most abstractly, preferences defined over multiagent allocation profiles have appeared. More
recently still, plausible objections to requiring that preferences be defined
over allocations alone (whether single or multiagent) have been voiced.
Agents care about decision-making procedures, some argue; the fairness of
a scheme for allocating commodities or the identity of who holds decision-
making power can directly affect an individual's well-being.

These last theoretical newcomers remain at the fringes of the discipline.
But, extrapolating into the future, there is every reason to believe that
expansions of what is theoretically admissible in preference orderings will
continue. Well-ordered preferences, not the specific field over which preferences are defined, are the critical feature of the ordinal tradition. Many
have objected that if economic theory is not wedded to a narrow, materi-
alistic theory of motivation then it necessarily falls into vacuity and tautology. To be sure, if the domain of choice were expanded to explain away any
and all instances of irrational choice, empirical confirmation would be short-
circuited; I discussed this difficulty in section 4.8. But the expansions that
have occurred are not this extreme; they have been few in number and discrete in nature. Contemporary preference theory continues to commit itself
to the claim that agents have a fixed ordering over *some* field of outcomes;
it is therefore not empirically vacuous.

The difficulty with enlarging the set of acceptable economic motivations
and refining the field of outcomes lies instead in the repercussions for the
completeness assumption. The typical reason for expanding the field of
choice is the discovery of a key, omitted characteristic or some previously
ignored complexity of a decision problem. In the mutations just cited,
economic theory has successively conceded that self-interest can be

51. See, e.g., Downey (1910) and Lewin (1996) for commentary.

propelled by manifold motives, that an agent may care about the effect of his or her actions on the welfare of others, and (less frequently) that symbolic and procedural attributes of choice affect an agent's well-being. But the mere enlargement of a choice problem hardly resolves the newly recognized complexities. Indeed, refinements of the field of choices make decision problems more demanding; incompleteness is all the more likely.

Treating the development of preference theory more abstractly, a pattern emerges. At first, a simple prescriptive account of decision making, such as hedonism, posits an external standard by which agents determine which actions are optimal. With time, the implausibilities of the prescriptive theory and the parts of the decision problem that previously had been ignored become apparent, and the theory is overturned. In its place, an ordinal theory simply assumes that agents are endowed with an ordering of their choices, omitting any explanation of how these orderings are constructed. A dilemma then appears: either continue to accept the older account, ignoring the cases it cannot cover, or adopt the new theory, which, since it fails to prescribe how decision making should be conducted, also fails to justify its assumption of completeness. The evolution of the theory of choice under uncertainty is a model application of this pattern; I discuss the parallels in a postscript at the end of this chapter.

A further consequence of the narrowing of the prescriptive content of preference theory has been to fuse all the more tightly what an agent chooses with what promotes the agent's welfare. Early neoclassical theory allowed a tentative separation of these concepts; as noted in section 4.4, some argued that agents erred when they discounted future relative to present utility or when they gambled at fair odds. Ordinal theory's rejection of prescriptive decision-making standards makes it much more difficult to allow that errors occur. Discounting has thus been reclassified as compatible with an agent's welfare; and gambling is now said to reveal that agents have convexities in their von Neumann–Morgenstern utility functions. Since agents in fact perform these behaviors, ordinalists have felt compelled to conclude that they both indicate preference and serve agents' interests.

Once the blanket prohibition on nonchoice theorizing is lifted—and I argued in section 4.8 that ordinalism must make this move—prescriptive accounts of individual welfare can no longer be dismissed out of hand. In reality, of course, people can be impatient and shortsighted; they fail to consider evidence and miscalculate probabilities; they reason speciously and invoke irrelevant considerations. A thorough incorporation of any of these propensities into preference theory would undermine the ordinalist equation of choice and welfare.

If the connection between choice and welfare is loosened, some decision-making anomalies appear less paradoxical. A consistent preference ordering is a goal that agents strive to construct, not a primitive with which they are naturally endowed. Complex environments must be deciphered; the similarities of seemingly different decision-making "frames" must be discovered; strategies for putting the future on a par with the present must be devised; rival goals must be weighed. In the meantime, the clock is ticking; decisions need to be made. Choices in these cases—even for the rational agent—are likely to be transitory signposts along the path of deliberation, not definitive judgments of preference inexplicably changing from moment to moment. Fully rational individuals may come to realize that certain actions are not serving their goals, and they may revise their behavior. The impatient can become more patient; gamblers may clarify their attitudes toward uncertainty and stop taking risks; the uncommitted come to verdicts about their ultimate values. Temporally inconsistent choice becomes the rule, not the exception.[52]

There are also spheres of decision making in which agents do not seek, or do not know how to obtain, global principles that resolve all conflict among competing aims. As demonstrated in section 4.10, the resulting incompleteness of preferences does not expose agents to identifiable harm. Economic theory therefore ought to distinguish between decision-making problems in which ordering criteria can be easily assembled from cases where they cannot. Many economic decisions fall into the former camp. Most prominently, when options can be ranked by their monetary return (and no other goals are involved), decision making is straightforward: wealth maximization prescribes the correct action. Or, to take an example from finance, many apparently complex portfolio decisions can be derived once an agent's preferences over the mean and variance of uncertain wealth are known. Early neoclassical economists thought pleasure could rank consumption options as straightforwardly as wealth ranks monetizable goals. This hope proved illusory. The consequence, so far unacknowledged by accepted theory, is that economic rationality must assume a less ambitious form. The psychological complexities of choice would then be easier to accommodate. When options are not ranked by preference, indecision and hesitation become authentic phenomena, not inexplicably emotive forms of indifference.

4.12 Postscript: choice under uncertainty

Uncertain choice has steadily become more important to preference theory; the agents of contemporary economics now routinely choose among bundles of state-contingent commodities. Since uncertain environments naturally induce preference incompleteness, they are a leading route by which the problem spreads into the mainstream of consumer theory. The development of the theory of uncertain choice is complex. My aim here is

---

52. Some of the changes in behavior I am discussing, but not all, can be characterized as instances of rational, Bayesian learning. Of course, with freedom to specify enough states of nature, any sequence of actions can be made consistent with the existence of a single, unchanged preference ordering. But, given the arguments in section 4.8, such a theory would be empirically empty.

simply to bring out one parallel to the evolution of traditional consumer theory.[53]

From the early neoclassical consumer theory of the late nineteenth-century to the von Neumann–Morgenstern model of the mid-1940s, uncertain events were described with objective probabilities, usually thought of as long-run frequencies of occurrence. The specification of objective probabilities allows these models to classify some actions as rational and others as irrational. To be concrete, consider the following elementary variant of expected utility theory. Let the items of choice be *lotteries*, each of which specifies a probability distribution $(\pi_1, \ldots, \pi_n)$, $\Sigma_{i=1}^{n} \pi_i = 1$, over a finite set of possible prizes, $A = \{a_1, \ldots, a_n\}$; the elements of A can be thought of as sums of money. Suppose that an agent has a complete, transitive ordering over lotteries satisfying the standard von Neumann–Morgenstern axioms of continuity and independence; his or her preferences over lotteries can then be represented by a function of the form $\Sigma_{i=1}^{n} \pi_i\, u(a_i)$.

In economic applications, the alternatives over which agents choose are often described differently. The world is described by a list of states, $(\omega_1, \ldots, \omega_s)$, with associated probabilities, $(\pi_1, \ldots, \pi_s)$, $\Sigma_{i=1}^{s} \pi_i = 1$. A *simple alternative*, a_j, specifies a prize, $a_j(\omega_i)$, in A as a function of the state. In fancier versions of the theory, an alternative can specify, for each ω_i, a lottery over the elements of A, not just a single a_i; call such alternatives *complex*. I suppose that preferences are state independent: as in the previous paragraph, agents are indifferent between alternatives that offer identical probability distributions over prizes, even if the labels of states at which prizes appear differ. Since alternatives specify all of the information provided by lotteries, it is easy to derive an agent's optimal ranking of alternatives: in the case of a set of simple alternatives, an agent should choose among the a_j so as to maximize $\Sigma_{i=1}^{s} \pi_i\, u(a_j(\omega_i))$. Preferences over lotteries thereby prescribe choices over a_j functions. The role played by objective probabilities in this theory is analogous to the role of hedonism in traditional consumer theory; each provides a prescriptive standard for determining optimal choices.

This treatment takes the probabilities of states to be exogenously given. In many cases, it makes little sense to suppose that states can be assigned objective probabilities. In response to this difficulty, postwar economic theory has increasingly turned to models of subjective uncertainty.[54] These theories eliminate the specification of probabilities but continue to assume that agents have complete and transitive preferences over alternatives. In fact, if an agent's preferences over complex alternatives satisfy continuity and independence axioms, and if, for any pair of states ω_i and ω_k, the agent's preferences over lotteries that deliver prizes at ω_i are identical to his or her

---

53. Levi (1986) also analyzes parallels between incompleteness in general and its appearance in theories of uncertainty.

54. Savage (1954) and Anscombe and Aumann (1963) are the most influential models; I follow the latter here.

preferences over lotteries that deliver prizes at ω_k, then the agent's ranking of the simple alternatives can be represented by a utility function of the form $\Sigma_{i=1}^{s} \bar{\pi}_i u(a_j(\omega_i))$, $\Sigma_{i=1}^{s} \bar{\pi}_i = 1$.

The numbers $\bar{\pi}_1, \ldots, \bar{\pi}_s$ are interpreted as the subjective probabilities the agent assigns to the states; they take the same values in all utility representations of the above form. Agents need not knowingly formulate numerical probabilities of the states—like all ordinal accounts, the theory is silent on the mental events underlying preference—but agents must make decisions that hinge on states' comparative likelihood. Consider an agent choosing between simple alternative a_j, which assigns a_1 to state ω_1 and a_2 to all other states, and alternative a_k, which assigns a_1 to ω_2 and a_2 to all other states. Given state independence, such a decision can depend only on whether the agent considers ω_1 to be more or less likely than ω_2 and on the relative psychological value of a_1 and a_2. This judgment need not determine a precise value for $\bar{\pi}_1/\bar{\pi}_2$, but—if the agent is not indifferent between a_1 and a_2—this ratio can be pinned down by considering the agent's ranking of complex alternatives offering lotteries of a_1 and a_2 at ω_1 and ω_2. Agents therefore act as if they had formed numerical probability judgments.

Models of subjective uncertainty are internally consistent; it is their assumption of completeness that is problematic. Agents want to choose among alternatives based on the likelihood of acquiring the prizes they desire. It may be that agents can form judgments of likelihood using only their own understanding of the factors determining which states will occur, but it is equally plausible that they cannot: the prescriptive mechanism at the core of the von Neumann–Morgenstern theory—the provision of objective probabilities of states—has been removed.[55] If agents are unable to gauge the likelihood of states, they will also be unable to rank the simple (or a fortiori the complex) alternatives.[56] Despite the manifest implausibility of completeness in this setting, the subjective theory nevertheless supposes that agents possess complete orderings.

55. I am only comparing the prescriptive content of subjectivist theory with that of von Neumann–Morgenstern theory; neither account prescribes orderings over those decisions for which uncertainty about states is irrelevant, e.g., the ranking of the elements of A received with certainty. For a discussion of a parallel incompleteness problem in von Neumann–Morgenstern theory, see section 5.1.

56. This drawback of the subjective model was an active subject of research in the 1950s. See Milnor (1954) for an overview and critique of proposed solutions; for a contemporary, philosophical account, see Levi (1986). The case presented in section 4.10, that there is no inherent irrationality in incompleteness, applies here; incomplete agents can hold to undominated status quo choices and thereby protect themselves against welfare-diminishing manipulations.

5

Historical Issues in Preference Theory

Cardinality and the Transition to Ordinalism

In the ordinalist caricature of the history of preference theory, economists prior to 1934 were confused about what could be inferred from choice behavior. Then, following the revelation of Hicks and Allen, unfalsifiable psychological assumptions were banished. In reality, early preference theory, with rare exception, did not claim that cardinal comparisons could be deduced from preference information alone; early neoclassical economists simply adopted a psychological theory in which agents form cardinality judgments. Moreover, as we saw in chapter 4, nonordinal properties of utility can sometimes advance theoretical coherence. Indeed, whenever nonordinal psychological premises have seemed plausible, economists have happily embraced them. Not only the original Jevonians but such forerunners of ordinalism as Irving Fisher and many postwar theorists have incorporated implicit or explicit cardinality assumptions. Thus the elimination of nonordinal properties of utility, in addition to being theoretically suspect, is historically only a partial truth.

For the first generation of neoclassical economists, cardinality was inseparable from a physiological understanding of pleasure and motivation. But when hedonism came under attack, early utility theorists compromised; while abandoning utilitarian psychology, they implicitly retained cardinal utility scales. Cardinality then no longer served much purpose; it neither justified any assumption on preferences over riskless choices nor was implied by any commonly held psychological model. At this point, early neoclassical theory can justifiably be accused of error; the ordinalists were right to complain that their immediate predecessors were pointlessly clinging to cardinality. But no broader principle should be inferred; when properly targeted, nonordinal theorizing can provide plausible psychological foundations for preference theory.

I discuss cardinality in reverse historical order, first providing a brief example of its survival in contemporary economics, and then confirming the consistency of early neoclassical usage. The final sections consider the initial moves to ordinalism and the last pre-1930s uses of cardinality.

5.1 Cardinality and cardinal measurability

Let us say that utility is *cardinally measurable* if the ratio of changes in utility experienced by an agent can be deduced from the agent's choices alone. Cardinality per se will refer to the capacity of agents to make cardinal comparisons. The difference between these concepts parallels the distinction in section 4.6 between the accuracy of a psychological theory and whether or not a theory can be tested solely with information about choice behavior. Keeping these ideas distinct is vital in the case of cardinality: cardinal measurability is a logical fallacy, cardinality is not.

As we will see, theorists prior to the 1930s did not uphold this distinction. Nor have postwar theorists always done so, particularly when considering the von Neumann–Morgenstern theory of choice under uncertainty. Expected utility functions resemble pre-1930s cardinal utility functions in that both are unique up to (increasing) linear transformations. Drawing on this fact, it was common in the 1940s and 1950s to conclude that von Neumann and Morgenstern had demonstrated that an agent's intensity of satisfaction could be inferred from his or her choices over lotteries or gambles. Seen as a rehabilitation of cardinal measurability, this conclusion is incorrect. Without additional psychological evidence, the cardinality of the von Neumann–Morgenstern utility function only lies in the fact that utility representations enjoying the mathematical convenience of the expected utility property are unique up to a linear transformation. A nonlinear transformation of a von Neumann–Morgenstern utility function (seen as a function on the set of lotteries, not lottery prizes) also represents an agent's ordinal preferences over uncertain prospects; it is just that the function that results does not represent the utility of lotteries as the mathematical expectation of the utility of the lottery prizes.

The simplest case occurs with a finite set of prizes, say $A = \{a_1, \ldots, a_n\}$. If u is a von Neumann–Morgenstern utility function and $p = (p_1, \ldots, p_n)$, $\sum_{i=1}^{n} p_i = 1$, is a typical lottery over A, then $U(p) = \sum_{i=1}^{n} p_i u(a_i)$ is the von Neumann–Morgenstern utility evaluation of p. Clearly, a nonlinear monotonic transformation of U, for example, $(\sum_{i=1}^{n} p_i u(a_i))^3$, represents the same preference ordering over lotteries, but the expected utility property disappears.

An expected utility measure of an agent's well-being need not track subjective feelings of satisfaction; hence, the von Neumann–Morgenstern theory in no way threatens the ordinalist claim that intensity of preference cannot be inferred from choice behavior alone. Suppose, for instance, that a_1 and a_2 are two quantities of money, with $a_1 > a_2$, and a_3 is an amount of money that some agent holds to be indifferent to the gamble of a_1 with probability .5 and a_2 with probability .5; a_3, therefore satisfies $u(a_3) = .5\, u(a_1) + .5\, u(a_2)$, where u is an expected utility function for the agent in question. If expected utility functions necessarily gauged cardinal satisfaction, an agent would be required to experience the gain in satisfaction from a move from a_2 to a_3 as equal to the gain in satisfaction from a move from a_3 to a_1.

Perhaps agents do assess their well-being in such a way. Implicitly at least, agents would then make cardinal comparisons, and their von Neumann–Morgenstern utilities would mathematically represent these judgments. But such a conclusion would be the product of additional assumptions or empirical information about agents and their feelings of satisfaction, not an inference from choice behavior alone.[1] Von Neumann–Morgenstern theory therefore does not threaten the ordinalist position on cardinal measurability.

While a correspondence between the subjective experience of well-being and expected utility constitutes an independent theoretical claim, it is not an implausible claim. When pondering risky decisions, agents often try to weigh increases in well-being against decreases. For example, when considering a gamble delivering a five dollar gain with probability 2/3 and a one dollar loss with probability 1/3, an agent might ask, "Is two-thirds of the satisfaction of a gain of five dollars greater or less than one-third of the satisfaction of a one dollar loss?" Such judgments are cardinal comparisons. Introspectively aware of this type of reasoning, many theorists tacitly equate expected utility and cardinal measures of well-being, and their intuition may well be empirically correct.

Indeed, without some such (extra-ordinal) account of how to deliberate about choice under uncertainty, the completeness assumption in von Neumann–Morgenstern would stand unjustified. In contrast to the theory of choice under certainty, therefore, cardinality can here provide pivotal psychological foundations.

As we will see, the distinction between cardinality and cardinal measurability carries a parallel importance in Irving Fisher's late nineteenth-century axiomatization of cardinality; the ordinalist rejection of cardinal measurability again emerges unscathed, but Fisher's psychological theorizing is nevertheless plausible.

5.2 Cardinality based on pleasure

Once diminishing marginal utility is uncoupled from cardinality (see section 4.7), cardinality no longer appears so central to the first generation of utility theorists. Among the myriad applications of diminishing marginal utility, claims that a good's marginal utility declines at a specific rate were rare. It was common to posit specific utility (or marginal utility) functions; and it is true that from a given utility function one can derive exact ratios

---

1. Many have emphasized that cardinal comparisons cannot be deduced from von Neumann–Morgenstern utilities; see, e.g., Luce and Raiffa (1957, pp. 22, 32).

of utility differences. But it would be farfetched to interpret the mere specification of a utility function as a commitment to cardinality. Since pre-ordinal theorists did not discuss which utility indices are psychologically accurate, it makes as much sense to infer that they believed that agents can assign unique utility numbers to changes in welfare or even to welfare levels.

Still, much of early utility theory employed implicit assumptions of cardinality. Consider Marshall's famous use of consumer surplus as a monetary measure of utility. Marshall supposed that an agent's willingness to pay for goods was an approximate gauge of changes in utility. Given this (nonordinal) psychological premise, coupled with restrictions on the size of the potential impact of price changes on the marginal utility of income, consumer surplus (the area under an agent's demand curve) can provide a rough estimate of changes in welfare.[2] Marshall proceeded to sum different agents' surpluses, which should extinguish any doubt that he implicitly took a cardinal view of individual well-being: if some nonlinear transformation were applied to a monetary measure of each agent's utility, and the outcomes summed, the resulting welfare ranking would generally differ from Marshall's consumer surplus ranking.

It is common nowadays to put an ordinalist spin on consumer surplus analysis. Consumer surplus is said to be an accurate welfare measure whenever preferences are representable by *quasi-linear* utility functions (i.e., functions linear in money income). But consumer surplus depends not only on income effects being small, but also on a supposition that quasi-linear representations of utility are accurate for welfare analysis. Without this nonordinal assumption, it is possible that some non-quasi-linear utility representation would be the appropriate function to use for welfare purposes.

Whatever the merits of his defense of consumer surplus, Marshall did not believe that the deducibility of cardinal comparisons from demand data was necessary for demand theory. Consumer surplus was a crutch used in welfare analysis; Marshall knew well that the derivation of consumer demand functions does not rely on the accuracy of consumer surplus. Marshall thus seems to have held that agents experience pleasure as a cardinal magnitude and that cardinal comparisons cannot systematically be inferred from demand behavior. There is, moreover, no reason to suppose that Marshall thought that cardinal comparisons could ever be deduced from market behavior alone. Drawing on introspection and sociological observation, Marshall argued that the marginal utility of money varies across agents and that agents with identical market behavior can experience different marginal utilities of money. Hence, it is implausible that Marshall could have simultaneously held that the approximate constancy of the marginal utility

2. Marshall (1890, pp. 740–741). Marshall's analysis closely followed Jevons (1871, pp. 140–142).

of money (which would allow market measurement of cardinal comparisons) could be inferred from choice data alone.[3]

There is a further interpretive wrinkle. Adopting Bernoulli's expected utility theory, Marshall held that risk-taking decisions *could* gauge the marginal utility of money and determine a utility function unique up to a linear transformation (1890, p. 741). Marshall thus anticipated the 1940s argument, discussed in the previous section, linking decision making under uncertainty to cardinality. Insofar as Marshall believed that a risk-based derivation of cardinal utility could proceed on a purely ordinal basis, he erred. Of course, Marshall did not spell out his precise psychological presuppositions. But even if guilty as charged, Marshall's oversight merely duplicates the error of 1940s von Neumann–Morgenstern theory.[4]

Like Marshall on riskless choice, Jevons's utility theory also combined implicit belief in cardinality with an ordinal view of measurability. Jevons certainly employed assumptions on utility functions that are preserved only under linear transformations. Jevons routinely assumed that utility functions are additively separable, and when describing agents for whom goods are perfect substitutes, he used utility functions where the ratio of marginal utilities of different goods is fixed.[5] Jevons's explicit comments on cardinality were guarded. "Far be it from me to say that we ever shall have the means of measuring directly the feelings of the human heart. A unit of pleasure or of pain is difficult even to conceive; but it is the amount of these feelings which is continually prompting us to buying and selling, borrowing and lending, labouring and resting, producing and consuming" [Jevons (1871, p. 13)]. Consistent with his periodic use of cardinal properties of utility, Jevons asserts here that individuals psychologically experience units (presumably cardinal units) of utility.[6]

Jevons went on to discuss measurability per se: "[I]t is from the quantitative effects of the feelings [i.e., from choice] that we must estimate their comparative amounts. We can no more know or measure gravity in its own nature than we can measure a feeling, but just as we measure gravity by its effects in the motion of a pendulum, so we may estimate the equality or

3. Marshall (1890, pp. 178–179). That income effects are small follows from the assumption that price changes induce small changes in the marginal utility of income; but small income effects do not imply an approximately constant marginal utility of income, since the latter is, in part, a nonordinal assumption. It is interesting that Edgeworth explicitly recognized that cardinal properties of utility were observationally inaccessible. See Edgeworth (1897, p. 117) and the discussion in section 6.2 in this book.

4. Marshall in fact went a little further and specified that the zero point for a utility function, which he thought should mark the dividing line between utility and disutility, occurs where an agent is consuming the necessities of life and no more. In the language of measurement theory, Marshall committed himself to a ratio scale, not just an interval scale.

5. See Jevons (1871, p. 128) and, for a different example of nonordinality, p. 55.

6. This conclusion is not contradicted by Jevons's remark (1871, p. 20) that "we can seldom or never affirm that one pleasure is a multiple of another in quantity." Jevons is here referring to the difficulty of specifying ratios of total utility (i.e., of constructing a ratio scale), not ratios of changes in utility.

inequality of feelings by the varying decisions of the human mind."[7] Jevons's remarks suggest that choice could only yield conclusions about indifference and strict preference ("equality or inequality of feelings"), not intensity of preference. Thus, like Marshall, Jevons seems to have believed in cardinality but not cardinal measurability.[8] And this makes sense. A cardinal account of units of satisfaction is a natural accompaniment to hedonism. But commitment to such a psychology need not be joined to a parallel (but false) claim of measurability.

The early neoclassical position appears complex because it combines assumptions on preferences with purely psychological hypotheses. Diminishing marginal utility and an approximately constant marginal utility of money are classic instances: each is a nonordinal psychological assumption that carries implications for choice behavior. Early utility theory evidently did not attempt to disentangle the parts of an assumption that can be inferred from choice behavior from the parts that cannot. Ordinalism's subsequent predominance has led the current-day prohibition of nonordinal properties to be imputed to the past and hence to the conclusion that early utility theorists were methodologically confused. It is more plausible to understand early neoclassical theory as making intelligible claims about economic psychology—hedonism and cardinality—that happen not to be testable with choice data alone.

5.3 The end of hedonism

All of the important criticisms of early utility theory made their first appearance prior to the 1930s. Although the early steps toward ordinalism were famously inconsistent, it is clear at least that by the early twentieth century denouncing hedonism had become a ritual exercise.[9] Partly in response to the external criticism of psychologists, virtually every major theorist from the 1890s onward opined that consumer theory need not rely on pleasure seeking as the sole motivator of economic behavior.[10]

Many have noticed the shift in Marshall's revisions of the *Principles*. It was only the Marshall of the initial editions who wrote that consumption delivers various amounts of pleasure. By the end, Marshall substituted

---

7. Jevons (1871, pp. 13–14). See also Jevons (1871, p. 19).

8. Stigler (1950) cites Jevons's claim that an individual's inverse demand function measures marginal utility as evidence of Jevons's belief in cardinal measurability. But Jevons (1871, pp. 140–142), like Marshall later, recognized that an approximately constant marginal utility of money was plausible only under limited circumstances. Moreover, his judgments of when the marginal utility of money is fixed rely on broad psychological considerations, not just on choice observations.

9. Stigler (1950) is the classic objection to the inconsistencies of pre-1930s moves to ordinalism.

10. See Lewin (1996) for a fascinating account of the criticisms of outsiders and the responses of economists.

"benefit" or "satisfaction" for "pleasure."[11] Marshall did not just swap labels: he speculated on the sociology of desire, on how the drive for social distinction shapes tastes, and on the dependence of preferences on social expectations. Marshall went out of his way to distance himself from physiological naturalism, arguing that it is not "sensuous craving" but social context that stimulates the desire for refined commodities. Marshall also rejected any form of Jevons's view that tastes are generated in an exogenous sphere demarcated from the rest of economic life. Economic development leads to the cultivation of novel capabilities and activities, which in turn propel consumption demand into new categories (toward, for example, highly crafted mechanical contrivances and skilled professional services). Marshall thus assigned no analytical priority to utility theory [(1920, bk. 3, chap. 2, particularly p. 90)]. But the interdependence of tastes and economic activity was a slow-working, long-run principle for Marshall. In the final edition of the *Principles*, preferences remain exogenous within the standard time frames of equilibrium analysis and, in the aggregate, obey a rough stationarity through time. This compromise is characteristic of utility theory in the first decades of the century and after the ordinal revolution as well. Preferences may well have complex, social origins, but—even without the clean line of separation provided by a physiological approach—are nevertheless taken to be temporally stable and fixed for analytical purposes.

Philip Wicksteed's *The Common Sense of Political Economy*, appearing in 1910, marks the distance traveled from Jevonian hedonism. Motivation, in Wicksteed's view, can encompass "all the heterogeneous impulses and objects of desire or aversion which appeal to any individual, whether material or spiritual, personal or communal, present or future, actual or ideal" (1910, p. 32). What matters is that goals are "comparable," that agents can prioritize diverse aims and decide how to trade off one goal against another. Having rejected hedonism as an explanation of decision making, Wicksteed felt no need to restrict utility theory to standard economic goods, as Jevons and Marshall had. Decisions dependent on ethical commitments were now an acceptable species of economic activity [Wicksteed (1910, bk. 2, chap. 1)].

Consistent with his understanding of motivation, Wicksteed saw preference as a "relative scale" representing only the preference or equivalence among different options. Preference in turn was equated with observable choice. Many of the details of Wicksteed's preference theory are consistent with these ordinalist views. Like Marshall before him, he usually represented consumer valuations of goods by monetary, not utility, equivalents. But cardinal statements about well-being are nevertheless scattered throughout Wicksteed's writings, reproducing the ambivalence of Marshall's use of cardinality. Wicksteed unabashedly referred to psychological units of satisfaction and to the potential divergence between monetary and

11. See Mitchell (1916), Stigler (1950), and Lewin (1996). Despite Stigler's claim, "utility" remains in place as a portmanteau word for the psychic rewards of consumption.

psychic measures of utility; more than any theorem, this distinction betrays a cardinal understanding of psychological measurement.[12]

As in Marshall's case, Wicksteed's cardinalism may have been intended as additional psychological theorizing, not as a claim about what can be inferred from market behavior. But Wicksteed's and the later Marshall's antihedonism undermined the obvious rationale for cardinality. Unmoored from any explicit psychology, the persistence of cardinality in Wicksteed and other early twentieth-century theorists began to seem like vestigial error.

5.4 Fisher: nonhedonistic cardinality

Wicksteed's utility theory was informal and did not explicitly analyze the cardinality of utility representations. Other economists near the turn of the century, notably Fisher and Pareto, did address the issue.

Fisher opened his *Mathematical Investigations in the Theory of Value and Prices* (1892) with an explicit rejection of the need to specify what motives underlie desire or preference; and utility, Fisher said, is only a method for denoting preference. Later in the work, and more distinctively, Fisher bestowed a new priority on indifference curves. Fisher represented indifference surfaces mathematically by their "lines of force," that is, the gradients of the utility function perpendicular to the tangent planes of indifference surfaces. Fisher argued that the significance of utility functions lay only in the direction of the utility gradients (or equivalently, therefore, in the indifference surfaces themselves). As proof, Fisher showed that Walrasian equilibrium allocations and relative prices are affected only by the direction, not the length, of agents' utility gradients. Consequently, "we may dispense with the total utility density and conceive the 'economic world' to be filled merely with lines of force."[13] At least with respect to price determination, only agents' patterns of preference and indifference matter.

Fisher simultaneously insisted that "utility is a quantity" when the utility of each good is independent of the quantities of other goods, that is, when the utility of goods is additively separable. Utility is a quantity, for Fisher, if there is an observational method that will determine an agent's marginal utilities up to a choice of the unit of measurement, that is, up to a multiplicative constant. Fisher's test of measurability is therefore that the ratio of any two marginal utilities (evaluated at possibly different consumption bundles) is uniquely specified. Given the equivalence of this property to uniqueness up to a linear transformation (see section 4.7), Fisher seemed to claim that an agent satisfying his independence assumption has a cardinally measurable utility function.

12. See, e.g., Wicksteed (1894) and Wicksteed (1910, bk. 2, chap. 2).
13. Fisher (1892, p. 88). In pointing to the transformations that preserve the direction of the gradients of utility functions, Fisher implicitly identified the same class of monotonic utility transformations that Hicks and Allen would employ in the 1930s.

In his early writing on measurability, Fisher considered violations of independence to be at least as likely as compliance. But later he asserted that independence is likely for broad categories of goods, which is all that his argument requires (1927, pp. 175–177). Ironically the proto-ordinalist Fisher thus seemed to end up as an explicit defender of measurability, outdistancing the founders of marginalism, supposedly the committed cardinalists, on this score. But let's look closer.

Fisher gauged an agent's marginal utility for some good j by the increase in the consumption of some other good i that is indifferent to an incremental increase in j. The marginal utility of good j at a different consumption level, or the marginal utility of some other good k, is ascertained by repeating the experiment with the same base consumption level of good i. Fisher then argued that the ratio of marginal utilities induced by these experiments is unaffected by the base consumption level of i, or indeed by which good serves as the comparison good.

A formal proof of Fisher's result is easy. Let $x_{i,j}(\Delta x_j, x_j)$ denote the increase in the consumption of i beyond a base level $\bar{x}_i$ that is indifferent to increases Δx_j of j beyond a base level x_j. The function $x_{i,j}(\Delta x_j, x_j)$ implicitly depends on $\bar{x}_i$, but, due to the independence assumption, it does not depend on the consumption of x_k, $k \neq i, j$. Fisher's measure of the marginal utility of j at consumption level $\bar{x}_j$ is then

$$\frac{\partial x_{i,j}(0, \bar{x}_j)}{\partial \Delta x_j}.$$

The independence assumption implies that there is a set of functions, $u_1(x_1)$, $\ldots$, $u_l(x_l)$, indicating the agent's utility for each of the economy's ℓ goods; $\Sigma_{j=1}^{\ell} u_j(x_j)$ is therefore an overall utility index for the agent. Fisher recognized that this set of functions is not uniquely specified. But for any such set of functions, $x_{i,j}(\Delta x_j, x_j)$ must obey

$$u_j(\bar{x}_j + \Delta x_j) - u_j(\bar{x}_j) = u_i(\bar{x}_i + x_{i,j}(\Delta x_j, \bar{x}_j)) - u_i(\bar{x}_i).$$

Differentiating with respect to Δx_j and evaluating at $\Delta x_j = 0$, we have

$$\frac{du_j(\bar{x}_j)}{dx_j} = \frac{du_i(\bar{x}_i)}{dx_i} \cdot \frac{\partial x_{i,j}(0, \bar{x}_j)}{\partial \Delta x_j}.$$

Similarly, the marginal utility of some good k (possibly the same as j) at consumption level $\bar{x}_k$ is

$$\frac{du_k(\bar{x}_k)}{dx_k} = \frac{du_i(\bar{x}_i)}{dx_i} \cdot \frac{\partial x_{i,k}(0, \bar{x}_k)}{\partial \Delta x_k},$$

and therefore,

$$\frac{\dfrac{\partial x_{i,j}(0, \bar{x}_j)}{\partial \Delta x_j}}{\dfrac{\partial x_{i,k}(0, \bar{x}_k)}{\partial \Delta x_k}} = \frac{\dfrac{du_j(\bar{x}_j)}{dx_j}}{\dfrac{du_k(\bar{x}_k)}{dx_k}}. \qquad (5.4.1)$$

Fisher's measured ratio of marginal utilities, the left-hand side of 5.4.1, is therefore equal to the ratio of marginal utilities derived from any additively separable utility representation of the agent's preferences. Moreover, since x_i does not appear on the right-hand side, the Fisher measure is indeed unaffected by the choice of comparison good or its base consumption level.

Although his formal result is correct, Fisher's interpretation of his result appears to commit the cardinalist sin of claiming that certain types of preferences are measurable. Fisher only calculated the ratios of marginal utilities that arise from additively separable utility representations. The representations implied by Fisher's method (i.e., the utility functions generated by integrating and then summing his marginal utility functions) could instead be cubed, for example, thereby eliminating additive separability and generating different ratios of marginal utilities. Fisher therefore did not demonstrate that utility is cardinally measurable, only that any application of *his* method yields the same set of cardinal comparisons. Agents with identical preferences that are representable by additively separable functions can, like any set of identical agents, offer conflicting cardinality judgments. In fact, since additive separability is a nonordinal property—it is not preserved by monotonic transformations—ordinally identical agents can even disagree about whether the utilities of different goods are in fact independent.

But rather than making an erroneous measurability claim, it is more plausible that Fisher was simply positing a nonordinal psychological property—that the satisfaction of each good is independent of the consumption of other goods. The utility functions that Fisher's method constructs would then indeed be the only utility functions (up to a positive linear transformation) that reflect agents' psychological experience of independence.[14] On this view, Fisher did not make illicit inferences from choice behavior; he simply was not following later ordinalist rules rigorously banning nonchoice information.

What then did Fisher demonstrate? He did not achieve the impossible, a proof of cardinal measurability, but he did show that a modest nonordinal assumption will imply that there is a unique, psychologically accurate cardinal utility function. An observer need not know an agent's cardinal comparisons or even that the agent consciously formulates cardinality judgments; only the knowledge that the psychological satisfaction an agent derives from some good is independent of the consumption levels of other goods is required. Cardinal comparisons can then be deduced from this fact and the agent's observable choices.

---

14. The ordinalist theorems specifying which ordinal preference relations can be represented by additively separable functions [see Debreu (1960)] are not relevant to the present issue of which utility representations are psychologically accurate. An agent might have preferences representable by a separable function but still not experience the cardinal comparisons generated by the separable utility representations.

Psychological independence is such a tangible and plausible assumption that even many ordinalists, despite their official methodology, have routinely accepted it. Hicks, in the mid-1950s, not only agreed that utility is measurable if some goods provide utility independently of the consumption of other goods, but also that preferences are empirically likely to satisfy this condition (1956, chap. 2). Hicks tempered his concession by insisting that utility is, in practice, unmeasurable since an outside observer could not know in advance which goods have independent utility. Still, Hicks effectively withdrew from the theoretical ground he and Allen staked out in the 1930s: agents can reasonably be assumed to experience cardinality.

Note that to deduce cardinal comparisons from choice behavior always requires a supplementary assumption about agents' (nonordinal) sensations of well-being. The cardinalist interpretation of von Neumann–Morgenstern theory, Marshall's theory of consumer surplus, and the current interpretation of Fisher all share this feature. In the von Neumann–Morgenstern case, expected utility functions are assumed to measure satisfaction; in Marshall, marginal utilities of money are posited to be constant; and in Fisher, agents must conform to psychological independence.

In closing, I should mention that Fisher did not always avoid the measurability fallacy. Following Auspitz and Lieben, Fisher (1892, p. 69) defined a pair of goods i and j to be complements or substitutes, depending on whether the marginal utility of one of the goods increases or decreases as a function of the consumption of the other good, that is, according to the sign of $\partial^2 u(x)/\partial x_i \partial x_j$. In accordance with his analysis of independence, Fisher recognized that a cardinal utility function is not specified when $\partial^2 u(x)/\partial x_i \partial x_j$ is nonzero (since additive separability is violated). But the only transformations that necessarily preserve the sign of $\partial^2 u(x)/\partial x_i \partial x_j$ are the linear transformations. Thus, in the very case where he claimed that utility is not cardinal, Fisher nevertheless implicitly asserted that only utility functions differing by a linear transformation are psychologically accurate. Given the distinction between cardinality and cardinal measurability, there is no logical difficulty in asserting that agents (with or without the independence property) form judgments of cardinality. The problem is that, under Fisher's definition, agents with identical ordinal preferences can differ about whether a pair of goods are substitutes or complements, a fact at odds with Fisher elsewhere considering complementarity and substitutability to be a property of indifference curves alone.[15] This slip offers one of the rare instances of an early utility theorist attempting to infer a nonordinal property of utility solely from preference information.

---

15. See Fisher (1892, pp. 70–71). Fisher's comment (p. 69) that a good's marginal utility "usually" diminishes with increases in quantity "but it may not" is indicative of similar difficulties. Is the "usual" case a product of additional nonchoice psychological information or a supposition that can be deduced from preferences?

5.5 The move to ordinalism

Fisher's suggestion for an economics beginning with indifference curves anticipated a full-scale principle in Pareto. Fisher continued to derive indifference curves from utility functions; Pareto in contrast used indifference curves as a formal starting point, attributing their status to being "given directly by experience." An ordered system of indifference surfaces can be assigned a utility index, but the choice of index has no greater meaning. Pareto also gave a more complete characterization of the set of utility indices representing a given preference ordering by stating a condition that implies that any utility transformation with a positive first derivative will not change the preferences represented.

Hicks and Allen drew directly on Pareto's "discovery" that utility is not measurable; they saw their own work as eliminating the remaining nonordinal elements from consumer theory. Hicks and Allen scolded Pareto for repeating Fisher's analysis of complementarity. Pareto had also reproduced Fisher's analysis of the measurability of utility, signed on (like all pre-Hicksians) to diminishing marginal utility, and, while doubting that agents can make exact cardinal comparisons, asserted that utility functions should reflect agents' ordinal ranking of utility differences. On the last point, Pareto declared: "Among the infinite number of systems of indices which we can have, we must retain only those which have the following property, namely, that if in passing from I to II the man experiences more pleasure than in passing from II to III, the difference between the indices of I and of II is greater than the difference between the indices of II and of III."[16] Why should utility indices reflect these experiences? Pareto did not say.

Pareto and his contemporaries may have thought that nonordinal properties of utility could be justified introspectively or on other psychological grounds. Certainly the survival of nonordinal assumptions, and cardinality in particular, is not by itself a sign of confusion about what can be inferred from preferences. But in the wake of hedonism's rejection, cardinality no longer seemed self-evident. Furthermore, although psychological independence might have supplied a substitute rationale for cardinality, the failure to explain the theoretical purpose of nonordinal assumptions left them vulnerable to criticism. In fact, as I argued in chapter 4, cardinality does not help to justify any of the standard assumptions of nonstochastic consumer theory. Thus, even though nonordinal assumptions—and psychological structure more generally—have their place in consumer theory, the scattered, unproductive persistence of cardinality assumptions gave the ordinalist proposal of complete extermination a prima facie credibility.

16. Pareto (1909, p. 192). In fact, as Lange (1934) argued [and as clarified by Samuelson (1938b) and Basu (1982)], if an agent has a continuous utility function, then all utilities that ordinally rank utility differences differ by linear transformations. The domain restriction necessary for this result [see Basu (1982)] is satisfied in standard commodity spaces.

Moreover, by the 1930s the attribution of greater significance to observable actions than to psychic states had long precedent. As we saw in section 5.2, Jevons held that feelings are not directly measurable and empirical estimates of changes in utility must be constructed from observations of choice. Similar sentiments resurfaced in Wicksteed, Fisher, Pareto, and many others. Jevons's comments do not by themselves imply that assumptions should be restricted to ordinal properties of utility or that purely psychological hypotheses have no scientific standing; and no economist prior to the 1930s was fully committed to such a methodology. But the lineage of supposing that choice has priority over psychological testament helped pave the way for the ordinalists' quick and decisive victory in the 1930s.

6

Paretian Welfare Economics

6.1 Introduction and overview

Social decisions involve gains for some individuals and losses for others. Utilitarianism faces this challenge head on: it aims for a complete set of evaluations that can judge all possible trade-offs among the well-being of agents. As an abstraction, utilitarianism delivers on its promise: it specifies an objective function that, when maximized subject to resource constraints, prescribes social decisions. But when confronted with concrete decisions, utilitarianism offers no constructive procedure for comparing agents' welfare.

Postwar welfare economics has tried to sidestep this difficulty by employing the concept of Pareto optimality: allocations are declared efficient if and only if no agent's welfare can be improved without harming some other agent. The welfare theorems of general equilibrium theory assert that Pareto efficiency can effectively discriminate among policy choices: if "distortions" of perfect competition are removed, the economy can reach a Pareto optimum. Laissez-faire policy recommendations are thereby affirmed.

In fact the conflict of individual aims cannot be eluded. Pareto efficiency can effectively rank social decisions only when policymakers possess a precise model of the economy. The early neoclassical recognition of the need for a method of weighing individual welfare is thus vindicated. Welfare theory consequently faces a painful dilemma: it needs a system for making interpersonal comparisons but cannot provide one.

The early neoclassical utilitarians confronted similar problems, since they could not, in practice, specify a complete ranking of social alternatives. Even when they took the extreme step of assuming that all individuals have the same preferences, lack of knowledge of the representative individual's cardinal comparisons hobbled the derivation of policy advice. Early neoclassical economists readily assumed that agents experience diminishing marginal utility. But for welfare analysis, diminishing marginal utility is not enough. Ranking policy options requires cardinality, which is both theoretically and practically inaccessible.

Unable to follow through on the utilitarian program, early neoclassical welfare theory—like postwar theory—tried to devise efficiency criteria that do not cardinalize or aggregate preferences. Most prominently, Pigou proposed that policymakers maximize the market value of output or "national income." But although value maximization provided early neoclassical economics with a workable efficiency concept, Pigou's justifications of the criterion were sketchy and at odds with his allegiance to utilitarianism.

The utilitarian consensus came under attack in the 1930s and rapidly crumbled. The so-called new welfare economics charged the early neoclassicals with foisting value judgments onto positive economic science. Although the accusation was imprecise—the preceding generation had in reality committed itself only to the most timid interpersonal comparisons of welfare—the discrediting of utilitarianism exposed the absence of a method for evaluating social decisions.

The subsequent search for a suitable welfare criterion took two forms. Bergson-Samuelson social welfare functions followed the utilitarian practice of positing a complete ranking of social choices, but without relying on hedonist or cardinalist psychology. However, the Bergson-Samuelson approach does not say how to construct welfare functions, and thus it suffers from the same defect of abstraction that plagued applied utilitarianism. With no way to adjudicate among rival social welfare functions, the Bergson-Samuelson approach can only recommend Pareto improvements unambiguously.

The other branch of the new welfare economics, compensation criteria, used the concept of potential Pareto improvements—Pareto improvements hypothetically achievable through income transfers—to order policies. Under one interpretation of compensation, the availability of potential Pareto improvements is checked by examining the sum of compensating or equivalent variations. Although a sum of variations can rank policies consistently, the orderings that result are not ethically plausible and do not correspond to intuitive notions of efficiency. Furthermore, despite initial appearances, sums of variations do not in fact test for potential Pareto improvements. Alternatively, potential improvements can be defined directly in terms of agents' allocations and welfare. Although the most famous of these criteria—due to Hicks and Scitovsky—are notorious for their logical contradictions, consistent orderings can in principle be constructed. But, as we will see, even if logically salvageable, compensationist rankings do not offer any policy-relevant advice not contained in a conceptually simpler test of Pareto efficiency.

Partly due to the failures of the compensation criteria, and partly because of the analytical breakthroughs of the welfare theorems of the 1950s, Pareto efficiency has emerged as the dominant welfare concept of postwar economics. The welfare theorems provide a stunning theoretical unity to previous analyses of first-best optimality. The traditional laissez-faire advice of economists can be justified, without the logical evasions or the intangible welfare judgments of utilitarian treatments. Even Pigou's recommendation that the value of output be maximized can be reinterpreted as a price test for Pareto optimality.

But while it dominates theory, economists frequently consider Pareto efficiency to be ethically flawed or practically unworkable. I argue that, properly formulated, Paretianism does not rank efficient allocations above inefficient but non-Pareto-comparable allocations—thus it does not make perverse value judgments—and it is not seriously impaired by real-world restrictions on the set of available policies. Rather, the prime difficulty of Pareto efficiency lies in its informational presuppositions. The fact that policymakers lack a fully specified model of the economy means that virtually any policy change can conceivably harm some agent. Moreover, the two prominent solutions to this uncertainty both fall short. One alternative posits ex ante preferences for each agent and then employs the standard definition of Pareto optimality; unfortunately, the construction of ex ante preferences requires a system for making interpersonal comparisons, thus undercutting the primary goal of Pareto efficiency. The other approach is to maximize expected social welfare. I show, however, that any policy is the maximum of some expected welfare function; all policy reform is therefore prevented. Hence, although Pareto optimality offers an explicit and internally consistent definition of efficiency, it cannot provide the value-free guide to policy making that economists have long pursued.

The impasse of postwar welfare economics thus uncannily duplicates early neoclassical dilemmas. The Bergson-Samuelson social welfare function, like utilitarianism, only provides a formal answer to the predicaments of social decision making. Pareto efficiency superficially appears to justify orthodox policy advice; but like Pigou's defense of maximizing the value of output, its rationale collapses under scrutiny.

6.2 Economic utilitarianism

Prior to the 1930s, the major English neoclassical economists were utilitarians. They held that economic policies should be decided by their effect on individuals' pleasure or utility, with one individual's gain or loss directly added to the gains and losses of others. Their view of aggregate welfare formalized philosophical utilitarianism and blended nicely with the early neoclassical account of individual decision making. Setting aside the troublesome issue of how to scale individual utility functions to make them interpersonally comparable, utilitarian welfare analysis used the same gauges of pleasure employed in the theory of consumer behavior.

When examining the distribution of welfare, early neoclassical economists took individual utility to be a function of income, a one-dimensional variable. The capacity to generate pleasure from income was thought to vary from person to person, but the effect of changing relative prices on this relationship was usually neglected. As in preference theory, diminishing marginal utility was pivotal. Consider a set of individuals of the same *type*, that is, agents who have the same functional relationship between income and utility. Diminishing marginal utility implies that at a utilitarian maximum all individuals of the same type should have the same income. Strikingly, no assumption about cardinality is needed for this result. What matters is that increments of income lead to progressively smaller increases in utility; the specific rate at which utility diminishes is irrelevant.

It is easy to see this point formally. Suppose there are n individuals of the same type, each with utility function $u(x_i)$, where x_i is i's income. Let e be the aggregate output to be distributed among the n agents. A utilitarian planner should choose wealth vectors $x = (x_1, \ldots, x_n)$ to maximize the social welfare function, $\Sigma_{i=1}^{n} u(x_i)$, subject to the constraints

$$\sum_{i=1}^{n} x_i \leq e,$$

$$x_i \geq 0, i = 1, \ldots, n.$$

If diminishing marginal utility—that is, $d^2u(x_i)/dx_i^2 < 0$—holds, the solution is defined by the equations

$$\frac{du(x_i)}{dx_i} = \frac{du(x_j)}{dx_j}, \text{ for all } i \text{ and } j,$$

$$\sum_{i=1}^{n} x_i = e,$$

Again assuming diminishing marginal utility, these equations are solved only when $x_i = e/n$, for all i. This result nowhere uses any cardinal property of utility: repeating the above argument after applying an arbitrary increasing concave—not just linear—transformation to the common utility function leaves the conclusion unaffected.[1]

Historically, two utilitarian objections to radical redistributions of wealth were broached. First, the heterogeneity of agents' capacities for pleasure can break the connection between redistribution and greater aggregate welfare. When maximizing aggregate welfare, utility functions have to be weighted or scaled in such a way that all agents' units of utility are comparable. Possibly, after adjusting the weights on individual utility functions to take into account the variations across individuals in the rate at which utility is produced, the bias toward equality could be eliminated. Edgeworth, for instance, argued that the status quo distribution was tolerably close to the optimal distribution: it so happens, Edgeworth claimed, that the

---

1. A terminological warning is necessary. *Cardinality* often refers to a restriction on the set of permissible additive social welfare functions: namely, if one of the utilities used in a welfare function is multiplied by a positive constant, then all other agent utilities must be multiplied by the same constant. Although the redistribution result still holds with concave rather than linear utility transformations, the same transformation must still be applied to all utility functions.

wealthy systematically derive more pleasure per dollar of income than the poor.[2] While other economists concurred that capacities for pleasure vary (most agreeing even that the rich have greater capacity), Edgeworth's defense of the status quo was exceptional: almost all early neoclassical theorists held that the direct effect of a moderate redistribution of wealth was to increase total utility.

The more serious objection to flattening the income distribution was that savings and labor supply would be adversely affected. Defenders of the status quo argued that taxes on profits diminish the return to savings, thus lowering capital accumulation and the size of future national income, and that income transfers to the poor depress labor supply and current output. Pigou's *The Economics of Welfare*, issued in various forms from 1912 to 1932, was the key early neoclassical attempt to grapple with the issue. Pigou labored to avoid the conclusion that the goal of redistributing wealth to the poor could be at odds with the dictates of economic efficiency. Economic policy can usually be constructed, he claimed, so that either national income increases without reducing the absolute income of the poor, or the income of the poor increases without any sacrifice of national income. Hence, he rejected poverty-relief policies that introduce distortions, for example, wage regulations, subsidies on goods chiefly purchased by the poor, and broad-based systems of transfer payments. He found such policies to be impracticable, dominated by other policies, or harmful to the poor in the long run. Pigou further claimed that those features of economic life that normally enhance output—increases in the supply of any factor, technical progress—do not lower the poor's absolute level of income and should therefore operate unimpeded.[3] Not surprisingly, Pigou's assertions met with periodic opposition. For example, some economists took issue with the claim that union restrictions on labor supply harm the working class and thus unambiguously lower total welfare [see, e.g., Wicksell (1901, pp. 78–79)].

Pigou's skewed perception of policy making and economic development cannot be attributed to Panglossian optimism or ideological bias alone. Early neoclassical utilitarianism, though it nominally posited a criterion that could weigh greater equality of distribution against losses in total output, had no explicit method for deciding these trade-offs. Pigou believed that, ceteris paribus, egalitarian income distributions are better than skewed distributions and that promoting growth is better than inhibiting growth. But on the rare occasions when he acknowledged that the goals of equity and growth conflicted, Pigou could only deliver intuitions about which policies are optimal, not justifications grounded in economic theory. With regard to

2. See Edgeworth (1881, pp. 76–82), which also cites the couplet

> Woman is the lesser man, and her passions unto mine
> Are as moonlight unto sunlight and as water unto wine.

with tentative approval. Edgeworth (1897) moved closer to the utilitarian mainstream.
3. These conclusions appear throughout Pigou (1932), particularly part 4.

guaranteeing a minimum income level, for instance, Pigou could only remark that policies that distinguish between the voluntarily and involuntarily poor and that impose work requirements on welfare recipients will lessen the disincentive effect on output. As to the optimal level of guaranteed income, Pigou had almost nothing to say; it should be set so that "the direct good resulting from the transference of the marginal pound transferred to the poor just balances the indirect evil brought about by the consequent reduction of [output]" (1932, p. 761). He conceded that the information necessary to convert this tautology into concrete advice was not "accessible."

Pigou's imprecision was symptomatic of deeply rooted problems in utility theory. Diminishing marginal utility implies only that redistribution of income (of individuals of the same type) is optimal when it induces no sacrifice of aggregate output; the utility gained by the poor is then always greater than the utility lost by the rich. When redistribution is costly, however, the cardinal information of the rate at which marginal utility diminishes is vital. Costly redistribution implies that the income gain of the poor is less than the income loss of the rich; hence any given move to income equality can lower welfare if marginal utility declines at a slow enough pace. A lack of information about cardinality can thus lead to a crippling incompleteness in policy advice.[4]

Our earlier model can be adjusted to make this point by letting aggregate output vary with the amount of redistribution. Let e_i denote agent i's initial endowment and let $f(x_i - e_i)$ denote the quantity of output lost as a function of i's level of taxation, that is, the extent to which i's consumption is less than his or her endowment. Total output is therefore

$$e = \sum_{i=1}^{n} (e_i + f(x_i - e_i)).$$

We assume that f is nonpositive, concave and, for $x_i - e_i < 0$, strictly concave. The concavity of f allows transferring wealth to become increasingly costly as the volume of transfers rises. For simplicity, but not implausibly, suppose that $f(x_i - e_i) = 0$ for $x_i - e_i \geq 0$.

It is easy to confirm that if u is differentiable it is never optimal to move from unequal wealth distributions to complete equality. Furthermore, under mild conditions, any status quo distribution of wealth is optimal for some $u(x_i)$ with diminishing marginal utility. To establish this result, it is enough to show that at the status quo any small distribution of wealth from the richest to the poorest individual can be welfare reducing. If $\bar{e}$ and $\underline{e}$ are the highest and lowest individual endowment levels, the change in welfare resulting from a small transfer, $\varepsilon > 0$, from the richest to the poorest individual is approximately

---

4. I am dissenting here from Cooter and Rapoport's view (1984, p. 527) that early neoclassical utility theory was "well adapted to the examination of propositions about material welfare."

$$\varepsilon\left[(1 - f'_-(0))\frac{du(\underline{e})}{dx} - \frac{du(\bar{e})}{dx}\right], \qquad (6.2.1)$$

where $f'_-(0)$ is the left-hand derivative of f at $x_i - e_i = 0$. If $f'_-(0)$ is strictly positive, it is clear that there is a u with diminishing marginal utility such that 6.2.1 is negative. (If u is approximately linear, $du(\underline{e})/dx$ and $du(\bar{e})/dx$ will be approximately equal.)

Pigou may have thought that the early neoclassical assumption of cardinality could resolve the difficulties of coming to definite policy judgments. If agents experience identical cardinal comparisons, the same set of utility functions—$u(x_i)$ and its positive linear transformations, $au(x_i) + b, a > 0$—represents each agent's cardinality judgments. It is credible in this case to assume that agents are of the same type, and that each agent should therefore be represented by the same utility function when maximizing social welfare. Independent of the linear transformation chosen, the resulting welfare function, $\Sigma_{i=1}^n (au(x_i) + b)$, generates the same complete ranking of allocations: hence, the trade-offs between the distribution and level of aggregate output can be evaluated.

But asserting that individuals experience the same cardinal comparisons is not enough. In order to specify the common utility function (or any of its linear transformations), the policymaker must know what those cardinal comparisons are. Given that cardinality judgments, if they even exist, are inherently private, the unwillingness of Pigou and others to posit particular cardinal utility functions comes as no surprise; any policy advice relying on such foundations would seem arbitrary and insupportable.

We can now see a further defect of early neoclassical utility theory, beyond those discussed in chapter 4. In consumer theory, cardinality served no analytical function; it just added psychological structure that was unnecessary for behavioral predictions or, after the rejection of hedonism, for the plausibility of the theory. In welfare theory, however, cardinal information about preferences is indispensable for ranking policy choices. The continuing inaccessibility of cardinality judgments thus marks the wholesale failure of the utilitarian approach; when finally cardinality had a concrete role to play, the needed particulars could not be provided.

It is also revealing that in welfare economics, just as in preference theory, the assumption of psychological concavity (see sections 4.7 and 4.9) drives the key early neoclassical theorems. The optimality of egalitarian redistributions—when they come at no cost in total output—only draws on the principle of diminishing marginal utility (which is equivalent to concavity in the present one-dimensional context). Recall that the formal result establishing the optimality of equality follows independently of which concave utility function represents agents of the same type; hence, only psychological concavity, not cardinality, need be assumed.

Even Edgeworth, the hard-line utilitarian, found cardinality to be hopelessly inaccessible. In his pathbreaking analysis of taxation and distribution, Edgeworth argued that taxation should be governed by the doctrine of *minimum sacrifice* rather than *equal sacrifice*: raising revenue for the government should minimize total disutility rather than equalize the utility losses of agents. Furthermore,

> there is a want of clearness in the reasoning from the principle of equal sacrifice, because in order to obtain any conclusion some assumption must be made as to the rate at which the increase of utility tends to diminish with the increase of means; while "to ascertain the exact relations between something psychical and something material is impossible." But the reasoning from the principle of minimum sacrifice assumes no exact relation between utility and means; it assumes only what is universally admitted, that utility does not increase proportionately to means, the Jevonian "law of diminishing utility."[5]

Edgeworth was right to recognize that equalizing sacrifice requires a cardinal utility scale and that this information is difficult, perhaps impossible, to assemble; but he did not realize that when taxes lower total output, the utilitarian principle of minimum sacrifice suffers from the same drawbacks.

There were early neoclassical schemes for measuring cardinal utility scales, for instance, Fisher's suggestion, discussed in section 5.4. Possibly such proposals lay behind Pigou's confidence that sufficient doses of empirical research would unravel the ambiguities of welfare policy. But even granting the viability of these schemes, utilitarianism faces further hurdles. So far we have followed the common early neoclassical presumption that agents are of the same type, a practice that is plausible when agents are ordinally and cardinally identical. Once we drop this pretense, utilitarianism not only requires a cardinal utility for each individual, but also a way to aggregate the cardinal utilities of different individuals. In principle, this problem can arise even when utility is a function of income alone: although ordinal preferences will coincide (as long as more income is preferred to less), cardinal comparisons can differ. Hence, in addition to positing a cardinal utility function $u_i(x_i)$ for each agent i, a planner needs to specify which positive linear transformation of u_i should be used in a sum of utilities. Once the multidimensional nature of consumption is acknowledged, a diversity of ordinal preferences will also appear; the need to cardinalize and scale agents' utility functions then becomes inescapable.

I discuss the challenge of comparing interpersonal welfare more extensively in section 6.5. For now, just note the considerable obstacles frustrating the utilitarian goal of constructing a ranking of social decisions.

---

5. Edgeworth (1897, p. 117). The quotation is from Henry Maine. Note that Edgeworth is suspicious only of drawing policy conclusions from cardinality. To use the language of chapter 5, Edgeworth acknowledges here that utility is not cardinally measurable, but he does not challenge the psychological reality of cardinality. He is therefore not advocating psychological concavity.

6.3 Early neoclassical definitions of efficiency

In response to the difficulties of cardinalizing and aggregating preferences, early neoclassical economists devised welfare criteria that omitted, or at least obscured, distributional issues and that did not rely on unobtainable cardinality information. Marshall used the area under demand curves—consumer surplus—as an estimate of agents' monetary valuations of goods. Consumer surplus is an unweighted sum of monetary valuations, and, as Marshall well understood, it ignores differences in agents' marginal utilities of money. Due to differences in agents' incomes, these differences arise even in the extreme case of all agents being of the same type. But Marshall reasoned that among large groups of agents differences in wealth and the capacity for pleasure "counterbalance" one another.[6] That is, different populations contain roughly the same distribution of individual types and income and hence translate money to utility at the same average rate. Even within the logic of neoclassical utilitarianism, Marshall's supposition is not enough. When comparing the effect of policy changes across communities, consumer surplus analysis needs to assume, for each income class and type, that monetary valuations change in the same proportion in all communities; otherwise, equal monetary measures of benefit will translate into utility at different rates. For instance, if the rich of community A regard increments to some good as worth only a small sum of money when compared to the rich of community B, equal changes in consumer surplus—say, in response to a government-engineered fall in this good's price—in the two communities will not represent equal changes in total utility; A's consumer surplus disproportionately represents the monetary valuations of the poor and therefore signals a larger change in satisfaction.

Pigou, in *The Economics of Welfare*, tried to separate efficiency and distribution issues. Like Marshall, Pigou identified welfare with sums of monetary valuations, which he referred to as the "national dividend" ("national income" in current terminology). Officially, he declared aggregate output at one point in time, say time 2, to have more national income than output at time 1 if, with a hypothetically fixed distribution of purchasing power across agents, agents assign greater monetary value to their time 2 consumption allocations than to their time 1 allocations.[7] For example, even though the distribution of income might worsen substantially from time 1 to time 2, if at an unchanged distribution of income the sum of monetary valuations were higher at 2, national income would (by definition) be larger. Pigou recognized that the fixed distribution of purchasing power could either be the time 1 or the time 2 distribution, and that each could generate a distinct

---

6. Marshall (1890, p. 152). To give consumer surplus as wide a berth as possible, I am ignoring the well-known discrepancies between areas under demand curves and sums of agents' monetary valuations; this difference adds further inaccuracies to consumer surplus analysis.

7. Pigou (1932, chap. 5). Pigou did not specify whether agents' valuations are calculated using period 1 or period 2 prices.

ranking of monetary valuations. But Pigou conjectured that empirically the two comparisons would usually rank output vectors in the same way. (In fact, there are an infinite number of possible comparisons, since any fixed distribution of purchasing power could be used.)

Pigou's definition was curious. What interest lies in fixing the distribution of purchasing power? Individuals can maintain their shares of national income and yet, due to changes in relative prices, experience either gains or losses in utility. Hence, due to differences in the marginal utility of income, a sum of changes in monetary valuations at the hypothetical income distribution can be positive even though the sum of utility changes is negative. Pigou should therefore have held the distribution of utility constant, not the distribution of purchasing power. (For a given distribution of utility, an increase in the sum of monetary valuations is equivalent to a Pareto improvement.) This point is so elementary that it is tempting to conclude that Pigou was trying to camouflage utilitarianism's need for unattainable psychological information. Knowing that the distribution of utility is fixed requires access to a cardinal utility function for each agent and a set of relative weights for these functions.

Pigou in any case quickly put his official definition aside. He conceded that even under the most optimistic scenarios his measure of national income, like Marshall's consumer surplus, depends on inaccessible valuations. (In fact, since Pigou's criterion uses hypothetical income distributions, his measure is even harder to check empirically than Marshall's.) Pigou concluded that, in practice, welfare comparisons must rely on index number measures of national income. Taking aggregate consumption and aggregate output vectors as equivalent, as a first approximation, Pigou asserted that if aggregate outputs at time 1 have less value than outputs at time 2, valuing both at time 2 prices, then one may infer that welfare at time 2 is greater than at time 1, and contrariwise when time 1 outputs have greater value than time 2 outputs. Pigou could provide a partial justification of his test when society consists of a single individual—if the time 1 consumption bundle is affordable at time 2's prices but rejected, the time 2 bundle must be preferred—but his reasoning about the many-individual case was hazy. Pigou again hypothetically fixed the distribution of purchasing power; even on this basis, however, he could not derive a link between his price test and aggregate monetary valuations.

Pigou recognized that since different points in time are analytically symmetrical, index number comparisons can be conducted with two sets of prices and that these measures need not agree. Suppose that at time 1 the ℓ-vectors of aggregate output y^1 and prices p^1 occur, and that at time 2 y^2 and p^2 occur. Then, for example, if

$$\sum_{j=1}^{\ell} p^1(j)y^1(j) < \sum_{j=1}^{\ell} p^1(j)y^2(j) \text{ and}$$

$$\sum_{j=1}^{\ell} p^2(j)y^2(j) < \sum_{j=1}^{\ell} p^2(j)y^1(j) \qquad (6.3.1)$$

hold simultaneously, no unambiguous ranking emerges.

Although Pigou acknowledged this paradox, he could ignore it: the policy prescriptions he wanted to defend did not compare national income intertemporally. Leaving aside some details about how to value resources saved for the future, Pigou's de facto criterion, often called *value maximization*, was to rank output vectors at any single time t according to their value at the prices that occur at t. Thus, if p^t is the price vector at t, a vector y' would be superior at t to the y^t that actually occurs if

$$\sum_{j=1}^{\ell} p^t(j)y'(j) > \sum_{j=1}^{\ell} p^t(j)y^t(j). \qquad (6.3.2)$$

A vector y^t is optimal if there is no feasible y' satisfying 6.3.2. Since only one price vector occurs at each point in time, the paradox of 6.3.1 is hidden. Pigou would have had to have asked whether, following a policy change from y^t to y', y^t yields higher value than y' at whatever prices occur with y'; he conveniently refrained from posing this question.

Pigou, and for that matter Marshall as well, instinctively viewed price as the accurate gauge of social value. Early neoclassical economics saw utility and real income as homogeneous and virtually synonymous substances. This tradition, in fact, underlay Pigou's interchange of the concepts of utility and purchasing power. If we ignore questions of justification and simply posit that an increment of a good adds to welfare in proportion to its price, then increasing the value of output will indeed be the proper way to augment welfare.

The practical advantages of value maximization were sizable. Pigou could claim that in the absence of countervailing considerations competition maximizes social welfare: the private pursuit of factor income will equalize a factor's price across different uses, guaranteeing that marginal value products are also equalized and hence maximizing the value of output. Pigou could thereby endorse Marshallian perfect competition policies, while eliminating Marshall's cumbersome (and inaccurate) calculations of monetary valuations.

Just as significantly, by examining deviations between private returns to factors and their marginal social value (their marginal contribution to the value of output), Pigou could catalog inefficiencies and prescribe, where appropriate, corrective "Pigovian" taxes and bounties and other institutional reforms. For example, when using a factor leads to a technological externality and diminishes costs of production for other producers, the market return to the factor will be less than its social return; Pigou then recommended subsidization.

But though Marshall and Pigou may have formalized and elaborated the content of orthodox policy advice, and even provided a veneer of scientific respectability, rigorous foundations were lacking. Even if we ignore questions of internal consistency, Marshall and Pigou's efficiency concepts were plainly inconsistent with their nominal adherence to utilitarianism. Consumption goods can readily be distinguished according to the wealth of their purchasers. Since Marshallian consumer surplus and Pigovian value maximization ignore this fact, they cannot be reconciled with utilitarian welfare maximization. Marshall and Pigou disguised their failure by arguing that their criteria accurately measure the welfare of single individuals; either by supposing that differences among groups average out or by hypothetically fixing the income distribution, they tried—unsuccessfully—to pass from the representative individual to society as a whole.

6.4 The rejection of utilitarianism

The utilitarian consensus would have had trouble surviving the ordinal revolution under any circumstances: with nonordinal properties of utility discredited, the cardinal utilities needed for utilitarian welfare analysis lost all theoretical respectability. Indeed, the new emphasis on observable choice behavior made any form of normative theory problematic. As it happened, the attack on utilitarianism—initiated by Lionel Robbins in 1932—slightly preceded Hicks and Allen's papers on preference theory. Robbins charged utilitarians with having no scientific basis for their policy advice; their conclusions relied on untestable interpersonal comparisons of welfare. Specifically, Robbins questioned the link between diminishing marginal utility and the optimality of leveling the income distribution. Redistributing income to a poor individual A from a richer individual B requires knowledge of their capacities for satisfaction, yet "there is no means of testing the magnitude of A's satisfaction as compared with B's" [Robbins (1932, p. 124)].

Robbins recognized that economists and others routinely form beliefs about other individuals' capacities for satisfaction; but these beliefs, Robbins claimed, are not objectively demonstrable findings. When later explaining the evolution of his position, Robbins related his reaction to the story of a Brahmin confronted with the utilitarian argument for equality:

> "But that," said the Brahmin, "cannot possibly be right. I am ten times as capable as that untouchable over there." I had no sympathy with the Brahmin. But I could not escape the conviction that, if I chose to regard men as equally capable of satisfaction and he to regard them as differing according to a hierarchical schedule, the difference between us was not one which could be resolved by the same methods of demonstration as were available in other fields of social judgement (1938, p. 636).

Finally, Robbins reasoned that even if an enterprising utilitarian managed someday to invent a hedonimeter, welfare economics would still fall short of scientific status. That societies should pursue maximum aggregate satisfaction is still a normative postulate and cannot be proved objectively.

Robbins's skepticism about interpersonal comparisons of utility had ample precedent. Jevons had been careful to point out that his theory did not depend on comparing "the amount of feeling in one mind with that in another." He saw no means by which such comparisons could be accomplished, since "the susceptibility of one mind may, for what we know, be a thousand times greater than that of another." Since the behavior of individuals of different "susceptibilities" can be identical, interpersonal comparisons of utility have no impact on economics as a positive science. Hence, "even if we could compare the feelings of different minds, we should not need to do so."[8]

Although Robbins largely replicated Jevons's position, the subsequent Marshallian era's confidence in the objectivity of interpersonal comparisons made Robbins's stance appear new.[9] Still, pointing out the distinctive character of interpersonal welfare judgments need not have impinged on the conduct of welfare economics. Robbins himself sympathized with the utilitarian tradition of weighting the interests of each person equally; equal weighting "is less likely to lead one astray" than other moral philosophies (1938, p. 635). Robbins also had no blanket methodological objection to introspection as a tool of economic science. Hence, had the utilitarian consensus otherwise been sustainable, Robbins's contribution would only have been to bring to light the (supposedly) suppressed moral and introspective premises of the Marshallian tradition. Dedicated Pigovians could have confessed their ethical beliefs and proceeded to prescribe the same policy judgments as before.

The destructive power of Robbins's position lay instead in the concurrent erosion of confidence in the raw materials of utilitarian psychology. The decline of hedonism had undermined the presumption that the psychological experiences of different individuals can be compared, and ordinalism subsequently challenged the status of cardinality. As we have seen, the abstract character of cardinality had already put the utilitarians in a vulnerable position. With no access to agents' cardinal comparisons, Pigou and his peers could justify rigorously only those limited recommendations guaranteed not to harm the poor. Once the ordinal revolution ended the practice of claiming that unavailable cardinality information was nevertheless psychologically real, the pretense that utilitarianism provided a complete ranking of social states became clear.[10] Thus, even if the argument that policy judgments require normative and introspective underpinnings was ultimately a platitude, Robbins brought the limited ability of economists to make interpersonal comparisons of utility into the open. Robbins's *Essay* revealed that the emperor had no clothes.

Roy Harrod was instrumental in exposing the precarious state of welfare theory. In 1938, he complained that Robbins had not only undermined the rationale of utilitarian income redistributions but of all policy prescriptions, even those that economists had dispensed for centuries. Harrod used the

---

8. Jevons (1871, p. 21). See also the passage by Edgeworth discussed in section 6.2.

9. See Cooter and Rapoport (1984) for a rich account of how an objective theory of needs underlay Pigou's explanation of welfare comparisons.

10. See, e.g., Kaldor (1939, p. 551): "And short of complete equality, how can the economist decide precisely how much inequality is desirable—i.e., how much secures the maximum total satisfaction?"

example of the repeal of the corn laws, which had once protected English agriculture against grain imports. Harrod contended that Robbins could not justify free trade since the removal of trade barriers inevitably diminishes the welfare of some agents (landowners, for example) and this harm could not be weighed against the gains of others. Robbins replied, as I indicated, that he concurred with the tradition of giving individuals equal weight in welfare decisions. But the precise derivation of policy advice now seemed mysterious. The commitment to weight individuals equally does not explain how to order social policies; some method of declaring which utility representations are "unweighted" and appropriate for interpersonal comparisons is necessary.

How then could social decisions, whether traditional or otherwise, be justified? Several welfare criteria put forward in the 1940s tried to answer this question, most prominently the social welfare functions of Bergson and Samuelson and the compensation criteria of Hicks and Scitovsky. Although each camp tried to provide a comprehensive set of policy rankings, in the end they both contributed to the postwar era's narrow focus on Pareto optimality.

6.5 Bergson-Samuelson social welfare functions

Abram Bergson's solution (1938) was simply to posit a functional relationship between the welfare of a community and the consumption of its individual members. Bergson's most general formulation allowed for public goods in addition to private consumption and permitted social welfare to vary independently of the welfare of individuals. But Bergson himself and most later writers subsequently restricted analysis to private consumption and required social welfare to be an increasing function of agent utilities. Letting the consumption of each agent i be represented by the ℓ-vector x_i, and letting $x = (x_1, \ldots, x_n)$ be the consumption profile of society's n individuals, a Bergson social welfare function is denoted $W(x)$.

Paul Samuelson, the most prominent backer of Bergson's theory, underscored the ordinal character of W. First, just as with individual utility functions, monotonic transformations of W do not alter the relative rankings of consumption profiles; no one of these representations is granted special standing. Second, Bergson-style welfare judgments do not presuppose that individuals are pleasure seekers or can make cardinal judgments of satisfaction intensity. Social decision makers can therefore base their rankings on a variety of psychological and philosophical models; they only have to devise judgments of the form "x is at least as socially good as x'." Indeed, if these "at least as socially good as" judgments are complete, transitive, and continuous, there will be a continuous function W that summarizes the judgments. If, furthermore, x is judged to be better than x' whenever x Pareto dominates x', W will be *individualistic*, that is, it will have the form $W(u_1(x_1), \ldots, u_n(x_n))$, where $u_1, \ldots, u_n$ are utilities for the n agents, and W is increasing in each of the u_i. Thus, even the requirement that social welfare is a function of agent utilities can be seen as a reflection of ordinal welfare judgments, not utilitarian psychology. Samuelson concluded that Bergson had cleansed welfare economics of its cardinalist origins.[11]

The Bergson-Samuelson approach provided explicit foundations for Pigovian policy advice. Recall that Pigou could not rigorously justify why prices measure social value; he assumed that they do, and derived policy rules on that basis. Bergson justified analogous policy rules from first principles. For example, Bergson showed that at a social welfare maximum the ratio of the physical marginal products of any pair of factors must be the same in all sectors of the economy, thus rationalizing the Pigovian rule that marginal value products should be equalized. Bergson's derivation, moreover, used only preferences and technology as data; it did not rely on prices or income as primitive concepts. As we will see in section 6.7, postwar welfare economics later completed Bergson's project, providing even deeper and more detailed foundations for Pigovian policy analysis.

On the other hand, Bergson-Samuelson welfare functions suffer from the customary defect of ordinal decision theory: they assume that options— here, allocations of commodities—are ranked rather than explaining how to construct rankings. Indeed, the potential incompleteness of social rankings is more pervasive than the comparable problem in individual decision theory. An individual's consumption purchases can often be justified by an appeal to desire or whim. But social alternatives raise questions of justice and equity, and therefore need to be ranked by impartial rules. Mere declarations of preference make little headway in disputes over distributive justice; to resolve social choice problems credibly, welfare functions must have a disinterested justification.

As we have seen, Pigou and his peers could make only limited and noncontroversial welfare judgments. The new welfare economics therefore did not dismantle a fully developed ranking of social alternatives. But the rejection of utilitarianism could hardly decide questions of social justice that the Pigovians themselves did not know how to answer; nor did a new method for aggregating preferences suddenly materialize. Bergson and Samuelson and other economists of the 1930s and 1940s shared the gentle egalitarian sentiments of preceding generations; but since they were equally in the dark about how to trade off individual gains and losses, they could not fill in the gaps left by the utilitarians. Indeed, as economic analysis became less aggregative, welfare judgments grew more problematic. When output is single-dimensional, at least the ideal outcome of egalitarian welfare maximization has a presumptive meaning: each individual should receive the

11. The ordinality of W refers to the multiplicity of functions that can represent a given social welfare ordering. Bergson welfare functions do rank the welfare gains of different individuals; in this sense, often employed in the social choice literature, a W does make cardinal comparisons.

same share of the single good. But when output consists of many goods, which allocation is the egalitarian optimum? A system for weighting individual preferences is indispensable.

The absence of an aggregation method has led to a credibility gap between policies that can be recommended by all individualistic social welfare functions and those that depend on the particular welfare function employed. The former lead to Pareto improvements and are the only policies that are "operationally significant," to use Oscar Lange's revealing expression (1942). The remaining policies help some individuals and harm others and are therefore recommended by only a subset of social welfare functions. A comparable distinction separates necessary conditions for social welfare maximization into two groups. The conditions that struck many as nonnormative were those that must be obeyed at the maximum of any individualistic social welfare function, for example, the equalization of individuals' marginal rates of substitution or the equalization of ratios of marginal products across sectors. Although written in the calculus of prewar theory, these and related requirements are simply necessary conditions for Pareto optimality. The second "normative" group are the interpersonal conditions specifying which Pareto optimum should be selected.

Samuelson has repeatedly stressed that full optimality is not achieved unless all conditions for social welfare maximization, including the interpersonal conditions, are satisfied. Indeed, given a social welfare function, non-Pareto optimal allocations will dominate some of the Pareto optima when the distribution of goods across individuals is judged to be sufficiently superior. But the absence of a tangible method for judging distributional equity has meant that Samuelson's pleas have rarely been heeded: simply recommending arbitrary Pareto optima appears to circumvent the logjam of interpersonal comparability. On the contemporary scene, the avoidance of particular social welfare functions is sometimes hard to see. Policy analysis often nominally posits a social welfare function; but typically, only results that are independent of the function maximized are considered definitive.

6.5.1 An example: Harsanyi social welfare functions

Ordinalism has often tried to avoid the problem of incomplete orderings by arguing that the necessity of choice leads preferences to be well defined (see section 4.10). Whatever the merits of this reasoning, it would seem to be inapplicable to social choice: no agent's observable choices weigh one person's welfare against another's. But the tradition of using choice to resolve valuation problems is so deeply ingrained that derivations of social welfare functions have nevertheless often tried to rely on carefully designed choice problems.

To illustrate the formidable difficulties of constructing neutral social welfare judgments, consider Harsanyi's (1953) use of von Neumann–

Morgenstern theory to justify additive social welfare functions. Harsanyi converts the problem of social welfare into a problem of individual choice by imagining a person who must choose the social allocation of goods in ignorance of which of society's n individuals he or she will be. A possible outcome is a pair of the form (i, x_i), indicating that the chooser ends up with the preferences and personality of individual i and the (possibly ℓ-dimensional) consumption bundle x_i. Harsanyi endows the chooser with von Neumann–Morgenstern preferences; let $u(i, x_i)$ be the von Neumann–Morgenstern utility of (i, x_i). Harsanyi requires that social welfare judgments be disinterested: the chooser should suppose that the probability of being any individual is the same, that is, $1/n$. The social welfare of $x = (x_1, \ldots, x_n)$ is therefore $\Sigma_{i=1}^n (1/n) u(i, x_i)$, which is a positive linear transformation of $\Sigma_{i=1}^n u(i, x_i)$. Let $\succeq_i$ indicate the (von Neumann–Morgenstern) preferences that individual i actually has. If preferences obey the *acceptance principle*—if, that is, the ex ante preference among options (i, x_i) and (i, x_i') and their probability mixtures always coincides with the $\succeq_i$ ranking—then each $u(i, \cdot)$ is a utility representation of $\succeq_i$ [see Harsanyi (1977, p. 54)]. Harsanyi thus arrives at an ordinal version of utilitarianism: even though individuals need not be pleasure seekers, and even if utility has no psychological meaning outside of summarizing preference, social welfare can always be represented as a sum of individual utility functions.

Does Harsanyi's hypothetical choice problem solve the riddle of how to make interpersonal comparisons of welfare? Although a person committed to particular values may be able to rank allocations and outcomes, Harsanyi requires that choosers do not know what values or personality they will ultimately have. Under these circumstances, the completeness of preference is highly dubious; agents would lack the very prerequisites of decision making. Harsanyi does not suggest how agents might form evaluations in the absence of a personality. Although he may seem to be obeying the ordinalist program of using choice to ground preference, Harsanyi cannot employ the trick of deriving preferences from observations of choice; anyone who might choose among social outcomes already possesses an identity. The meaning of preference behind the veil of ignorance therefore remains obscure.

Even if we put aside these doubts about the completeness of personalityless preference, Harsanyi provides no reason to believe that different individuals would construct the same hypothetical preferences. Valuations require appraisal of the nature and depth of competing goals and are therefore shaped by individuals' disparate histories. For example, a committed environmentalist might deem the appreciation of unspoiled nature to be a more profound satisfaction than physical pleasure, while a hedonist might think that the contemplation of nature is a mirage fabricated for the idle. Hence, when imaginatively placing themselves behind the veil of ignorance, both types of people have reasons to conclude that their enjoyment of their most-valued options is the more intense experience, and therefore deserving of greater weight ex ante.[12]

More generally, Harsanyi's proposal cannot settle disagreements about how to make interpersonal comparisons of welfare. Having an ex ante preference relation means being able to make judgments of the form: "I prefer having preferences $\succeq_i$ with a vector of goods x_i to having preferences $\succeq_j$ with vector x_j," as well as subtler judgments involving probabilistic choice. But if someone can say that i experiences more welfare with x_i than j with x_j, then presumably ex ante he or she would choose to be i with x_i rather than j with x_j. Conflicting welfare judgments therefore translate into conflicting ex ante preference judgments; no progress is made by translating questions of interpersonal comparability into the language of decision theory.

The difficulties of making or coming to consensus about interpersonal comparisons leads to a corresponding indeterminacy of social welfare functions. In principle, any set of von Neumann–Morgenstern utility representations of society's n preference relations could represent an ex ante judgment of individuals' capacities for satisfaction. If $\{u(1, x_1), \ldots, u(n, x_n)\}$ is one set of representations, then, as long as $a_i > 0$ for all i, so is $\{a_1 u(1, x_1), \ldots, a_n u(n, x_n)\}$. Consequently, $\sum_{i=1}^{n} a_i u(i, x_i)$ is a social welfare function obeying the acceptance principle.

Presumably a group of individuals could agree to exclude at least some of these social welfare functions. If two individuals j and k have the same von Neumann–Morgenstern preferences, and in the absence of any reason to deem either individual more capable of satisfaction, it is reasonable to require that $a_j u(j, x_j) = a_k u(k, x_k)$ when $x_j = x_k$. But beyond this rarely applicable rule, general guidelines for restricting the set of admissible social welfare functions are hard to devise. We are left with the dissatisfying conclusion that, even if agents can agree to exclude some welfare functions, economic theory cannot characterize these restrictions formally. Thus, if we ignore the case of identical agents, the only changes in allocations that can be endorsed unambiguously are the changes recommended by all possible social welfare functions, that is, the Pareto improvements. And under mild restrictions, essentially every Pareto optimum is the maximum of some Harsanyi social welfare function.

6.6 Compensation criteria

The need for policy advice that does not depend on contentious and highly abstract interpersonal comparisons of welfare lay behind the development of compensation criteria, the main branch of the new welfare economics. In his brief but influential contribution of 1939, Nicholas Kaldor tried to come to grips with the fact that policy changes usually harm some individuals.

---

12. Arrow (1977) emphasizes precisely this disparity of information as a reason why individuals' welfare judgments diverge (indeed for a weaker form of social welfare judgment than that which Harsanyi considers).

Kaldor argued that a policy can be recommended if, by redistributing wealth from gainers to losers, it is "*possible* to make everybody better off than before, or at any rate to make some people better off without making anybody worse off."

Kaldor and other compensationists did not deny that policy making has a political and ethical dimension. But like Robbins, Kaldor felt that economists had no special expertise in judging distributions of welfare: whether losers "should in fact be given compensation or not, is a political question on which the economists, *qua* economist, could hardly pronounce an opinion." Kaldor hoped that the compensation principle would nevertheless rescue Pigou's separation of increases in economic efficiency from changes in distribution. In the compensationist vision, economic science should bracket ethical questions and rank economic arrangements solely on the basis of their efficiency. Politicians and philosophers, in their corner, would debate the principles of distributive justice and decide which of the most efficient allocations should be instituted.

Given that Harrod had initiated the crisis of how to justify policy advice, Kaldor naturally applied his welfare criterion to Harrod's claim that a defense of free trade must rely on interpersonal comparisons of utility. Free trade is unambiguously superior to agricultural protection, Kaldor countered, because losers under free trade—primarily landowners—can be compensated for any loss of income by transfers from the rest of the community. Kaldor supposed that a move to free trade does not change aggregate nominal income; the income decline of losers therefore exactly equals the income gains of winners and transfers can return each agent's nominal income to its ex ante level. But since the domestic price of grain falls, each agent can now afford greater consumption and is better off. The traditional free trade prescription is thereby reaffirmed.

Steeped in Pigovian thinking, Kaldor treated real income and utility as homogeneous, interchangeable concepts. In reality, both a move to free trade and transfers of wealth across agents will, by altering the pattern of demand, change the prices of consumption goods. Consequently, even if transfers keep the distribution of income constant, it is a virtual certainty that some individuals—those disproportionately purchasing goods with increased prices—will be worse off. Kaldor, in contrast, assumed that free trade would raise national income in the Pigovian sense. Since he viewed the different distributions of welfare that can arise from a single endowment of resources as embodying the same level of income, Kaldor held that an increase in national income could be reshuffled without loss of utility to generate a Pareto improvement. The Pigovian inheritance also explains Kaldor's puzzling assertion that free trade and other standard policy recommendations lead to increases in "physical productivity"—even when technology is unchanged. Greater physical productivity was simply shorthand for a per capita increase in Pigovian income.

Hicks, in a long sequence of articles, tried to clarify the meaning of compensation. Curiously, the first of Hicks's proposals, written later in 1939, conforms most closely to current-day thinking. "Let us define an *optimum* organisation of the economic system as one in which every individual is as well off as he can be made, subject to the condition that no reorganisation permitted shall make any individual worse off." Hicks went on to offer one of the best informal characterizations to date of Pareto optimality.[13] Since Pareto optimality only uses preferences and technology as primitive concepts, Hicks avoided any Pigovian concept of real income in his definition of efficiency.

But Hicks held that Pareto optimality constitutes only a portion of welfare economics. Since first-best optimality can rarely if ever be achieved, Hicks reasoned that rankings of nonoptimal allocations are indispensable. Indeed, it is the attempt to build second-best rankings that distinguishes 1940s welfare economics from the postwar reliance on Pareto optimality as the sole test of efficiency. Kaldor's paper suggested that the compensation principle provided a way to build such a ranking. Two major systems followed his lead. The next two subsections demonstrate the failure of these attempts to supplement Pareto efficiency; readers willing to take this on faith can proceed to section 6.7.

6.6.1 Hicksian variations: cost-benefit analysis

In *Value and Capital* (1939), Hicks developed Marshall's consumer surplus into a more accurate monetary measure of the gain or loss an agent experiences when prices change. Hicks refined these measures in the early 1940s, inventing the compensating and equivalent variations. With compensation criteria in the air, a sum of Hicksian variations provided an obvious way to test the capacity of gainers to compensate losers.[14]

Sums of variations can in principle generate consistent rankings of both optimal and nonoptimal allocations. Let $u_i(x_i)$ be an arbitrary utility function for each individual i and let $e_i(p, u_i)$ be the corresponding expenditure function, that is, the minimum quantity of income necessary for i to achieve utility level u_i at prices p. If we fix p arbitrarily, say at $\bar{p}$, $e_i(\bar{p}, u_i(x_i))$ is a (money-metric) utility function for i, since, for any $\bar{p}$, e_i is monotonically increasing in the u_i argument. Hence $\Sigma_{i=1}^{n} e_i(\bar{p}, u_i(x_i))$ is a legitimate Bergson-Samuelson social welfare function, indeed one taking the utilitarian sum of utilities form. Consequently $\Sigma_{i=1}^{n} e_i(\bar{p}, u_i(x_i))$ generates a transitive ordering of allocations $x = (x_1, \ldots, x_n)$ that ranks Pareto-superior allocations above Pareto-inferior allocations.

With the appropriate choice of $\bar{p}$, the $\Sigma_{i=1}^{n} e_i(\bar{p}, u_i(x_i))$ ranking of allocations will match the ranking of policies given by the sum of equivalent variations. Associate with each government policy the price vector p' that

---

13. In the Anglo-American literature, Hicks (1939a) was preceded by Lerner (1934) and Hotelling (1938).

14. Hicks (1941) contains Hicks's proposal to use variations to measure compensation payments. For later developments, see Hicks (1942, 1943, 1946).

results from the policy, and let p^1 denote the current status quo price vector. Let $x_i(p)$ be i's demand function. (For convenience I have suppressed the income argument; alternatively, let income be derived from endowment sales.) Agent i's *equivalent variation* is defined as

$$e_i(p^1, u_i(x_i(p'))) - e_i(p^1, u_i(x_i(p^1))),$$

which equals the change in income when prices are p^1 that allows an agent to achieve the utility obtainable when prices are p'. Summing, we have

$$\sum_{i=1}^n e_i(p^1, u_i(x_i(p'))) - \sum_{i=1}^n e_i(p^1, u_i(x_i(p^1))).$$

Hence a ranking of p' vectors according to the aggregate equivalent variation is equivalent to a ranking by $\sum_{i=1}^n e_i(p^1, u_i(x_i(p')))$—the $\sum_{i=1}^n e_i(p^1, u_i(x_i(p^1)))$ term being the same constant for all p'. Setting $\bar{p} = p^1$, an equivalent variation ranking of policies thus leads to the ranking implied by the Bergson-Samuelson social welfare function $\sum_{i=1}^n e_i(\bar{p}, u_i(x_i))$.

Hicksian variations are alive and well today in cost-benefit analysis. In day-to-day usage, sums of monetary valuations are compromised by inconsistent rules for choosing the base prices, $\bar{p}$, in $e_i(\bar{p}, u_i(x_i))$. First, the aggregate compensating variation, often used in applied work, amounts to a ranking of alternative price vectors p' according to the function $\sum_{i=1}^n e_i(p', u_i(x_i(p^1)))$. However, $e_i(p', u_i(x_i(p^1)))$—the amount of income, when prices are p', that allows an agent to achieve the utility obtainable when prices are p^1—need not ordinally rank the p' according to i's preferences. The function $e_i(p', u_i(x_i(p^1)))$ uses a different base-price vector p' for each policy; but e_i, if seen as a function of the x_i associated with p', is not a utility function for i.[15] Consequently, policies ordered by the aggregate compensating variation need not rank p'' above p' when p'' Pareto dominates p'.

Second, even when equivalent rather than compensating variations are used, rankings calculated at different dates will yield distinct orderings if current prices are used as base prices at each date: letting p^1 and p^2 be the status quo price vectors at dates 1 and 2, the ranking of policies p' generated by $\sum_{i=1}^n e_i(p^1, u_i(x_i(p')))$ and $\sum_{i=1}^n e_i(p^2, u_i(x_i(p')))$ will typically not be the same. In fact, beginning from a status quo with prices p^1, a move to p^2 can be recommended, but then, after arriving at p^2, a return to p^1 can be recommended. In symbols,

$$\sum_{i=1}^n e_i(p^1, u_i(x_i(p^2))) > \sum_{i=1}^n e_i(p^1, u_i(x_i(p^1)))\ \text{and}$$

$$\sum_{i=1}^n e_i(p^2, u_i(x_i(p^1))) > \sum_{i=1}^n e_i(p^2, u_i(x_i(p^2)))$$

can hold simultaneously.

---

15. That is, fixing p^1, consider the function of x_i given by $e_i(x_i^{-1}(x_i), u_i(x_i(p^1)))$, where $x_i^{-1}(x_i)$ is i's inverse demand function. See Chipman and Moore (1980) and Chipman (1987) for more on this point.

In one sense, these problems are only technical glitches: an equivalent variation ranking using a single vector of base prices at all dates generates no contradictions. But the frequency of base-price inconsistency reveals the arbitrariness of using $e_i(\bar{p}, u_i(x_i))$ functions in a sum of utilities. Using money-metric utility functions can only be justified by an assumption that, for each agent, the welfare generated by the goods that a unit of money buys is the same. Since rationales for this assumption are never provided, current prices produce a money measure of utility that is just as intuitive—or counterintuitive—as the money measures produced by other dates' prices.

In addition, despite the internal inconsistency, current prices conveniently rationalize the allocations generated by perfect competition. The Marshall-Pigou tradition used current prices to gauge social welfare in part because undistorted competition then maximizes social welfare. Cost-benefit analysis relies on modern-day versions of the same result: undistorted perfect competition maximizes the sum of equivalent variations, but only when market prices are used as base prices. This is due to the fact that with the utility functions $e_i(\bar{p}, u_i(x_i))$, the marginal utilities of income of the agents are identical (and in fact equal to 1) if $\bar{p}$ are the prices agents face on the market. If base and market prices do not coincide, marginal utilities of income will generally differ across agents and redistribution of income will be called for. Consequently, if one set of prices were declared to be the once-and-for-all vector of base prices, the conclusion that (undistorted) perfect competition leads to optimality would be lost. Even more embarrassing, the need to redistribute wealth would undermine the claim to be measuring efficiency rather than distribution. The internal consistency of Hicksian variations thus comes at considerable conceptual and ideological cost.

Hicksian variations and cost-benefit analysis are heirs of sorts to Marshall's vision that consumer surplus analysis would provide a practical implementation of utilitarianism. But Marshall understood that an exact utilitarian justification of consumer surplus requires that all agents have the same marginal utility of income. As we have seen, Marshall could not accept such an assumption, which would have been at odds with utilitarian intuitions about diminishing marginal utility. Hicksian variations sweep away these misgivings. Assigning each agent the same marginal utility of income by fiat, cost-benefit analysis tries to evade the egalitarianism of the utilitarian tradition.

The logic of compensation also does not justify the use of money-metric utility functions. The size of a sum of monetary valuations does not indicate how the set of feasible allocations would change if the hypothetical compensations were paid. Income transfers change relative prices, thus invalidating any variational measure of the amount of money agents must receive in compensation. Hence, even if one endorses the ethics of compensationism, a sum-of-dollars ranking cannot be rationalized. That such rankings can be made internally consistent does not alter this fact.

6.6.2 Output comparisons

I turn to the second and more important theory of compensation. In 1940, prior to his rehabilitation of consumer surplus, Hicks tried to compare the welfare potential of aggregate output vectors. By focusing on the set of consumption allocations achievable from a given output vector, Hicks gave the first clear interpretation, in real rather than monetary terms, of how compensation can rank second-best policies.

Hicks's ranking of output vectors, and other similar rankings, depend in part on how output is allocated, either before or after a change in policy. In order to keep notation uniform, we have little choice but to consider orderings of output allocation pairs.[16] For any ℓ-vector of aggregate outputs y, call the allocation $x = (x_1, \ldots, x_n)$ a *distribution* of y if $\Sigma_{i=1}^n x_i = y$, and call x a *Pareto distribution* of y if, in addition, there is no distribution of y that Pareto dominates x.[17] An output allocation pair is therefore denoted (y, x), where x is a distribution of y. (Including y is redundant, since $y = \Sigma_{i=1}^n x_i$, but notationally convenient.)

Suppose we wish to compare (y^1, x^1) and (y^2, x^2). Hicks (1940) defined y^2 as having more real income than y^1 if there is no distribution of y^1 leaving all agents at least as well off as at x^2. This definition has the advantage that an index-number comparison can test for an increase in income. Let p^1 denote the prices of the consumption goods at time 1 and p^2 the prices at time 2. If

$$\Sigma_{j=1}^\ell p^2(j)y^2(j) > \Sigma_{j=1}^\ell p^2(j)y^1(j), \qquad (6.6.1)$$

Hicks claimed that y^2 must have more real income than y^1.

Although Hicks did not provide much in the way of proof, the first welfare theorem makes the argument easy. Suppose, to the contrary, that there is a distribution of y^1, say x', that leaves all agents as well off as at x^2. Then, for each agent i (and assuming preferences are locally nonsatiated),

$$\Sigma_{j=1}^\ell p^2(j)x_i'(j) \geq \Sigma_{j=1}^\ell p^2(j) x_i^2(j).$$

Summing these n inequalities and using the definition of a distribution, we have

$$\Sigma_{j=1}^\ell p^2(j)y^1(j) \geq \Sigma_{j=1}^\ell p^2(j)y^2(j),$$

which contradicts 6.6.1.

Unfortunately, even if the inequality

$$\Sigma_{j=1}^\ell p^1(j)y^2(j) > \Sigma_{j=1}^\ell p^1(j)y^1(j),$$

16. On this point, see Chipman and Moore (1978), which also provides an excellent overview of compensation criteria.

17. Output is a misleading but commonly used locution: all goods that affect agents' utilities, including leisure, must be included in output.

also holds, y^1 can simultaneously have more real income than y^2; that is, there may not be any distribution of y^2 leaving all agents as well off as at x^1. Hicksian real income comparisons are therefore not unambiguously defined; I provide an example momentarily.

Still, the index-number test was the most significant result of the new welfare economics of the 1940s. Hicks reestablished a connection between Pigovian value maximization and welfare improvements, and even mimicked some aspects of Pigou's justification of index numbers; both proposals utilize the potential allocations that can be achieved through redistribution. But Hicks dropped all references to the mysterious concept of purchasing power and stated explicitly that Pareto improvements constitute the relevant potential allocations.

Scitovsky (1941) offered an interpretation of Kaldor's original proposal which, although differing in the details from Hicks, also applied the logic of compensation to output vectors. On Scitovsky's reading of Kaldor, (y^2, x^2) is superior to (y^1, x^1) if x^1 is a Pareto distribution of y^1 and there exists a distribution x' of y^2 that Pareto dominates x^1. Although it is an injustice to Kaldor, I follow tradition and call this ranking the *Kaldor criterion*.

The Kaldor criterion has the inconvenience of being able to rank as inferior only output vectors that are Pareto optimally distributed.[18] But even putting aside this drawback, say by considering only Pareto optimal distributions, a moment's reflection reveals that the Kaldor criterion and Hicks's ranking need not coincide. To take the most trivial example, consider a two-agent, two-good economy in which agent 1 only desires good 1 and agent 2 only desires good 2. If y^2 has more of good 2 and less of good 1 than y^1—that is, $y^2(2) > y^1(2)$ and $y^2(1) < y^1(1)$—there can be no distribution of y^2 that Pareto dominates $\hat{x}^1 = ((y^1(1), 0), (0, y^1(2)))$ and no distribution of y^1 that Pareto dominates $\hat{x}^2 = ((y^2(1), 0), (0, y^2(2)))$. Hence, by Hicks's criterion, y^1 has more real income than y^2, and y^2 has more real income than y^1, generating the ambiguity mentioned earlier. Since $(y^1, \hat{x}^1)$ and $(y^2, \hat{x}^2)$ are evidently unranked by the Kaldor criterion, the Hicks and Kaldor orderings need not agree.

The situation is easy to represent with *utility possibility sets* (i.e., sets of achievable utility vectors defined relative to some fixed specification of utility representations).[19] For the utility functions $u_1(x_1) = x_1(1)$ and $u_2(x_2) = x_2(2)$, figure 6.1 depicts the utility possibility sets, $U(y^1)$ and $U(y^2)$, achievable through distributions of y^1 and y^2. Clearly the ambiguity of the Hicks ranking and its nonoverlap with the Kaldor criterion will continue to hold with less extreme preferences that smooth the boundaries of $U(y^1)$ and $U(y^2)$.

---

18. If we did not require x^1 to be a Pareto distribution, y^2 could have less of each good than y^1 and yet (y^2, x^2) could be superior to (y^1, x^1).

19. We always suppose that utility is freely disposable, i.e., if some point $(u_1, \ldots, u_n)$ is in a utility possibility set, then so is any point $(u_1', \ldots, u_n')$ with $u_i' \leq u_i$ for all i.

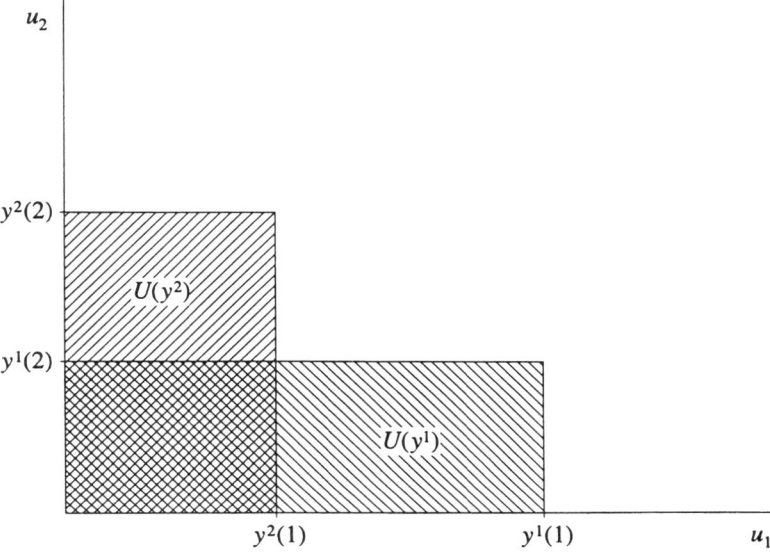

Figure 6.1 The divergence of the Hicks and Kaldor orderings

The incompleteness of the Kaldor criterion would by itself be a relatively minor shortcoming. But, as Scitovsky famously pointed out, the ranking suffers from the same embarrassing defect as the Hicks approach: it is possible for (y^2, x^2) to be Kaldor superior to (y^1, x^1) and for the reverse ranking to hold. This is illustrated in figure 6.2, drawn from Samuelson (1950). Thus, neither Hicks's output ranking or the Kaldor criterion provides an unambiguous ranking of output vectors. Scitovsky therefore proposed that Kaldor be amended: (y^2, x^2) should only be considered superior to (y^1, x^1) if, in addition to there being a distribution of y^2 that Pareto dominates x^1, there is no distribution of y^1 that Pareto dominates x^2. Hence, under the Scitovsky amendment, (y^1, x^1) in figure 6.2 is not ranked relative to (y^2, x^2).[20]

As Samuelson (1950) subsequently argued, Scitovsky's repair work scarcely frees the Kaldor criterion of all inconsistencies. The raison d'être of Kaldor's program was to segregate efficiency analysis from distributional judgments. But Scitovsky's ranking critically depends on the distribution of welfare. Referring again to figure 6.2, y^2 would be superior to y^1 if $\hat{x}$ rather than x^2 were the distribution of y^2. In addition, and perhaps more

---

20. The Scitovsky criterion can also be defined in the following, more compact way. Let $\succeq_S$ be the relation over output allocation pairs defined by $(y^2, x^2) \succeq_S (y^1, x^1)$ if and only if there exists a (y^2, x') such that x' leaves all agents as well off as at x^1. The strict relation $\succ_S$ is defined from $\succeq_S$ in the standard way as $(y^2, x^2) \succ_S (y^1, x^1)$ if and only if $(y^2, x^2) \succeq_S (y^1, x^1)$ and not $(y^1, x^1) \succeq_S (y^2, x^2)$. It is immediate that $(y^2, x^2) \succ_S (y^1, x^1)$ is equivalent to (y^2, x^2) being superior to (y^1, x^1) by the Scitovsky criterion defined above.

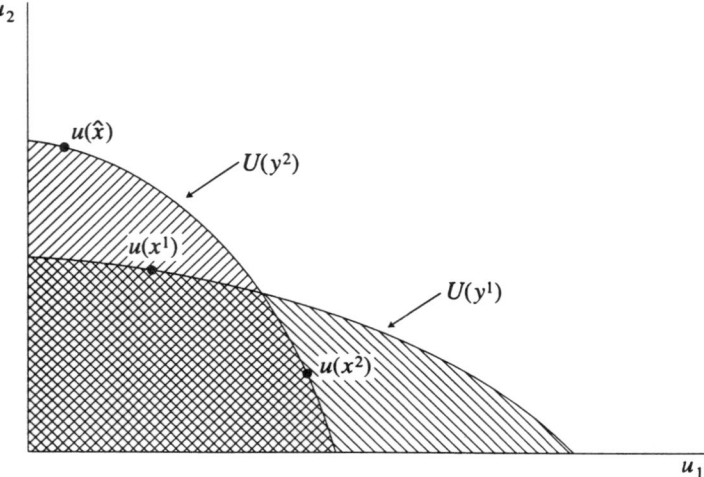

Figure 6.2 The inconsistency of the Kaldor criterion

disturbingly, it is easy to construct cases where the Scitovsky ordering is intransitive, that is, where (y^1, x^1) is superior to (y^2, x^2), (y^2, x^2) is superior to (y^3, x^3), but (y^3, x^3) is superior to (y^1, x^1).

Samuelson, although hostile to the compensation paradigm, concluded that the only consistent compensationist output ranking would be to judge y^2 weakly superior to y^1 if and only if, for any distribution x^1 of y^1, there is some distribution x^2 of y^2 at which all agents are at least as well off as at x^1. Call this ranking the *Samuelson output criterion*: it is equivalent to the utility possibility set $U(y^2)$ containing $U(y^1)$. Naturally, y^2 is strongly superior to y^1 if, in addition, there is some x^2 that achieves a vector of utilities that is not an element of $U(y^1)$.

Samuelson's proposal has the virtue of not making any reference to the actual consumption of agents; it is a pure ranking of output vectors, independent of the distribution of welfare. Also, it is easy to confirm that Samuelson's output criterion is transitive. On the other hand, output vectors will usually be unranked. For instance, if one agent prefers the entirety of y^1 to the entirety of y^2 and another agent has the reverse preference, y^1 and y^2 will not be ordered. Hence, with a large and diverse set of agents, virtually the only output vectors that will be ranked are pairs where one vector contains at least as much of every good as the other. As Samuelson noted, ranking output vectors in this case was never under dispute; the gymnastics of compensationist reasoning are therefore not worth the bother.

With the benefit of hindsight, it is clear that the difficulties above stem from the very project of trying to rank output vectors. Kaldor originally proposed to rank policies, but the primary interpreters of Kaldor unfortunately identified policies with the particular vectors of output the policies happen to generate. Consider again the compensationist argument for the superiority of free trade. Kaldor argued that with appropriate redistributions of income a protectionist status quo can be Pareto dominated. Without the redistributions, however, the free trade composition of output will shift toward the goods that happen to be desired by those who gain under free trade; and there is no reason for this vector of goods to be ranked superior to the status quo by the Kaldor or Scitovsky criterion or by the Samuelson output criterion. A workable compensation test must consider the entire set of allocations that a policy can achieve as redistributions of income vary.

Samuelson pursued this reasoning, extending his output criterion to sets of output vectors. Let us say that the set of output vectors Y^2 is (weakly) superior to the set Y^1 by the *Samuelson policy criterion* if and only if, for every x^1 that is a distribution of some y^1 in Y^1, there is a distribution x^2 of a y^2 in Y^2 that is weakly Pareto superior to x^1.[21] In other words, any allocation achievable with Y^1 is (weakly) Pareto inferior to some allocation achievable with Y^2: to paraphrase Samuelson, 2 can do everything 1 can do—and better. Of course, Y^2 is strictly superior to Y^1 when the above definition holds and, in addition, Y^1 is not weakly superior to Y^2. Analogous to the output criterion, the superiority of Y^2 over Y^1 is equivalent to $U(Y^2)$ containing $U(Y^1)$, where $U(Y^i)$ is the set of agent utility vectors obtainable from the y in Y^i.

Samuelson's policy criterion is easily applied to the free trade versus protection example. Let Y^P be the set of outputs that can be produced at the status quo competitive equilibrium when a given set of protective import tariffs is present and let Y^F be the set of outputs that can be produced when tariffs are eliminated. Include in Y^F the output vectors that occur in competitive equilibrium when consumer wealth is determined either by initial endowments or by lump-sum redistributions of those endowments; if desired, Y^P can also contain the outputs that occur when endowments are redistributed. If no distortions, such as externalities, are present, if markets are perfectly competitive, and if the country in question is a price-taker on world markets, it is easy to show that Y^F is superior—and typically strictly superior—to Y^P by the Samuelson policy criterion. (In fact, in this example, the Samuelson policy criterion is needlessly complicated: the set of aggregate consumption vectors attainable with free trade contains, and usually strictly contains, the consumption vectors attainable under protection. Thus, no mention of preferences is necessary to conclude that free trade has an efficiency advantage.)

The Samuelson policy criterion seems to provide the distributionally neutral and internally consistent ranking that the compensationists had been seeking. Yet it had little historical influence, either in theoretical work or practical affairs. Why? As the free trade versus protection example makes clear, the obvious applications of Samuelson's criterion do nothing

---

21. This is also the KHS ordering of Chipman and Moore (1971, 1978).

more than claim that a policy leading to a Pareto optimum is superior to policies leading to non-Pareto optimal allocations. In principle, one could also construct intermediate sets of outputs whose associated utility possibility sets contain the distorted status quo's utility possibility set and are contained by the fully efficient utility possibility set. Such sets are awkward constructions: in the free trade versus protection case, a partial reduction of tariffs need not lead to a utility possibility set containing the status quo utility set. And no Hicksian index-number test can cut through the complexity; such tests at best measure the welfare potential of pairs of output vectors, not sets of output vectors. Still, with carefully chosen combinations of tariff changes and endowment redistributions an intermediate utility possibility set could be assembled. But in addition to being difficult, such a calculation would be pointless. For policy purposes, the only pertinent question is how to move from a distorted status quo to the Pareto-efficient frontier. Policies leading to allocations that can be Pareto dominated by other policies should never be chosen and therefore do not need to be characterized. Ranking nonoptimal policies can only offer a commentary on what might have been necessary, or, when making comparisons with the past, an index of whether output has expanded.

What of the argument of Hicks and other compensationists that the infeasibility of first-best allocations makes a ranking of second-best policies imperative? On closer inspection, Hicks's argument does not call for a ranking of second-best policies but only for a Pareto efficiency test of second-best policies. Given a complete model and an arbitrary set of policy tools, the set of achievable allocations can always be calculated. Any allocation not on the Pareto frontier of this constrained set of achievable utilities is inefficient and should therefore be rejected. This logic applies whether the set of achievable allocations contains all physically conceivable allocations or a second-best subset; factoring in restrictions on policy availability does not lessen the futility of ranking options that a policymaker would never select.

The Pareto efficiency paradigm is hardly problem-free: declaring policies to be inefficient based on the fiction of a completely specified model is suspicious, and I examine this methodology in detail in section 6.8. But the difficulty of partitioning allocations into Pareto efficient and inefficient sets is paralleled by an analogous complexity in ranking inefficient allocations. The knowledge required to construct policies ranked by the Samuelson policy criterion is just as formidable as what is needed to calculate the constrained Pareto optimal frontier. The two approaches are therefore equally vulnerable to the criticism that they require unrealistically detailed information.

6.7 The postwar consensus

Pareto efficiency not only incorporates the policy-relevant substance of the compensation criteria, and with less effort: it can also claim to resolve the decades-long search for a consistent definition of economic efficiency. By identifying a set of optimal allocations, the Paretian position avoids the distributional questions that Marshall and Pigou had wanted to but did not know how to ignore. Allocations are Pareto efficient if and only if they maximize some individualistic social welfare function. Consequently, any policy recommended by any of the standard normative goals of neoclassical economics is Pareto efficient; and the Pareto inefficient policies will be rejected by any of these standard objective functions. Moving to the Pareto frontier still presupposes value judgments—for instance, preferences must be assumed to reflect individual welfare—but the most controversial judgments, interpersonal comparisons of welfare, are unnecessary.

Historically, it was the welfare theorems of general equilibrium theory that secured Pareto efficiency's ascendancy. The Pareto optimality of competitive equilibria had earlier been discussed in continental general equilibrium theory (by Pareto among others); and in England, Pareto efficiency was implicit in the claim that equilibria (without externalities or other distortions) are utilitarian maxima. What was new from the late 1930s onward was the careful mathematical scrutiny of Paretian and social welfare optima, which exposed the depth of the connection between optimality and market equilibrium. Bergson's maximization of social welfare functions in particular made the parallels between the marginal equalities describing Pareto efficiency and market equilibrium transparent.

Pre-1950s treatments still had technical weaknesses: even Lange (1942), the best of this era, made extensive and unnecessary use of the calculus and assumed implicitly that each agent consumes positive quantities of all goods. The independent papers of Arrow and Debreu in 1951 repaired these weaknesses. More profoundly, they allowed the Pareto efficiency of competitive equilibria (the first welfare theorem) to be separated rigorously from the fact that any Pareto optimum can be instituted through an equilibrium with income transfers (the second welfare theorem). This distinction revealed the simplicity and generality of the first theorem: the Pareto efficiency of competitive equilibria does not hinge on convexity or differentiability but only on agents facing the same set of prices and the almost trivial assumption that preferences are locally nonsatiated.

The welfare theorems stand as the cornerstone of postwar normative economics, and the Arrow and Debreu proofs contain perhaps the best-known arguments in the history of formal economics. Part of the attraction of the theorems is that they seem to justify the sweeping market reforms that economists have long advocated. In an economy without externalities, any restriction on competition will lead to a Pareto-inefficient allocation; and although a pure move to competition will likely harm some agents— for example, factor owners previously sheltered from competition—the government can in principle redistribute income so as to leave no individual worse off.

Pareto efficiency could also resurrect Pigou's equation of efficiency with value maximization, though as a test for optimality rather than as a method for comparing arbitrary pairs of output vectors (as Hicks had also hoped would be possible). Suppose that all agents face the same prices, that no consumption externalities are present, and that the output vector y, distributed as x at prices p, is such that $\Sigma_{j=1}^{\ell} p(j) y(j)$ is at least as great as $\Sigma_{j=1}^{\ell} p(j) y'(j)$, for all possible alternative output vectors y'. Then a slight rewording of the argument in subsection 6.6.2 justifying Hicks's index-number comparisons shows that x must be Pareto optimal. (Since profit maximization guarantees that $\Sigma_{j=1}^{\ell} p(j) y(j)$ is maximized, this claim amounts to a restatement of the first welfare theorem.) Conversely, if there is a y' such that $\Sigma_{j=1}^{\ell} p(j) y'(j)$ is greater than $\Sigma_{j=1}^{\ell} p(j) y(j)$ (and if utility functions are differentiable), then aggregate outputs a small distance from y in the direction of y' can be distributed so as to Pareto dominate x [see, e.g., Varian (1984, sec. 7.5)]. Maximizing the value of output is thus sufficient and almost necessary for Pareto optimality.

The practical significance of these results is admittedly cloudy. Suppose that the government has some influence over the economy's aggregate outputs, say through infrastructural investment. Confirming that the value of output is maximized requires comparisons with the value of all possible alternative output vectors. And comparisons of a small number of output vectors say very little: for instance, changing from a y distributed as x at prices p to a y' with a lesser value at p can move the economy from a Pareto-inefficient to a Pareto-efficient allocation.[22] Furthermore, as will be clear in the next section, knowing that the value of output is not maximized does not mean that a policymaker can calculate any of the Pareto-improving policies. Hicks's dream of basing policy decisions on uncomplicated index-number comparisons therefore cannot be salvaged. But these practical limitations do not eradicate the achievement of providing a rationale for the welfare properties of value maximization. The basis of centuries of orthodox economic advice had seemingly been unearthed: postwar welfare theory can claim the discovery that Pareto optimality, not aggregate utility, underlies the concept of economic efficiency.

Restricting value maximization to characterizing Pareto optima also clears up the index-number paradoxes. Recall from section 6.3 that Pigou had noticed that there could be two price-output combinations, (p^1, y^1) and (p^2, y^2), such that y^2 will have more value than y^1 when valued at p^1, but less value than y^1 when valued at p^2. To Pigou, this implied that y^1 simultaneously has more and less real income than y^2. From the Paretian perspective, there is no puzzle. If both y^1 and y^2 are feasible in both periods (and if utilities are differentiable and the feasible set is convex), neither is Pareto

---

22. Of course, it must be that at the prices p' that occur with the new allocation, $\Sigma_{j=1}^{\ell} p'(j) y(j)$ reaches a maximum at y'. Also, even if y maximizes the value of output at p relative to all other output vectors (and is therefore allocated as an efficient x), a y' with lesser value at p can still lead to a (different) Pareto-efficient allocation.

optimal; therefore no ranking of y^1 and y^2 is proposed. An index-number test for Pareto optimality is less useful than a complete ordering of output vectors, but at least internal consistency is salvaged.

6.8 Problems with Pareto optimality

Some common complaints directed against Pareto efficiency are easy to counter. Initially the criterion was faulted for not identifying a unique optimum and, when the status quo is inefficient, for not specifying which Pareto improvement should be chosen [Samuelson (1947, pp. 243–244), Arrow (1951a, p. 37)]. Although Pareto efficiency does only identify a set of optima, it was never intended to settle all policy disputes. In his original compensation proposal, Kaldor aimed to segregate efficiency questions, on which economists could appropriately pronounce, from the harder distributional decisions that must be resolved politically. The same rationale applies to Pareto efficiency. As long as sufficiently many policies are rejected as inefficient, economics can still claim a meaningful, though not overly ambitious, role in social decision making.

A related, more frequently voiced objection charges the Pareto approach with violating its own credo that distributional judgments are off limits. Policies, it is said, should be judged in terms of the allocations they induce. A Pareto optimum therefore cannot be recommended over an inefficient allocation unless the former is a Pareto improvement over the latter. This reasoning attacks a flawed (but not uncommon) formulation of the Pareto approach. Pareto optimality identifies a *set* of efficient allocations and does not pretend to rank non-Pareto comparable allocations. Politicians may not choose to institute Pareto improvements when eliminating Pareto inefficiencies, but they could if they wished. (There is no reason, it should be noted, for a government maximizing a social welfare function to choose a Pareto improvement when a policy constraint is removed and a larger set of utilities becomes accessible.) Paretians may seem naive in imagining that political authorities' policies are guided by well-specified plans. But they can retort that one portion—the economist's portion—of ideal governance is to characterize what is efficient and what is not.

Finally, it sometimes has seemed that Paretian welfare economics presupposes an improbable array of policy tools. Most conspicuously, governments do not make lump-sum transfers; they redistribute only with imperfect devices, such as wealth and income taxes, that depend on agents' behavior and therefore warp incentives. This objection suffers from two problems. First, even with a reduced set of redistributive instruments conceivably it could still be possible to declare a large number of policies Pareto inefficient. Second, and more fundamentally, lump-sum transfers are usually not institutionally proscribed; rather, they are informationally inaccessible. Governments must use behavior-dependent rather than lump-sum policies because it is only by observing agents' actions—for example, their consumption decisions—that governments can learn agents' characteristics and thus whom to transfer income to and at what rate.

Indeed, the Pareto approach's information requirements are its critical weakness. Far from having too many options to choose from, policymakers typically cannot reach the Pareto optimum they most prefer or devise Pareto improvements. The problem is often masked by common interpretations of the welfare theorems. The second welfare theorem states that any Pareto optimum can be reached through wealth redistributions and competitive markets. The relationship between wealth distributions and the optimum achieved may be complex, but it still seems as if reaching a desired optimum is straightforward: if governments can transfer wealth, the optimal policy is contained in the set of feasible policies.

But both the optimum chosen and the policy that reaches it vary as a function of agents' preferences. Consequently a policymaker who is ignorant of agents' characteristics will not be able to design the required wealth transfers. Suppose that a policymaker's uncertainty can be described by an exhaustive list of states of nature. Each state specifies a complete model of the economy; in an exchange setting, for instance, each state is a vector of agent preferences and endowments. The policymaker wishes to institute a particular Pareto optimum at each state, perhaps determined by maximizing a social welfare function; consequently at each state there is a well-defined distribution of wealth—say, a rearrangement of initial endowments—at which the optimum is a competitive equilibrium. Since the optimal distribution of wealth will vary with the unknown characteristics of agents, no state-invariant policy can achieve the targeted optimum in all states. The usefulness of the second welfare theorem is therefore severely qualified. If policymakers know agent characteristics, as the second welfare theorem seems to suppose, markets would be superfluous for allocating resources; the government could simply dictate the desired allocation. On the other hand, when policymakers do not know agent characteristics, the information needed to devise the appropriate income transfers is missing. The policy recommendations implied by the second welfare theorem are thus either dispensable or unobtainable.

Similar difficulties confound Pareto improvements. Consider a policymaker facing a status quo distorted by excise taxes and subsidies—for simplicity, suppose that any surplus revenue is distributed lump sum to consumers. The first welfare theorem reports that abolishing the taxes and subsidies will lead to a Pareto optimum. But the elimination of taxes will change relative prices and thus typically harm some individuals. The second welfare theorem assures us that transfers exist that can compensate the losers. But, once again, policymakers do not have the preference or demand information to determine who the losers are or the size of the appropriate transfers. Yet if Pareto improvements are not in fact calculable, labeling the status quo as "distorted" is suspect: the status quo is not Pareto inefficient from the policymaker's limited-information perspective. The ability of the

Pareto criterion to discriminate among policy choices is therefore jeopardized: if all policies are efficient, no guidance is provided. When all or most policies are efficient, let us say that *policy paralysis* obtains.

Remarkably little attention was paid to the informational basis of Pareto efficiency in the first years of postwar equilibrium theory. This was due, no doubt, to the disproportionate emphasis on models in which perfect competition could be identified as distortion-free. Even a policymaker with little or no information about agents' characteristics can then achieve first-best Pareto optimality: in the tax example, simply set taxes to zero, independent of agents' preferences. The dilemmas of policy design become more obvious when constraints on policy tools leave some distortions irremediable. The theory of the second best, pioneered by Lipsey and Lancaster (1956), shows that if some distortion cannot be removed then not even constrained (second-best) efficiency will be achieved by letting markets operate unimpeded. For instance, if an excise tax on some good is institutionally constrained to be nonzero, then optimal excise taxes on other goods will generally also be nonzero and depend in complex ways on the specifics of preferences. The last, reassuring nostrum of the welfare theorems vanishes: no simple laissez-faire policy will achieve even second-best Pareto efficiency.

Why were the Lipsey and Lancaster results considered so alarming? If a complete model of the economy were available, the complexity of policy construction would only be a technical hurdle. The constrained maximization of social welfare functions or the derivation of the set of second-best Pareto optima would remain well defined. Indeed, extensive literatures have pursued both these programs. In the absence of a complete model, however, second-best theory exposes the dilemmas of policy design. No policy, no matter how subtly crafted, can achieve either first- or second-best Pareto efficiency at all states.

Can the informational problems of the Pareto program be overcome? Recall that with a complete model, a Pareto-efficient allocation can be characterized either as an allocation at which no agent can be made better off without making someone worse off or as an allocation that maximizes some individualistic social welfare function. The two most prominent extensions of Pareto efficiency to environments where the policymaker is uncertain about the model refine these definitions.

The first option retains the assumption that each agent's well-being can be described by a single preference ordering. Each agent's preferences must therefore be defined ex ante, that is, prior to the resolution of the policymaker's uncertainty; if the von Neumann–Morgenstern theory is employed, an expected utility function can then be assigned to each agent. As we will see in a social-choice example in the next section, this strategy does discriminate adequately among policy options: arbitrary policies are usually inefficient. But the goal of avoiding interpersonal comparisons of welfare is sacrificed. Since the policymaker does not know agent preferences, each ex ante ordering must rank the choices an agent would hypothetically make if uncertain about what preferences he or she will have. Even if a policymaker could construct these rankings, the orderings would embody judgments about the relative value and intensity of different preference relations. Our earlier discussion of Harsanyi's model, in subsection 6.5.1, underscored the drawbacks of choice behind the veil of ignorance. Indeed, although they apply only to the potential preferences of one agent at a time, the current ex ante preferences are constructed on the same principle as Harsanyi social welfare functions: they both posit von Neumann–Morgenstern preferences in which the objects of choice include the prospects of having various personalities. Consequently, disagreements about how to make interpersonal comparisons will reappear in the choice of which ex ante preference relation to employ. Thus, to make this option workable, consensus about how to make interpersonal comparisons is required.

The second alternative declares policies efficient if they maximize some expected social welfare function. An expected welfare function is a probability-weighted sum of the social welfare occurring at each state. Each such function incorporates a system of welfare comparisons: for each preference relation occurring at one or more states, an interpersonally comparable utility function must be specified. Neutrality with respect to interpersonal comparisons is maintained by permitting optimal policies to maximize an arbitrary expected welfare function; *any* system for weighting individual utility functions is permissible.

Expected welfare maximization suffers from the opposite difficulty of ex ante preferences: large numbers of policies, and often all policies, are optimal. Loosely speaking, if the uncertainty facing the policymaker is substantial, then it is probable that any move from the status quo will harm some agent in at least one of the states. Hence, for any given policy change, some expected social welfare function that heavily weights the preferences of the harmed agents will reject the change. In fact, in the social-choice model in the next section, each policy option maximizes some expected welfare function: complete policy paralysis occurs.

The policy paralysis phenomenon arises in concrete economic contexts. Consider again an economy with arbitrary excise taxes and subsidies. The standard full-information welfare theorems argue that some combination of zero taxes and lump-sum transfers will Pareto dominate any status quo with nonzero taxes. As I have stressed, informational limitations make these policies problematic. But beyond this negative reasoning, an arbitrary status quo vector of excise taxes has positive advantages: taxes change relative prices in ways that systematically benefit certain preference relations. For instance, a low relative price for some good will disproportionately benefit those potential agents who prefer that good. It would be better of course to transfer wealth directly to those agents—or, more accurately, those preference relations—that the government wishes to benefit. But in the absence of the information needed to devise these transfers, tax-induced changes in relative prices can efficiently target the right preference relations; in expectation, the agents with the favored preferences will gain.[23]

The two options of positing ex ante utilities and maximizing expected welfare converge in practice. Policy recommendations that depend on how preferences are aggregated into ex ante utility functions will appear to be artifacts of the policymaker's opinions about interpersonal comparisons. Just as with the Bergson-Samuelson approach, only the conclusions that are independent of the aggregation method will be authoritative. But any policy that is the maximum of some expected welfare function is a Pareto optimum relative to some system of ex ante preferences. Hence, if we try to purge interpersonal comparisons from ex ante preferences, the policy paralysis conclusions of expected welfare maximization reappear.

Note that both ex ante preferences and expected welfare maximization take the policymaker's uncertainty to be a fixed feature of the environment. Perhaps policymakers can establish a strategic environment in which agents will reveal their private information, or where agents at least have an incentive to act in ways that allow social decisions to depend on their private information. Theories of implementation and mechanism design have actively pursued these possibilities. A full evaluation of these literatures is beyond the scope of this chapter, but certainly it is unrealistic to think that policymakers must accept their ignorance as a fait accompli. It is equally implausible, however, to imagine that strategic manipulations can eliminate model uncertainty; and the policy paralysis dilemma can arise with even small amounts of such uncertainty.

Once the depth of the policy paralysis problem is recognized, the mission of the new welfare economics of the 1940s becomes easier to fathom. Hicks recognized that first-best Pareto optimality is not a useful tool for policy analysis. And while he did not point to informational complexity as the fatal weakness of the Pareto approach, Hicks grasped the importance of having an informationally parsimonious procedure for classifying policies. Hicks thought that Pigovian index-number comparisons could meet this need. Unfortunately, as we saw in section 6.6, binary comparisons of the value of output do not provide a test of any well-defined welfare criterion.

6.9 Policy paralysis: a social-choice example

A simple model of social choice illustrates the dilemmas of Pareto efficiency.[24] Imagine a policymaker who can choose a pure policy option

---

23. The optimal taxation problem is treated in more detail in Mandler (1996b). I show that the set of policies that are the maximum of some expected social welfare function is large in the sense of being an open set. Some policies can be rejected due to fact that the preferences of some agents can be ex ante identical from the vantage point of a policymaker with model uncertainty; hence, some redistributions from a better-endowed agent to a worse-endowed agent are recommended.

24. This section draws freely on Mandler (1996a).

from the set $A = \{a_1, \ldots, a_m\}$ or a probability mixture, $q = (q_1, \ldots, q_m)$, $\Sigma_{i=1}^m q_i = 1$, of the elements of A. Each individual $j = 1, \ldots, n$, has von Neumann–Morgenstern preferences over the pure and mixed policy choices, summarized by the utility function $v_j(a_i)$; the utility of q to agent j is therefore $\Sigma_{i=1}^m q_i v_j(a_i)$. Naturally, any increasing linear—or, strictly speaking, affine—transformation of v_j is also an expected utility representation of j's preferences. Let an *assignment* of utilities be a vector of functions $u = (u_1, \ldots, u_n)$ where for each j, u_j is some increasing linear transformation of v_j. Corresponding to each assignment is the additive social welfare function $W_u(q) = \Sigma_{j=1}^n \Sigma_{i=1}^m q_i u_j(a_i)$.[25] Since multiplying each v_j by an arbitrary positive constant yields an assignment, the welfare functions generated by assignments includes not only the unweighted sums of utilities but also the weighted sums.

Suppose first that the policymaker knows the primitives of the economy with certainty. A Pareto-efficient policy is then defined in the standard way as a q such that no q' is weakly preferred to q by all agents and strictly preferred by at least one agent. The equivalence of the Pareto optima and the policies that maximize some social welfare function holds in this model. See figure 6.3, which depicts a utility possibility set U for a two-agent model. Each vertex in the figure denotes the utilities of the two agents for one of the pure policies; the entire set additionally contains the utilities achievable through mixed policies. The Pareto optima are the northeast frontier of U (and the q that reach these points are independent of the utility assignment used to construct U). Since the level set of any social welfare function W_u is a negatively sloped straight line in figure 6.3, the maximum of any W_u is a Pareto optimum. Conversely, if we fix the representations used to construct the utility possibility set, any negatively sloped line corresponds to the level set of some W_u; hence, each point on the Pareto frontier, for example, $\bar{u}$, is the maximum of some welfare function. Consequently, a policymaker applying a Pareto efficiency standard could instead decide to consider only those policies that maximize some W_u.

When policymakers know the model, Pareto efficiency forcefully discriminates among policy options. If the utility possibility set U has a nonempty interior, almost every policy will be Pareto inefficient: in figure 6.3, for example, any policy placing positive probability weight on each of the pure policies is inefficient. In typical two-agent models, all policies can be Pareto efficient only if there are two or fewer pure policies. More generally, if the number of pure policies (m) is greater than the number of agents (n), utility possibility sets typically have nonempty interior, and hence

---

25. I use additive welfare functions because of Harsanyi's (1955) theorem that social preference relations should be representable as a sum of agent utilities. Harsanyi's key axiom is that the social preference relation must obey the von Neumann–Morgenstern assumptions, which—since our social choices are lotteries—is plausible here. Of course, since it is the ordering underlying $\Sigma_{j=1}^n \Sigma_{i=1}^m q_i u_j(a_i)$ that matters, any monotonic transformation of $\Sigma_{j=1}^n \Sigma_{i=1}^m q_i u_j(a_i)$ could serve equally well.

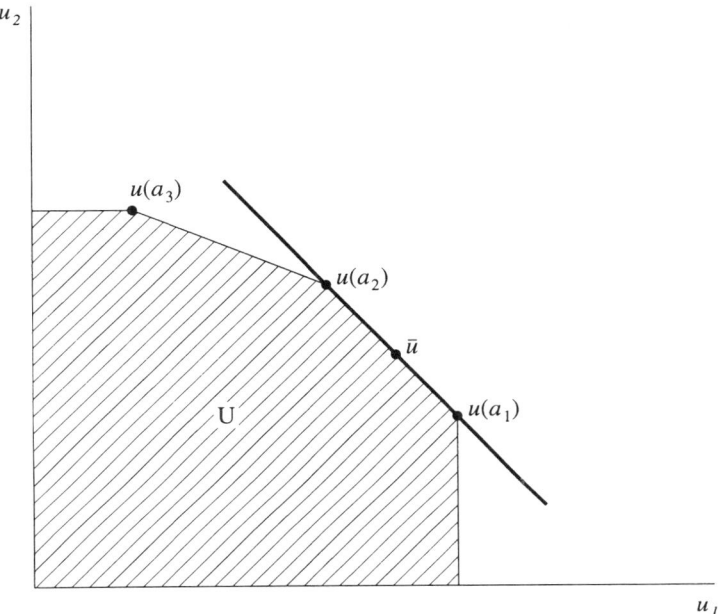

Figure 6.3 Effective policy discrimination with no uncertainty

almost all of the achievable utility points are Pareto inefficient.[26] Moreover, the condition that m is larger than n is easy to satisfy. Although economic models differ in some respects from social-choice models, the set of allocations can be interpreted as a set of policy options. In an exchange economy with ℓ commodities, the dimension of the set of allocations, which is analogous to m, is $\ell(n - 1)$; this number is larger than n if $n \geq 2$, $\ell \geq 2$, and $\ell + n \geq 5$. Thus, when policymakers directly determine allocations, mild restrictions imply that most options are Pareto inefficient.

A policymaker who is uncertain about the parameters of a model faces more difficult decisions. Suppose the policymaker has a state space, $\Omega = \{\omega_1, \ldots, \omega_s\}$, where each state specifies von Neumann–Morgenstern preferences over the policy choices for each of the n agents. Let $v_j(\cdot, \omega_k)$ denote an arbitrary utility function for j at ω_k. The probabilities for the s states are denoted $\pi = (\pi_1, \ldots, \pi_s)$, with each $\pi_k > 0$ and $\Sigma_{k=1}^{s} \pi_k = 1$.

The ex ante preference approach imagines that each agent j faces hypothetical uncertainty over Ω as well as A. Let each j's ex ante preferences be represented by a von Neumann–Morgenstern utility function $u_j^*(a_i, \omega_k)$. The utility of a pure policy a_i is therefore $\Sigma_k \pi_k u_j^*(a_i, \omega_k)$, and the utility of a

---

26. This is only a generic result: the utility possibility points associated with the pure policies must not lie in the same affine subspace.

mixed policy q is $\Sigma_i \Sigma_k q_i \pi_k u_j^*(a_i, \omega_k)$. (We are assuming that the policy-maker must randomize among pure policies in such a way that the outcome a_i is independent of ω_k.) Although it does not bear directly on the policy paralysis question, it is natural to suppose that Harsanyi's acceptance principle holds, that is, for each ω_k, let $u_j^*(\cdot, \omega_k)$ be an increasing linear transformation of $v_j(\cdot, \omega_k)$.

If the policymaker can specify ex ante preferences, policy analysis is straightforward. The previous definition of Pareto efficiency applies without amendment: a policy q is efficient if and only if there is no q' that each agent weakly prefers and that one or more agents strongly prefers to q. Since we have simply replaced each number $u_j(a_i)$ with the number $\Sigma_k \pi_k u_j^*(a_i, \omega_k)$, the geometry of when utility possibility sets have nonempty interior is unchanged: hence, if $m > n$, almost all policies are inefficient. Policy paralysis does not occur.

Access to ex ante preferences also guarantees that policy recommendations are not overturned by a small amount of uncertainty. Suppose a policymaker begins with a one-state model specifying a preference ordering for each j, represented by $v_j(a_i)$, and recommends a policy q' that leaves every agent strictly better off relative to a status quo policy $\bar{q}$. The policymaker then realizes that an additional $s - 1$ states are possible, each with small probability. Each j's ex ante preferences are then represented by a function $u_j^*(a_i, \omega_k)$, where ω_1 denotes the state at which the original one-state model occurs. By applying the appropriate increasing linear transformation, set $u_j^*(\cdot, \omega_1) = v_j(\cdot)$. Given u_j^*, if π_1 is sufficiently near $1, \Sigma_k \pi_k u_j^*(\cdot, \omega_k)$ will be "close" to $v_j(\cdot)$. Since this conclusion holds for all j, a move from $\bar{q}$ to q' will still benefit each agent.[27]

As discussed in the previous section, ex ante preferences make welfare comparisons among preference relations. Ex ante preferences are complete: that is, for any two policies, q and q', one policy is weakly preferred to the other. Hence, even if two of j's possible ex post preferences disagree about how to rank q and q', the ex ante preferences chosen by the policymaker dictate a decision for j about how these options should be ordered. Correspondingly, ex ante utilities for j are highly restricted: they must be increasing linear transformations of $\Sigma_k \pi_k u_j^*(\cdot, \omega_k)$. The Pareto optima identified by the ex ante preferences can therefore only be the maxima of welfare functions using this restricted set of utilities.

We therefore consider a more permissive form of welfare maximization. To define an expected welfare function, utility functions for each of the possible ex post preference relations are necessary. An *ex post assignment* of utilities specifies a

$$u_{\omega_k} = (u_1(\cdot, \omega_k), \ldots, u_n(\cdot, \omega_k)) \text{ for } k = 1, \ldots, s,$$

27. This conclusion requires fixing the u_j^* and letting π_1 converge to 1; for any fixed π, there will be a perturbation of additional states and a specification of u_j^* that will lead $\bar{q}$ and q' to be non-Pareto comparable.

where each $u_j(\cdot, \omega_k)$ is some increasing linear transformation of $v_j(\cdot, \omega_k)$. (It is natural to require additionally that identical preference orderings, whether they appear at one state or at different states, be represented by the same $u_j(\cdot, \omega_k)$.) Given an ex post assignment u_{ω_k}, the social welfare of the policy q at ω_k is $\Sigma_j \Sigma_i q_i u_j(a_i, \omega_k)$ and the expected welfare of q is $\Sigma_k \Sigma_j \Sigma_i \pi_k q_i u_j(a_i, \omega_k)$.[28] Consequently, a policy q is an *expected welfare maximum* if there is a u_{ω_k} such that for all q',

$$\sum_k \sum_j \sum_i \pi_k q_i u_j(a_i, \omega_k) \geq \sum_k \sum_j \sum_i \pi_k q_i' u_j(a_i, \omega_k).$$

Ex post utility assignments remove the restrictions on utility representations imposed by ex ante preferences. Any set of utilities representing each j's ex post preferences can be used to designate j's overall welfare in an expected social welfare function, not just linear transformations of the vector $(u_j^*(\cdot, \omega_1), \ldots, u_j^*(\cdot, \omega_s))$. Consequently, policies that are Pareto efficient according to the ex ante preferences maximize some expected social welfare function, but—as long as the ex ante preferences are held fixed—the reverse implication does not hold.

Conceivably, even if expected welfare maximization validates more policies than ex ante Pareto efficiency, a large set of policies could still be declared inefficient. And clearly, under some circumstances, some policies fail an expected welfare maximization test. If every potential agent prefers a_i to $a_{i'}$, then any policy placing nonzero probability weight on $a_{i'}$ will not maximize any expected welfare function. But with no restrictions on the preferences policymakers believe possible and with sufficiently many states, every policy is the maximum of some expected welfare function. The logic of this result is easy to grasp. If the policymaker is uncertain about agents' preferences—and there is no restriction on ex post utility assignments—it is as if the policymaker knew the model but there were ns agents: each of the standard Pareto optima in a certainty model with these ns individuals is the maximum of some expected welfare function in the uncertainty model.[29] Furthermore, if among the ns preference relations more than m of the preferences can be set arbitrarily, then generally each possible q will be a Pareto optimum of the model with ns agents. (Recall that in a certainty model, the efficacy of Pareto efficiency hinges on the number of agents being less than m, the number of pure policies.) Thus, even if n is less than m, the great variety of potential agents can cause each mixed policy to be the maximum of some expected welfare function in the model with uncertainty. Policy paralysis obtains. Moreover, since our conclusion does not depend on the probabilities of the states (as long as they are nonzero),

---

28. Social welfare functions as I have defined them correspond to Hammond's "ex-post welfare functions." See Hammond (1983) and the references cited therein.

29. Although the utilities of potential agents in expected welfare functions are multiplied by π_k's, ex post utilities can be scaled linearly, and therefore the set of welfare maxima ignoring the π_k's coincides with the set of probability-weighted maxima.

policy paralysis only requires that the policymaker believe that a large diversity of agents is possible, not likely.

6.10 Conclusion

The inability to go beyond noncontroversial interpersonal comparisons of welfare has remained a constant of neoclassical welfare economics. Utilitarianism imagines a complete social welfare ordering, but does not stipulate a constructive decision procedure. Robbins, Kaldor, and Hicks were therefore right to claim that the utilitarians did not provide a scientific analysis of distribution: they provided very little analysis at all. A fortiori, the same complaints apply to Bergson-Samuelson social welfare functions. The desire for a distributionally neutral method of policy evaluation is therefore understandable. The currently popular proposal, Pareto optimality, makes some theoretical headway. Unlike Pigou's suggestion that efficiency be defined relative to hypothetically fixed distributions of purchasing power, Pareto optimality is defined unambiguously and has a clear rationale. And at least in some abstract settings, Pareto efficiency can provide rigorous foundations for laissez-faire policy criteria (e.g., value maximization). But as a general theory of policy analysis, Paretianism fares poorly: it cannot simultaneously discriminate among policy choices and remain free from interpersonal comparisons.

Postwar welfare economics thus closely reproduces the dilemmas encountered by the early neoclassicals. In both eras, some theorists posited an abstract ethical criterion, which, although nominally complete, cannot in fact dispense policy advice. Both eras also proposed theories of efficiency that appear to justify traditional economic policy rules. In reality, neither era's justifications hold up to analytical scrutiny.

Meanwhile, applied welfare economics continues to use the empirical yardsticks championed by Marshall and Pigou. Cost-benefit analysis evaluates projects by comparing sums of monetary valuations with costs; aggregate welfare is still measured by the (deflated) market value of national income. Notwithstanding the flaws of the available justifications, economists still take discrepancies between price and marginal cost or restrictions preventing factors from moving to higher-value uses to be inefficiencies. Given the dilemmas of welfare theory, it may seem that applied economics has little alternative but to stick to unfounded but workable tools. But a few provisos temper such a discouraging conclusion.

Some of the priorities that are arbitrary from the vantage point of formal welfare theory can still be evaluated in the broader political and social terrain. I argued in sections 6.8 and 6.9 that a distributionally neutral concept of efficiency is unattainable. Under mild conditions, any policy is efficient in the sense of maximizing a bona fide (expected) social welfare function. Hence, even policies that distort according to a value maximization standard efficiently serve some social objective. The breakdown of a value-free definition of efficiency may therefore seem to imply that all policies are equally valid.

But the objectives served by arbitrary policies are often perverse. Consider again the example of optimal commodity taxes. Even without access to fully specified social welfare functions, some tax policies—subsidizing health care, for instance—can easily be defended by credible piecemeal welfare judgments. But arbitrary subsidies or tax credits designed to line the pockets of the politically well connected are harder to rationalize. Such policies arise from the mechanics of power, not from an attempt to increase the welfare of agents with a particular type of preference relation or with low wealth. Nor is it easy to link such policies after the fact to defensible welfare judgments.

Possibly, therefore, many of the policies long attacked by economists as inefficient could still be rejected. But rejection must be on the grounds that these policies serve noxious goals, not that they prevent potential Pareto improvements. In fact, when pressed, economists often defend laissez-faire regimes on the grounds that the only alternative is to politicize the allocation of wealth, leading to results that are both unfair and impoverishing. Such arguments, whether right or wrong, rely on fragmentary welfare judgments, not on a spurious efficiency concept or globally defined welfare functions.

The Paretian view that interpersonal comparisons are inherently unjustifiable has stifled the development of welfare judgments. The early neoclassical principle of diminishing marginal utility permitted at least the limited result that, ceteris paribus, income equality is superior to inequality. Furthermore, although the early neoclassicals could not judge how much output should be sacrificed to achieve greater equality, they at least identified the potential conflict in aims and conceded (sometimes grudgingly) that neither goal automatically takes precedence. Indeed, the most perceptive early neoclassical economists realized that utilitarianism does not sanction unadjusted applications of consumer surplus analysis or value maximization.

In contemporary economics, on the other hand, the fiction that maximizing the value of output is efficient makes distributional objectives seem like extraneous distortions. The ordinal revolution is partly to blame for this change: the claim that any nonordinal property of utility is suspect demotes all interpersonal comparisons, even those rooted in the plausible psychology of diminishing marginal utility. Overturning ordinalism's narrow view of preference would help to determine the interpersonal comparisons that can command consensus and help to validate them as genuine economic goals.

7

A Positive Rate of Interest?

7.1 Introduction

Economists were once obligated to explain why the rate of interest or profit is normally positive. The flow of net income to owners of capital was too analytically and socially prominent for classical and early neoclassical theorists to ignore. The postwar theory of value diverges from the traditional pattern; although economists continue to assume that interest rates are positive, theorists no longer actively investigate the underlying causes. Nor does postwar theory implicitly contain a convincing explanation. Partial accounts have surfaced as the by-product of other research programs, but as we will see, a satisfactory account of positive interest cannot be extracted from contemporary work.

Debate over interest and capital flourished in the early neoclassical era, drawing in Austrian followers of Böhm-Bawerk, English Marshallians, and American marginal productivity theorists. Convincing explanations for why interest rates are positive were difficult to construct; early neoclassical theorists had to invent ingenious restrictions on intertemporal preferences and technology. Postwar theory rejects the early neoclassical innovations, which now seem dispensable given the shift in research agenda. But when seen in light of their original purpose, the early neoclassical proposals—even if unconvincing—reemerge as adroit and well aimed.

Classical explanations of the profit rate rested on two principles: first, savers accumulate capital only if offered a positive rate of return, and second, an economy can evade diminishing returns to capital investment by specializing in manufacturing. The neoclassical revolution removed both of these arguments from the menu of acceptable reasoning. A correlation between savings and positive interest rates now had to be reconciled with the utility calculus, and, since labor was no longer considered a produced good, diminishing returns became an inescapable fact of economic life.

164

Early neoclassical theorists proposed two alternatives. First, agents were hypothesized to undervalue the utility of future consumption relative to present consumption, that is, to be impatient. Second, the output of production processes was assumed to be an increasing function of the amount of time expended. The former argument commanded the larger following, but the latter argument, although closely identified with Austrian capital theory, also circulated broadly. Both provoked exhaustive and heated debate; in marked contrast to factor price theory, early neoclassical interest theory enjoyed little unity or resolution. Indeed, no other topic in the history of economic theory is more steeped in controversy and invective.

Behind the quarrels, the project of demonstrating that real interest rates are normally and substantially positive gave the competing schools a common mission. Nevertheless, early neoclassical interest theory could not deliver its desired theoretical goal. As we will see, agent impatience and the productivity of time-consuming investments have manifest limitations: depending on the time pattern of endowments, zero or negative interest rates need not choke off the demand for savings, and the Austrian view of technology is empirically precarious.

Absorbed in its own theoretical concerns, early postwar general equilibrium theory rarely tried to explain why interest rates are positive.[1] Initial research concentrated on finite horizon models, which can only cope awkwardly with intertemporal issues. But later the capital theory of the 1960s and the infinite-horizon general equilibrium theory of the 1970s, although not expressly designed to explain the sign of interest rates, tacitly addressed the issue. Models with infinitely lived agents generalize the impatience assumption of early neoclassical theory and clarify when impatience can lead to positive interest rates. But though internally consistent, infinite horizon models do not offer a credible theory of the link between present and future, and they cannot be rescued by the common overlapping-generations-with-bequests interpretation.

Although contemporary equilibrium theory has largely bypassed the positive interest rate question, the topic is not prohibited in principle. Postwar theory is not staked to the proposition that the positivity of interest ought not to be explained. Indeed, as we will see, further structure could be added to standard models to incorporate an explanation.[2]

Before proceeding to the substance of the argument, a few conceptual distinctions are needed. First, to make interest rates analytically tractable, I use models with a single real interest rate rather than a multiplicity of commodity rates. Prior to Hicks's popularization of the intertemporal equilibrium model in the 1930s, most economists followed the same practice.

1. Perhaps this period was influenced by the stagnationist views of Alvin Hansen and some other early Keynesians, who argued that equilibria with full employment often do not exhibit positive interest rates.

2. Malinvaud (1953), a classic of postwar intertemporal theory, was close enough to the early neoclassical era to make a brief effort in this direction.

Even Irving Fisher, who repeatedly emphasized that there are as many interest rates between two time periods as choices of *numéraire*, in the end produced an aggregated theory of interest.[3] A single real rate (for any given pair of time periods) can arise in two ways: in models with only one good per period—in essence, Fisher's approach—and in steady-state equilibrium. In the latter case, since relative prices remain fixed through time, the real rate is independent of the choice of *numéraire*. I use both approaches, although the single-good models are used largely to simplify exposition.

Second, although microeconomic theory no longer tries to explain when or why interest rates are positive, models with zero or negative interest rates nevertheless seem suspicious to contemporary eyes. Perhaps this intuition rests on the fact that in aggregate models with no population growth, a negative steady-state interest rate implies that equilibrium is Pareto inefficient and violates the golden rule. Since consumption would be larger at a zero interest rate, negative interest rate equilibria seem paradoxical. I do not want to challenge either the empirical perception that capital accumulation has not yet reached the golden rule watershed or the suspicion of models with negative or zero interest rates. Contemporary and early neoclassical theory concur on these intuitions. My purpose is to examine whether they can be theoretically justified.

Third, early neoclassical economists held that the interest rate was not just positive but substantially positive. This distinction is slippery—economic theory lacks even a vague sense of quantitative magnitude. But, particularly to the Austrian tradition, the difference was important; the early neoclassicals hoped to demonstrate that under normal conditions capitalists and rentiers earn a substantial income. Whenever possible, I interpret "substantially positive" to mean that interest rates have a (strictly) positive lower bound; hence, models permitting interest rates arbitrarily near zero fall short of the early neoclassical goal.[4]

Fourth, I do not distinguish between interest and profit rates. Although the rates differ systematically, both classical and neoclassical economists have held that they are causally linked and move in tandem; pure theory has therefore often ignored the distinction. The riskiness of production allows real capital investment to earn a premium over the risk-free rate of return; since the arguments under consideration apply to the risk-free rate, they establish the positivity of both types of rates. Theory has similarly

---

3. See Fisher (1907, chap. 5); the subsequent chapters also use a unidimensional (single-good) definition of income. Early neoclassical theorists commonly conceded that a negative rate of interest can arise with a careful choice of *numéraire* and time period: if a good's nominal price rises at a rate greater than the nominal interest rate—e.g., strawberries between summer and winter—the real rate of return in terms of that good will be negative. Such examples were seen as somewhat exotic, however.

4. To get a feel for how large "substantially positive" is, note that the golden rule interest rate equals the population growth rate. Growth theorists of the 1960s therefore commonly regarded an interest rate larger than the population growth rate as the normal case.

disregarded the difference, due to taxation or financial intermediation, between borrowing and lending rates. Whatever its merits, I follow this practice as well and treat these rates as interchangeable. [But note that this distinction implies that the technological arguments of section 7.5 may not be enough to demonstrate that the (lending) rate earned on financial investments is positive.]

Finally, I do not consider the robustness of the standard single-sector models of capital theory. Early neoclassical theorists instinctively thought in single-sector terms and embraced many of the parables later formally articulated by the Solow model, for example, that the steady-state interest rate varies inversely with capital intensity and per capita consumption. Perhaps the paradoxes of capital aggregation can be understood as a substantive critique of aggregative neoclassical theory. But these difficulties do not bear on the basic organizing concepts of early neoclassical capital theory—impatience and the roundaboutness of production—or on whether these concepts can explain the "nature" of interest. Moreover, the coherence and adequacy of early neoclassical ideas can be evaluated independently of the shakier, aggregative parts of capital theory. For example, one can use impatience as an argument for positive interest rates without having to uphold single-sector Solow growth theory.

7.2 The classical position

Classical economists held that savings are forthcoming only when rewarded by a positive rate of return. The interest rate must then be positive in the long run; a negative or zero rate shrinks the capital stock, diminishing labor demand and contracting the quantity of land under cultivation. With wage and average land rental rates consequently decreasing, the profit rate must increase. Reductions in the capital stock continue until interest and profit rates move into positive territory.[5]

The link between positive interest rates and savings was supported by two distinct considerations. In the first, the classicals maintained that for savings to occur, owners of wealth must be compensated for "abstaining" from current consumption. John Stuart Mill cast this point in remarkably neoclassical terms: savings decisions stem from agents' psychological comparisons of current and future needs. Given this premise, Mill simply presumed the rate of interest would be positive.[6] Supplementing this logic, the

---

5. For more on this mechanism, see the discussion in section 3.5 of postclassical arguments for factor price determinacy.

6. See Senior (1836, pp. 58–60) for the classic exposition of savings as abstinence; a systematic connection between abstinence and the rate of interest is missing, however. Though Ricardo does not use the word abstinence, he also stressed that savings require that a net gain be earned. See Ricardo (1817, p. 122). As for Mill, see Mill (1848, bk. 1, chap. 11, and bk. 2, chap. 15, sec. 2). Unlike Senior, in Mill the link between abstinence and the rate of interest is unambiguous.

availability of money provides savers, in the absence of inflation, with a low-risk asset with a zero rate of return. Consequently, all other investment vehicles must earn at least a zero rate of return (and risky investments in production have to earn a positive rate of return).[7]

The second argument drew on the classical understanding of the savings behavior of different classes. Laborers in classical theory are not wealthy enough to save, and landlords, although rich enough, lack the middle-class virtues of thriftiness and frugality. The primary source of savings is therefore the profit income of capitalists. If, as Ricardo claimed in one extreme moment, the only source of investment is profits, total capital investment over any sufficiently lengthy time period must be less than total profits.[8] Consequently, if the rate of profit were negative and total profits therefore shrinking through time, the capital stock would ultimately have to fall. As above, wages and land rents would fall until the profit rate became positive again.

This point is simple enough, but it may help to phrase it in terms of the steady states of the Solow growth model. In Solow growth theory, the stock of labor is fixed and aggregate output can therefore be modeled as a function of the capital stock alone. In a classical setting, land is the ultimate scarce resource and labor is elastically supplied in the long run. Consequently, we may still think of output, at least in the long run, as a diminishing-returns function of the capital stock alone. (In the short run, of course, classical theory allowed labor supplies to be supplied inelastically.) Therefore let aggregate output at time t be a strictly concave function, say f, of the amount of capital available, say k_t. Capital can either be thought of as the physical capital of the Solow model, or, more in the spirit of classical analysis, as a measure of "doses" of capital and labor jointly applied. The simplest interpretation of all is to suppose that k_t is just the real wage payments advanced to workers at time $t - 1$ at some fixed (presumably subsistence) wage rate.

Capital at t can be augmented by reducing consumption at $t - 1$. Specifically, suppose one additional unit of k_t costs one unit of output at $t - 1$. If an increment of k_t returns $f'(k_t)$ units of output and $(1 - \delta)$ units of capital (which can be exchanged, unit for unit, for output) at t, the net rate of return r on such an investment is defined by

$$(1 + r)1 = f'(k_t) + (1 - \delta),$$

and so

$$r = f'(k_t) - \delta.$$

The variable δ is the rate of capital depreciation; when capital consists only of wage advances, δ equals 1. Implicitly, landowners (and any other owners of fixed factors) receive $f(k_t) - f'(k_t)k_t$. Gross investment at t is defined by

---

7. This seems to be the implicit argument in Smith (1776, chap. 9).
8. Ricardo (1822, p. 234). See Hollander (1979, p. 325).

$$i_t = k_{t+1} - (1 - \delta)k_t. \qquad (7.2.1)$$

Suppose, following the classical logic discussed above, that gross investment is less than gross profits: $i_t < f'(k_t)k_t$. In a steady state, where the capital stock remains unchanged through time, $k_t = k_{t+1}$. Hence, given 7.2.1, $f'(k_t) - \delta > 0$. Thus, although a large capital stock can certainly lead to a negative or zero rate of interest in the Solow model, the rule $i_t < f'(k_t)k_t$ will eventually preclude this result.

A class sociology of savings behavior thus reinforced the psychological argument linking savings and positive interest rates. Indeed, as long as capital accumulation was tied to capitalists as a social class, classical economists did not need to distinguish rigorously between the above two arguments, or even to examine the precise causal link between profits and investment. Whether the psychological motive for savings diminishes as the rate of return falls, or whether a fall in the rate of return reduces capitalists' income and thus diminishes the supply of new savings, the same relationship between savings and the profit rate was sustained. Under any scenario, a positive rate of profit was a sine qua non of capitalist growth.[9]

The reasoning discussed so far only addresses the longest-run forces governing the interest rate. Moreover, these considerations only support the weak conclusion that the interest rate is positive; any stronger result about the magnitude of interest rates must adduce additional arguments. Classical economists conceded that theoretically the rate of interest would descend to a low (but still positive) rate if the economy reached the so-called stationary state. But the stationary state was a conjecture (see section 3.2), not a description of probable conditions. Except possibly at a distant point in the future, other forces keep the interest rate significantly away from its long-run theoretical minimum.

First, technical advances in agriculture can allow the economy to satisfy growing demands for food without extending the margin of cultivation. The full force of diminishing returns can thus be kept at bay. In a similar vein, food imports can give capital and labor supply room to grow without necessitating any expansion of the agricultural sector. In both cases, the scarcity of the fixed resource of the classical system—agricultural land—is sidestepped, and as a consequence, the accumulation of capital need not drive the rate of profit down to near zero.

The first argument can be crudely approximated in the Solow model: technical progress can be seen as increasing $f'(k)$ for each k, thus increasing $f'(k) - \delta$. The second argument is intrinsically multisectoral, however, since it relies on the fact that there are some sectors—in particular, manufacturing—that use only inputs that are elastically supplied at given prices. Imports can then permit capital to accumulate without flowing into sectors

---

9. See Hollander (1979, chap. 7) for a discussion of the varied evidence concerning Ricardo's analysis of the connection between investment and the profit rate.

that utilize fixed inputs and thus experience diminishing marginal returns. Of course, this latter argument only postpones the difficulty; diminishing returns reappear when considering the growth of the world economy as a whole.

7.3 Early neoclassical interest rate theory

The abstinence theory of interest, with its emphasis on utility and psychological desire, was a natural match to neoclassical economics. But where the classicals could simply assert that interest rates must be positive in order for net savings to be generated, a neoclassical analysis of intertemporal choice had to employ the highly structured language of utility theory. This fact had two consequences. First, since utility maximization was meant to be a universal description of economic behavior, all agents, not just those identified as capitalists, can engage in intertemporal substitution: workers and rentiers could now be potential savers. Second, once the connection between utility and saving was explored in detail, it became clear that agents could, under the right circumstances, want to save even in the face of zero or negative rates of return. In early neoclassical language, saving involves a comparison of the current marginal utility of income with the anticipated future marginal utility of income; saving at a zero interest rate will occur when the latter happens to exceed the former. We will explore this point in more detail; for now, simply note that utility theory weakened both of the long-run classical arguments for a positive interest rate.

Neoclassical economics also, mercifully, brought the Malthusian tradition of treating labor as a producible good to an end. With labor a fixed or quasi-fixed resource, diminishing returns to capital investment became, theoretically speaking, an economywide phenomenon. All production now used scarce resources; hence, the international division of labor no longer offered a route by which domestic production could specialize in "constant returns" sectors. The accumulation of capital can therefore potentially proceed to the point where its net marginal return is negative—in the Solow model's language, to a k such that $f'(k) - \delta \leq 0$.

To sum up, all of the key arguments that allowed classical economists to conclude that interest rates are positive were threatened by the new theoretical program: (1) all agents were now potential "capitalists," (2) when the marginal utility of future income is sufficiently high, saving can occur at a zero or negative interest rate, and, on the technological side, (3) the marginal returns to investment can drop beneath any prespecified level.

New arguments were therefore necessary. Eugen von Böhm-Bawerk, whose *Positive Theory of Capital* (1889) was the richest source of innovation, asked why interest—positive interest—exists. He proposed three causes. First, Böhm-Bawerk contended that agents are generally wealthier in the future than in the present; present goods consequently have a higher marginal utility than future goods. Hence, if agents were to face a nonpositive interest rate, they would in the aggregate desire to borrow, which is inconsistent with equilibrium. Second, even if agents are as well provided for in the present as in the future, agents "systematically undervalue" their future wants, due to a lack of willpower or ignorance and uncertainty about the future.[10] In the face of nonpositive interest rates, this myopia leads agents to supplement current consumption at the expense of the future; to check the demand for loans, a positive interest must prevail.

Böhm-Bawerk's third and most controversial cause of interest was that "lengthier" or more "roundabout" production processes produce more output than less time-consuming processes utilizing the same level of resources. In the typical Böhm-Bawerkian parable, labor (perhaps with other "original" factors) can be used to produce consumption directly, or can be used indirectly to first produce intermediate inputs:

> Firewood can very easily be obtained by simply gathering up dry twigs or breaking off small branches. A short circuitous path of production leads to the making and using of a stone axe. A longer path leads to the digging of iron ore, the gathering of the fuel and tools needed for smelting, the production of iron from the ore, of steel from the iron, and finally from the steel a well-sharpened axe. To go into it at greater length we might mention that the mining requires ingenious machinery and rolling stock, the smelting calls for efficient blast furnaces, the shaping and sharpening of the axe necessitate the building of special machinery. Going still further back we see that these machines in turn call for other factories and machinery, and so on [Böhm-Bawerk (1889, pp. 83–84)].

More circuitous methods can always be employed; and as the quantity of time used in production increases, so does the quantity of final output produced (per unit of original factor input). Böhm-Bawerk concluded that current resources, since they can be devoted to the lengthier production techniques, are more valuable than future resources. Once again, equilibrium requires that present goods command a premium over future goods.

Böhm-Bawerk's account was and is confusing, in part because each cause was forced into the awkward present versus future goods schema. When criticized, Böhm-Bawerk gave no ground, however, insisting on both the accuracy and logical independence of each of his three causes. (Böhm-Bawerk founded capital theory's legacy of obstinate and overly subtle debate.) Concerning the first cause of interest, Böhm-Bawerk acknowledged that agents can have more resources in the present than in the future, and even that such agents might predominate in the economy as a whole. But he countered that present goods will still command a premium over future goods since many present goods, in particular money, are durable and can therefore serve future needs as effectively as present needs. In modern terminology, a durable good can function as an asset or an investment vehicle. Böhm-Bawerk's defense of his first cause therefore reduces

---

10. Böhm-Bawerk (1889, p. 268). For Böhm-Bawerk's overall theory, see the remainder of book 4, chapter 1.

to the claim that assets with a zero real rate of return exist, and hence savers need not resort to investments with a negative rate of return. (A similar classical argument arose in section 7.2.) Note that this backup argument provides no grounds for concluding that interest rates are strictly positive.

The third cause for interest was also poorly formulated. As Fisher argued at great length (1907, chap. 4), future resources can be used in the same more lengthy (and thus, in Böhm-Bawerk's view, more productive) production processes that current resources can be used in. Therefore, unless by assumption we use a positive interest rate to discount future goods, it is unclear why future resources should have lesser value than current resources. But Böhm-Bawerk's underlying idea is clear enough. If an agent desires wealth at some future date rather than at present—and intertemporal technology conforms to Austrian assumptions—the agent will earn a higher rate of return by devoting present resources to productive investment than by trading current resources one for one for future output. Again, it is more in keeping with contemporary language to describe current resources invested in production as a form of investment. On this understanding, Böhm-Bawerk's third cause boils down to the assertion that, due to the productivity of time-consuming techniques, current resources can always be invested at a positive rate of return.

In sum, Böhm-Bawerk presented two types of considerations: (1) either due to the fact that agents ex ante are relatively underendowed with present goods or due to myopia, a zero or negative interest rate would lead to an excess demand for borrowing, and (2) either through the storage of durable goods or the net productivity of time-consuming production processes, assets and production processes earning at least a zero and typically a substantially positive rate of return are available. Böhm-Bawerk contended that when either of these considerations applies, interest rates will be positive in equilibrium.

These arguments were not unique to Böhm-Bawerk. In fact, despite the bad blood between the Austrian and American schools of capital theory, both camps concurred on these two analytical mechanisms. Irving Fisher, the other luminary of early neoclassical interest theory and the leading figure of the American school, anticipated much of modern intertemporal economics.[11] He argued that agents' intertemporal marginal rates of substitution are equalized in equilibrium and that this common rate will equal the marginal rate of intertemporal technological transformation, a principle that is still the centerpiece of textbook interest rate theory. When addressing the early neoclassical concern with why interest rates are positive, Fisher offered distinctly Böhm-Bawerkian arguments. First and foremost, analogously to Böhm-Bawerk's assumption of myopia, Fisher proposed that agents are systematically impatient. Second, Fisher concurred with Böhm-Bawerk that the storability of durable goods ensures that most

---

11. For Fisher's overall theory, see Fisher (1907, 1930).

commodity interest rates have a floor of zero. And finally, though officially distancing himself from Böhm-Bawerk's third cause, Fisher agreed that the length of the process of production can usually be increased so as to expand total productivity (although not to the extent that Böhm-Bawerk imagined).[12] The availability of high productivity roundabout technologies in turn raises future consumption relative to present consumption, lowering the marginal utility of future consumption compared with the marginal utility of present consumption. This "endogenous" impatience thereby contributes to the positivity of interest rates. Thus, whether explicitly or implicitly, Böhm-Bawerk and Fisher agreed on the causal impact of roundabout production.

Still, particularly in earlier versions of his theory, Fisher gave impatience the lion's share of attention. But this emphasis, although it lends a contemporary flavor to his work, weakens Fisher's argument. Let us define an agent to be *impatient* if, at a constant consumption stream, small increases in current consumption are preferred to small increases in future consumption. Consumers who are impatient in this sense and endowed with a constant income stream will then borrow at zero or negative interest rates. Hence, since equilibrium requires no positive borrowing in the aggregate, interest rates must be positive. But impatient agents with endowments that decrease through time may well desire to save even at a negative rate of return. Consequently, although impatience (or myopia) may make positive interest more likely, it cannot ensure the conclusion.

Furthermore, Fisher conceded that some agents show ample foresight about the future (unlike Böhm-Bawerk, who based myopia on irrationality and lack of self-control). He therefore ought to have acknowledged the possibility of saving at a zero interest rate. Instead, Fisher simply maintained a discount of the marginal utility of future income relative to current income as an undefended primitive. All agents—even those who anticipate a diminishing income stream, face no uncertainty, and plan for the future—borrow at a zero interest rate. Variations in foresight, uncertainty, and the time pattern of endowments only determine how near the ratio of future to current marginal utility of income is to one.

In contrast, Böhm-Bawerk and the Austrian tradition—whatever the merits of their positive theorizing and forgiving their theoretical clumsiness—grasped the dilemmas of interest rate theory. Böhm-Bawerk recognized that an agent with relatively large current income, even if

12. All of these points are made in Fisher's brilliant *The Rate of Interest* (1907). For impatience (here called time preference), see chapter 6; for the connection between storage and nonnegative interest rates, see chapter 5, section 5; and for the existence of productive roundabout processes, see chapter 4, section 2. Although many Fisherian elements have no counterpart in Böhm-Bawerk—including the famous treatment of the optimality of maximizing the present value of an income stream—much of Fisher's work, by his own admission, builds a unified framework for what are ultimately Böhm-Bawerkian concepts. Most of these ideas (but not all, as we will see) end up considerably clearer in Fisher's hands.

myopic, may want to defer consumption into the future; negative rates of return then become possible. Partly for this reason, Böhm-Bawerk saw the need for a third, technological cause for interest.

In addition to its inadequacy as an explanation of positive interest rates, impatience was attacked as theoretically untenable. Psychological discounting directly contradicted the early neoclassical equation of individual rationality with an (unweighted) summing of the utility of consumption goods; foes lambasted using the deus ex machina of irrationality to patch a weak theory. Most famously, Schumpeter deemed any assumption that agents undervalue the future, whether as a direct supposition or as justified by myopia, to be an offense "against the rules of economic reason (1912, p. 35)." Impatience smuggles a positive interest rate bias into utilitarian psychology; hence, even if descriptive of some behavior, Schumpeter could not admit discounting as a primary theoretical building block. Frank Knight, the last of the major American critics of Böhm-Bawerk's theory, reiterated many of Schumpeter's arguments, remarking that complete rationality "certainly means indifference to time in consumption," and even wondering if savings decisions are in fact governed by utility maximization.[13]

Schumpeter and Knight, working within the paradigm of early neoclassical interest theory, did not doubt the need to explain why interest rates are positive. Their objections to impatience were aimed at Böhm-Bawerk's specific theory. Schumpeter instead argued that entrepreneurs, motivated by lucrative innovations, continually enlarge the demand for loans and thereby prop up interest rates.[14] Knight, although he did not spell out a clear logic, believed that technology ensures that increments to the capital stock always yield a positive net return.[15]

Schumpeter's and Knight's criticisms did not carry the day; the orthodox position on impatience was vigorously defended, most actively by Böhm-Bawerk's followers.[16] But the complaints directed against impatience indicate the difficulty of devising a convincing case for interest rate positivity and further justify Böhm-Bawerk's desire to retain a supplementary technological argument. Since impatience survives as a standard assumption of contemporary intertemporal economics, I first turn to the modern scene

13. Knight (1936, p. 635; see also pp. 627, 636). In Knight (1934, p. 272) he wrote that "there is literally no 'sense' in the notion of an inherent reluctance to postpone, or preference of present to future enjoyment, as a general principle embedded in human nature, rational or sentimental."

14. See Schumpeter (1912, chap. 5) and Negishi (1989a, chap. 8, sec. 4) for a sympathetic interpretation of Schumpeter. Negishi's analysis indicates that a positive interest rate is more likely in the presence of technological progress; but zero and negative interest rates remain possible under suitable endowment assumptions.

15. Although a productivity theory of interest is commonly ascribed to Knight—see, e.g., Kuenne (1963, chap. 4, sec. 3a) which also discusses some of the challenges of interpreting Knight—it is difficult to extract a complete account from Knight's writings. But see Knight (1941) for a concise treatment.

16. Von Mises (1949, chap. 18), arguing that impatience is actually a consequence of rational behavior, is eloquent on this score.

and an explicit analysis of the adequacy of the impatience approach before coming back to Böhm-Bawerk's technological basis for interest in section 7.5.

7.4 Contemporary interest rate theory and the impatience assumption

The standard postwar general equilibrium model is not an ideal setting for interest rate theory. The finiteness of the total number of goods, which entails an artificial terminal date to economic activity, makes it difficult to incorporate steady states. Relative prices consequently vary through time, and so no single rate of interest connects any two time periods. And none of the assumptions of the finite-horizon Arrow-Debreu model, whether on preferences or technology, imposes temporal characteristics on commodities. Hence, even when a single interest rate is well defined—say, there is only one good per time period—no conclusion about the sign, let alone magnitude, of interest rates can be drawn.

In fact, the interest rate in a general equilibrium model is only defined relative to an interpretation of when each good appears. Consider a model with goods $i = 1, \ldots, T$ in which agents meet at one point in time to trade for delivery of all goods, current and future; let $(p_1, \ldots, p_T)$ be a vector of equilibrium prices. If each good appears at a distinct period, and the commodity labels 1 through T reflect the forward flow of time, then the interest rate between period i and period $i + 1$ is $(p_i/p_{i+1}) - 1$.[17] Alternatively, if the commodities are interpreted to appear in reverse sequence—T being the first period, and 1 the last—then the interest rate between the period at which good i appears and the period at which good $i + 1$ appears is $(p_{i+1}/p_i) - 1$. Consequently, if a strictly positive interest rate between some pair of time periods appears in one interpretation, a strictly negative interest rate between some other pair of periods will appear in some other consistent interpretation. This ambiguity is not a flaw; the Arrow-Debreu model is not designed to say anything about interest rates. Indeed, this very fact indicates the distance between the prewar and postwar climates in interest rate theory.

Models without an arbitrary end to economic activity can impose more structure on interest rates. The most powerful technique, first applied by the mathematician Frank Ramsey in 1928 to an optimal planning problem, assumes that some agents have an infinite planning horizon. Ramsey did not place a discounting or impatience assumption on his model's objective function; indeed, he maintained that in a normative model of planning, discounting future utilities is "ethically indefensible."[18] Ramsey's paper

---

17. The gross amount of the period $i + 1$ good purchasable with one unit of the ith period good, say R, is defined by $Rp_{i+1} = p_i$. Since the net rate of return r earned on such a trade is defined by $1 + r = R, r = (p_i/p_{i+1}) - 1$.

18. Ramsey (1928, p. 543). The practice "arises merely from the weakness of the imagination."

remained an isolated experiment until the study of optimal growth took off in the 1950s and 1960s. Some of the renewed work continued Ramsey's maximization of undiscounted sums of utility.[19] But the Ramsey approach faces conceptual hurdles; the lack of discounting can easily lead optimization problems to have no solution.

For instance, in the so-called cake-eating problem, a fixed sum of wealth (cake) is to be consumed over an infinite number of periods. Let c_t indicate the consumption of cake in period t. Normalizing units so that the cake has size 1, we must have $\Sigma_{t=0}^{\infty} c_t = 1$. If an undiscounted sum of per-period utilities, $\Sigma_{t=0}^{\infty} u(c_t)$, is maximized and u is strictly concave, a positive c_τ for any τ cannot be optimal. At a sufficiently distant date—where c_t must be near 0—the marginal utility of consumption will be larger than at τ. Since never consuming any cake is also not optimal, the cake-eating problem has no optimal solution. Due to this and similar problems, analyses of infinite-horizon decision making have concentrated on objective functions that discount future utility or that otherwise exhibit impatience.[20]

To see how infinite-horizon theory can generate positive market interest rates, we turn to models where intertemporal decisions are made by decentralized agents rather than by a planner.[21] The key features of the infinite-horizon model arise in relatively simple examples. Consider an exchange economy with one consumption good per period and a finite number of agents. Beginning at an arbitrary time period 0, each agent j faces a sequence of prices

$$p = (p_0, p_1, \ldots, p_t, \ldots)$$

extending into the infinite future and has the endowment

$$e^j = (e_0^j, e_1^j, \ldots, e_t^j, \ldots) \geq 0.$$

Agent j's income is therefore $\Sigma_{t=0}^{\infty} p_t e_t^j$. Agent j chooses a consumption vector,

$$x^j = (x_0^j, x_1^j, \ldots, x_t^j, \ldots),$$

to maximize an intertemporal utility function of the form,

$$\sum_{t=0}^{\infty} (\beta^j)^t u^j (x_t^j),$$

subject to the budget constraint $\Sigma_{t=0}^{\infty} p_t x_t^j \leq \Sigma_{t=0}^{\infty} p_t e_t^j$. The number β^j, which we assume to be strictly positive, is agent j's rate of time preference; j *discounts* future utility if $\beta^j < 1$.

---

19. See, for example, von Weizsäcker (1965) and Gale (1967).

20. Cass (1965) and Koopmans (1965), which demonstrate that the capital stock converges in a single-sector model, were important in showing that models with discounting are well behaved. Magill (1981) reviews the literature on the existence of optimal solutions and concludes, as others have, that impatience is the natural sufficient condition for existence.

21. The classic model of an infinite-horizon, finite-agent intertemporal general equilibrium economy is Bewley (1972). See also Peleg and Yaari (1970).

If there are J agents, equilibrium occurs when p is such that agents choose x^j that satisfy $\Sigma_{j=1}^J x^j \le \Sigma_{j=1}^J e^j$. As a matter of definition, the per-period interest rate between the initial period and any period t, say r_t, is given by

$$\left(\frac{p_0}{p_t}\right)^{\frac{1}{t}} - 1 \qquad (7.4.1)$$

where the positive root of (p_0/p_t) is taken.[22] (Although p_t, e^i_t, and x^i_t are scalars, most of the following remarks extend to models with many goods per period; p_t, e^j_t, and x^j_t are then vectors and $p_t e^j_t$ and $p_t x^j_t$ can be read as inner products.)

The mere assumption that agents face a single intertemporal budget constraint imposes severe constraints on the sign of interest rates. Suppose that e^j has some positive lower bound; that is, assume there is a $k > 0$ such that $e^j_t \ge k$, for all t. Then, in order for j's income, $\Sigma_{t=0}^{\infty} p_t e^j_t$, to be finite, p_t must converge to 0. Consequently, for all t sufficiently large, r_t is strictly positive; the interest rate is, in this sense, asymptotically positive. Furthermore, in a steady state—where p_t/p_{t+1} equals some fixed positive constant for all t and each agent's consumption is constant across time—we must have $p_{t+1} < p_t$ for all t. Hence all r_t are positive (and in fact equal).

It may seem remarkable that the budget constraint alone, without any explicit assumption of impatience, can imply that interest rates are positive. The sleight of hand is that in order for the infinite-horizon model to have an equilibrium, some form of agent impatience is usually necessary. If agent j does not discount future utility, that is, if $\beta^j \ge 1$, then he or she faces a dilemma similar to that arising in the cake-eating problem. Consumption goods in the distant future become arbitrarily cheap (since $p_t \to 0$). Consequently j ought to defer consumption indefinitely, which obviously is not optimal either. When $\beta^j < 1$, in contrast, the utility of consumption in the distant future receives a progressively smaller (and asymptotically zero) weight in j's intertemporal utility function; indeed, if β^j is small relative to the rate at which p_t declines, j's decision-making problem has a well-defined solution.

The infinite-horizon general equilibrium model, with its key ingredients of agent impatience and infinite-horizon budget constraints, delivers the result that interest rates are positive. Whether interest rates can be expected to be *substantially* positive is more subtle. In our example, it is true that if all agents discount future utility at the same rate, say β, then the steady-state interest rate will be large to the extent β is small. One of the first-order conditions facing each j in a steady state (where x^j_t and r_t are constant for all t) is $1/\beta = p_t/p_{t+1}$; thus a small β—agents who are highly impatient— implies a large r_t. But when agents' rates of time preference are well

---

22. Reasoning as before, the gross amount of the tth-period good purchasable with one unit of the 0th-period good, say R_t, is defined by $R_t p_t = p_0$. Since r_t is defined by $(1 + r_t)^t = R_t$, we have 7.4.1.

dispersed, and thus some j likely has β^j near 1, only those agents with the largest β^j (call this $\bar{\beta}$) consume in amounts that do not converge to 0 as t increases.[23] Above and beyond the absurdity of this feature of the model, r_t approaches $1/\bar{\beta} - 1$, which is likely to be near 0. (The steady state may be a long time coming, however; with a dispersion of rates of time preference, the model might still predict that r_t is substantially positive for long time spans.)

Does the infinite-horizon model adequately explain the positivity of interest rates? There are two conspicuous reasons for doubt. First, investing a given quantity of goods in production may, as a pure matter of technology, always return a larger quantity of goods in the future, thus setting a lower bound for the interest rate. Indeed, Austrian theory makes just such a claim about technology. This twist cannot be directly incorporated into a model of pure exchange, but the difficulty can be glimpsed by prohibiting ad hoc interest rates below some technologically determined value, say $\bar{r} > 0$. Equilibrium can now fail to exist. If some agent psychologically discounts future utility at a rate smaller than $\bar{r}$, another cake-eating problem appears. Increments to savings will always yield a future utility payoff larger than the utility sacrifice of foregoing current consumption, making an optimal allocation of wealth, and hence equilibrium, impossible. As an explanation of positive interest rates, impatience in the infinite-horizon model is thus at odds with the technological explanations we consider in section 7.5: when the technological explanation is operative, the infinite-horizon model need not have an equilibrium.[24]

The second difficulty is the obvious one. The assumption that agents have budget constraints that extend into the infinite future cannot be taken with complete seriousness. Indeed, only insofar as the infinite-horizon model can link successive generations through altruistically motivated bequests does it have a claim to plausibility (and even then, a remote one).[25] In the bequest model, each generation of agents receives utility from the welfare of its descendants; working recursively, each agent effectively has an infinite-horizon utility function. The option of leaving wealth to one's offspring gives agents the opportunity to spend current wealth on this infinite stream of post mortem consumption.

Unlike the infinite-horizon budget constraint model, however, the bequest model only contingently ties agents to the future, and zero or negative interest rates can therefore occur. If agents discount the utility of their

23. The fact that only the most patient consumer has positive asymptotic consumption is well recognized; see Bewley (1982).

24. Are technologies in which an increment to capital can induce an unbounded expansion of wealth intrinsically unreasonable? Reflection on such questions quickly degenerates into armchair speculation on the finiteness of the world (or even the universe). Suffice it to say that for the problems at hand it is only necessary that agents believe that capital investments can return unbounded streams of wealth.

25. The bequest model is due to Barro (1974).

descendants—and such an assumption is necessary to avoid the cake-eating problem—no wealth will be transferred to offspring at a zero or negative interest rate; the link into the indefinite future can thus break down. Recall that when budget constraints take the infinite-horizon form, negative interest rates do not occur because they lead to unbounded personal wealth; loosely speaking, the value of endowments becomes arbitrarily large in the distant future, and agents will attempt to spend this wealth in the present, preventing the existence of equilibrium. In the bequest model, on the other hand, the smallest sum that agents can bequeath is zero, not negative; consequently agents are prevented from transferring their descendants' wealth into the present. Negative interest rates, as we will see, can therefore occur.[26]

Of course, many agents do leave wealth to their offspring, possibly even for the reason that the bequest model proposes—the utility they derive from the welfare of their descendants. It might therefore be tempting to argue that since, as a matter of empirical fact, agents effectively do have an infinite-horizon budget constraint interest rates must be positive. But this argument would not explain why the world finds itself in a positive-bequest, positive-interest equilibrium. The phenomena are not under dispute; the challenge is to find a plausible model that necessarily generates positive interest rate equilibria. Moreover, given the fact of positive interest rates, that agents leave wealth to their descendants is to be expected. Therefore, even if positive bequests and positive interest rates necessarily accompany one another, it may be that the latter is causing the former rather than vice versa; the fact of bequests does not validate the bequest model as an explanation of positive interest rates.

Whether due to these difficulties or to more fundamental doubts about altruistic utility functions, we must look beyond infinite-horizon theory to the other major branch of current-day intertemporal economics, the original overlapping generations model, in which agents live for only a finite amount of time and have no active altruistic linkage to their descendants. As the following example illustrates, the overlapping generations model can easily generate steady states with a nonpositive interest rate—even when agents discount consumption in their later periods of life.[27]

---

26. That linking agents to the future requires positive bequests is given due emphasis in Barro's original paper. A substantial literature studying the conditions under which bequests are operative has since developed; for a sample, see Drazen (1978) and Weil (1987). I am ignoring the transfer of wealth from later to earlier generations through gifts, also first discussed in Barro (1974). In addition, see Abel (1987).

27. That negative interest rates can arise in the overlapping generations model is well known, particularly in exchange economies. See Samuelson (1958) and Gale (1973) for analyses of the exchange case. I follow the production model of Diamond (1965), with the exception of allowing capital to depreciate (excluded in Diamond only for the sake of simplicity). With no depreciation, positive interest rates follow solely from the fact that the marginal product of capital is positive. I deal with technological arguments for positive interest later; an absence of depreciation is not a particularly plausible version of the thesis.

Example

In the simplest overlapping generations economy with production, a typical agent $j = 1, \ldots, J$ lives for two periods and derives utility $u^j(x_1^j, x_2^j)$ from consumption in each period. The agent sells an endowment of labor in the first period and uses the proceeds to purchase x_1^j and capital k. Capital is then sold in the second period to purchase x_2^j. Agent j therefore faces the budget constraints $x_1^j + k \leq wl^j$ and $x_2^j \leq (1 + r)k$, where $(1 + r)$ equals the receipts earned from selling a unit of capital held for one period and l^j is j's labor endowment. Combining the two budget constraints, we have $x_1^j + x_2^j/(1 + r) \leq wl^j$. Clearly, agents desiring to consume in their second period will purchase capital independently of the sign of r. If, for example, $u^j(x_1^j, x_2^j) = \ln x_1^j + \beta^j \ln x_2^j$, then x_1^j will equal $wl^j/(1 + \beta^j)$ and j's demand for capital is therefore $wl^j - wl^j/(1 + \beta^j) = wl^j(\beta^j/(1 + \beta^j))$. All that is necessary for a negative r is that at some w, the aggregate steady-state demand for capital leads to a capital-labor ratio with a sufficiently low marginal product of capital. Of course, the r generated in this way also must be compatible with w in the sense that firms earn zero economic profits at w and r. Recall from our discussion of the Solow model that $r = f'(k) - \delta$, where f indicates output as a function of the capital stock (with the fixed factor, labor, now held fixed at $\Sigma_{j=1}^J l^j$) and δ is the depreciation rate. Setting $k = \Sigma_{j=1}^J wl^j(\beta^j/(1 + \beta^j))$, any production function such that $f'(k) - \delta < 0$ and $w = f(k) - f'(k)k$ yields the desired result. The latter condition ensures that w and r are consistent with firm profit maximization. The world may well yield parameters such that $r > 0$, but the case $r \leq 0$ is certainly not pathological. ∎

The example reinforces Böhm-Bawerk's intuition that multiple arguments for the positivity of interest rates are needed. When, as in the example, agents anticipate that their future income will be small, they will save even if interest rates are low or negative. Böhm-Bawerk's first cause for interest thus does not operate and the second cause, impatience, need not outweigh the desire to save. I therefore turn to the technological case for why marginal investments should always have a positive rate of return.

7.5 Technological arguments for a positive interest rate

The possibility of storing goods through time, which briefly arose in our discussion of Böhm-Bawerk and Fisher in section 7.3, supplies a rudimentary technological case for why interest rates should be positive. Fisher in particular put great stock in the fact that money can be costlessly stored (without deterioration) and that savers therefore need not resort to assets with a negative nominal rate of return.[28] As Fisher recognized, however, a

---

28. See, e.g., Fisher (1907, chap. 5), which is also the source of the arguments to follow.

positive money rate of interest can translate into a negative real rate if returns are deflated by a nominal price that is rising through time. He therefore also applied the storage argument to physical commodities. To use Fisher's own example, if the price of wheat is expected to rise at a rate greater than the nominal interest rate—that is, if the "wheat rate of interest" is negative—investors will borrow money, purchase wheat for storage, and then sell the wheat in the future, making positive economic profits. Fisher concluded that a negative wheat rate of interest cannot arise in equilibrium. This argument seems to leave the issue up in the air; as both Fisher and Böhm-Bawerk acknowledged, the storage argument does not apply to goods that are costly to store (such as wheat, it should be noted) or to perishable goods. But at least in a steady state, it is only necessary that *some* durable good can be stored at zero cost. Since relative prices in a steady state stay constant through time, storing such a good earns a zero real rate of return independent of the price or set of prices used to deflate nominal investment returns.

But storage cannot lift real interest rates strictly (let alone substantially) above zero. For Böhm-Bawerk, the fervent anti-Marxist, it would not do for interest rates to be nil and for the heroic capitalist to be reduced to tending a storage depot. The grail of Austrian capital theory therefore was to demonstrate that marginal investments of capital generate a net addition to society's wealth.

Why should investments always yield a positive net return? As we have seen, marginal productivity theory by itself provides no rationale.[29] Böhm-Bawerk's answer was to expand the set of productive factors: in addition to the original factors, land and labor, an infinite diversity of capital goods is available. Böhm-Bawerk and his followers distinctively saw capital goods as original factors that have been invested or "stored" for various lengths of time. Each final output is therefore the product of original factors applied at various dates; recall the Böhm-Bawerk parable quoted in section 7.3. Moreover, Böhm-Bawerk assumed that as the time profile of original factor usage lengthens—holding fixed the total quantity of original factors applied at all dates—the amount of final outputs harvested increases.

Böhm-Bawerk measured the length of a production process by the *average production period*, which is a weighted sum of lengths of time between when original inputs are applied and when final output appears. The weights are given by the ratio of the quantity of input used to the total

---

29. One can always simply posit a sufficient array of productive investments; for example, we could assume that there are production activities producing a vector of outputs that is larger in every component than the vector of inputs consumed (with no nonproduced goods, such as natural resources, required). Alternatively, as discussed in footnote 27, we could assume that capital always has a positive marginal product and does not depreciate. The challenge is to devise a more compelling story. Exogenous productivity growth, it should be noted, is not enough. But see Negishi (1989a, chap. 8, sec. 4) for an analysis of interest rates under labor-augmenting technical change.

quantity of the input used at all dates [Böhm-Bawerk (1889, pp. 86–87)]. Since the average production period is defined separately for each original input, Böhm-Bawerk did not provide an unambiguous gauge of the time structure of inputs. As it happened, he primarily applied his measure to labor, which he saw as the chief input.

Böhm-Bawerk's view of technology suffers from numerous flaws, which furnished critics with ammunition and, worse, drew attention away from his critical (and more defensible) assertions. I simply mention these difficulties and move on to the essence of the positive interest rate claim. First, the Austrian approach assumes that each quantity of final output can be attributed to a uniquely defined flow of original inputs. Joint production is therefore excluded; if an input stream generates more than one output, there will be multiple ways of assigning inputs to the outputs produced.[30] Second, Böhm-Bawerk not only asserted that greater time can be allocated in ways that boost productivity, but also insisted on the dubious historical claim that almost all technological advances have in fact been the outgrowth of more time-consuming processes (1889, p. 82). Finally, we come to the point that drew the most fire: Böhm-Bawerk's use of the average production period to measure capital intensity. Even when output can be reduced to a well-defined stream of original factor inputs, the inherently multidimensional character of a time path of inputs cannot be captured by a single number. The average production period can behave perversely as a function of other parameters of the economy; for example, as interest rates fall, the average production period of optimally adopted techniques can fall rather than rise. And increases in the average production period need not correlate with increases in average factor productivity.

But at the heart of Böhm-Bawerk's system, untouched by these criticisms, is the connection between productivity and the consumption of time. Wicksell's formulation of Austrian capital theory greatly clarifies this link (1901, vol. 1, pt. 2, chap. 2–3). Wicksell rejected Böhm-Bawerk's hazy claims that production processes are longer or shorter overall, consequently dropping the average production period, and used differentiable production functions to describe technology. But Wicksell retained the Austrian emphasis on the expanded roster of capital goods and on the productivity of long-lived inputs. Indeed, he stressed the compatibility between time-dated capital goods and the growing consensus around marginal productivity.[31]

Wicksell also wisely chose to study interest rates in the context of steady states. He grasped that positive interest rates will not arise in any and all time frames. Given an arbitrary array of capital goods, few opportunities to transfer resources productively to specific dates in the future may be present; it is only relative to the indefinite future that positive rate of return

30. See Hicks (1973) for a discussion of this point.
31. Böhm-Bawerk and other early Austrians in contrast were hostile to the "American" idea of marginal productivity. See, e.g., Böhm-Bawerk (1909, 1912, chap. 7).

investments might be abundant. Wicksell realized that steady states are the natural mathematical setting in which to embed this principle.

Wicksell's simplest model allows original inputs to be invested, or stored, for only one time period. Let output be a differentiable, increasing, concave function F of $N = (N_0, N_1)$ and $L = (L_0, L_1)$, which are vectors of "current" and "stored" inputs of labor and land, respectively. I assume there is one firm with the production function F; of course, if F exhibits constant returns to scale, total output could instead be produced by many small firms, each endowed with the same technology. The function F reports the maximum output obtainable from (N, L); behind F there may be processes using only current inputs and other processes using both current and stored inputs. If output can be stored, for example, $F(N, L)$ may originate from maximizing the sum of outputs from two distinct production functions, $F^0(N_0^0, L_0^0)$ and $F^1(N_0^1, N_1; L_0^1, L_1)$, subject to $N_0^0 + N_0^1 = N_0$ and $L_0^0 + L_0^1 = L_0$.

Equilibrium can be described in two equivalent ways. In the first, firms directly purchase labor and land in the initial period and add another dose of labor and land to their goods in process in the latter period. Producers face factor prices w and p_L for labor and land in the two periods and the interest rate r; I normalize the output price to 1. Factor prices are not distinguished by date because of the steady-state assumption. Discounted profits are then

$$\frac{1}{1+r}(F(N, L) - (wN_0 + p_L L_0)) - (wN_1 + p_L L_1).$$

Letting subscripts denote partial derivatives, producer equilibrium requires

$$F_{N_0} = w, \ F_{N_1} = (1 + r)w, \text{ and}$$

$$F_{L_0} = p_L, \ F_{L_1} = (1 + r)p_L, \tag{7.5.1}$$

when all four inputs are in use. Therefore,

$$r = \frac{F_{N_1}}{F_{N_0}} - 1 = \frac{F_{L_1}}{F_{L_0}} - 1. \tag{7.5.2}$$

In Wicksell's words, "interest is the difference between the marginal productivity of saved-up labor and land and of current labor and land" (1901, p. 154).

This interpretation has the same firms storing labor and land and producing final output. Wicksell, in contrast, awkwardly interpreted the storage of labor and land as separate investment activities producing distinct commodities. Let stored labor and land have the prices w_1 and p_{L_1}. Saving one unit of labor, for example, costs w and earns w_1 when the stored labor is sold to final output producers. The equation $(1 + r)w = w_1$ defines the interest rate earned on this investment. Since profit maximization for output producers implies $w = F_N$ and $w_1 = F_{N_1}$, we return to the first equality in 7.5.2. The second equality can be derived in the same way.

Although only the above equilibrium conditions directly bear on the relationship between technology and interest, we sketch a completion of the model. If labor and land are inelastically supplied at levels $\bar{N}$ and $\bar{L}$, and if F produces the only final output in the economy, steady-state market clearing for factors is given by

$$N_0 + N_1 = \bar{N}, \text{ and } L_0 + L_1 = \bar{L}. \qquad (7.5.3)$$

At a point in time, N_1 and L_1 are fixed by past decisions; N_0 and L_0 are applied to these stocks to produce current output, while $\bar{N} - N_0$ and $\bar{L} - L_0$ are invested in the initial stages of tomorrow's output production. We then have the six equations in 7.5.1 and 7.5.3 to determine N_0, N_1, L_0, L_1, w, p_L, and r. Although Wicksell was somewhat confused on this point, a degree of freedom remains since we have not yet specified intertemporal preferences.[32] Since infinite-horizon consumers would by themselves lead to a positive interest rate—making the technology-interest rate connection moot—an overlapping-generations description of agents is the natural way to generate an additional demand condition to close the model; we omit the details, but see sections 7.4 and 2.7.

Following Böhm-Bawerk's lead, Wicksell hypothesized that a shift of a small amount of labor or land from current to stored forms "tends in many cases" to increase total product (1901, p. 153). Formally, assume that in equilibrium,

$$F_{N_1} > F_{N_0} \text{ and } F_{L_1} > F_{L_0}. \qquad (7.5.4)$$

Due to 7.5.2, the interest rate must be positive. Wicksell was well aware that as production becomes more capital intensive—that is, as N_1 and L_1 increase relative to N_0 and L_0—diminishing marginal productivity will lead F_{N_1}/F_{N_0} and F_{L_1}/F_{L_0} to decrease; therefore 7.5.4 might not hold. As in the single-capital good Solow model, a sufficiently large accumulation of capital in the current two-vintage model can lead to a zero or negative interest rate.

To forestall this possibility, Wicksell deployed the standard Austrian gambit: as interest rates fall, producers construct and employ capital goods of even greater time intensity. Although he only presented the cases of two- and three-period vintages of capital equipment in detail, Wicksell explicitly recognized that a general positive interest rate conclusion hinges on there being an abundance of capital vintages. If only a few types of capital are available, the accumulation of capital can so diminish the marginal productivity of capital goods that the rate of interest will have to be zero or negative; with a multiplicity of potential capital goods, on the other hand, a large accumulation of capital need not drive marginal products so low.

I turn therefore to a more general model where production can potentially use vintages of stored labor and land of arbitrarily long duration. Input vectors are now sequences, $N = (N_0, N_1, \ldots) \geq 0$ and $L =$

---

32. Garegnani (1990) adduces a broader significance to Wicksell's confusion.

$(L_0, L_1, \ldots) \geq 0$. Assume that (N, L) implicitly defines a (finite) age, denoted $T(N, L)$ or simply T, for the oldest type of capital used in production; otherwise, the distance in time between initiation and completion of production would be unbounded, and output would never appear.[33] Böhm-Bawerk called T the "absolute production period"; formally, it is the least integer such that for all $t > T, N_t = L_t = 0$. The production function is again denoted F and is assumed to be increasing, concave, and differentiable.[34]

When considering production using the inputs (N, L), profits are given by

$$\frac{1}{(1+r)^T} F(N, L) - \sum_{i=0}^{T} \frac{1}{(1+r)^i}(wN_{T-i} + p_L L_{T-i}).$$

For each i (including $i > T$), the first-order conditions necessary for (N, L) to be a maximum are

$$F_{N_i} \leq w(1+r)^i \qquad (= \text{if } N_i > 0),$$
$$F_{L_i} \leq p_L(1+r)^i \qquad (= \text{if } L_i > 0). \tag{7.5.5}$$

An equilibrium with respect to producer optimization occurs when N, L, and r satisfy 7.5.5. If factors continue to be inelastically supplied at levels $\bar{N}$ and $\bar{L}$, equilibrium in factor markets now requires $\sum_{i=0}^{T} N_i = \bar{N}$ and $\sum_{i=0}^{T} L_i = \bar{L}$. When both N_i and N_{i+1} are used in positive amounts, $r = F_{N_{i+1}}/F_{N_i} - 1$; thus 7.5.2 is a special case of 7.5.5.

Wicksell's model clarifies how the Austrian assumption that time is productive can be reconciled with the fact that actual producers do not use all potential vintages of capital equipment. Even though older capital goods may have a greater physical marginal product than factors of more recent vintage, the older factors need not be constructed or employed. As 7.5.5 indicates, in order for a capital good to be used, its discounted marginal product must be at least as large as the relevant original factor price. Thus, for some N_i, for example, F_{N_i} can be large but the corresponding inequality in 7.5.5 can still be satisfied with strict inequality if i is large and r is positive.

A positive interest rate theorem requires an explicit assumption that lengthier vintage factors are more productive than more short-lived factors. Suppose, therefore, for any (N, L), that either

---

33. Produced inputs can, under certain circumstances, be modeled as a stream of original inputs extending into the infinite past. At this point, however, produced inputs are not included in the model; I indicate later how they can be incorporated.

34. We define F only at those (N, L) with a finite number of nonzero entries. Formally, F is constructed from a sequence of functions, $f_n: R_+^n \to R, n \geq 0$, where each f_n denotes the output generated from any (N, L) such that $N_t = L_t = 0$ for all $t > n$. For all $n, m > 0$, assume $f_n(N_0, \ldots, N_n; L_0, \ldots, L_n) = f_{m+n}(N_0, \ldots, N_n, 0, \ldots, 0; L_0, \ldots, L_n, 0, \ldots, 0)$. Then, $F(N, L)$ is defined as $f_{T(N,L)}(N_0, \ldots, N_{T(N,L)}; L_0, \ldots, L_{T(N,L)})$. Of course, the derivative of F w.r.t. N_i (or L_i) is calculated using the function $f_{\max[i, T(N,L)]}$. Also, we mean F to be increasing in the strong sense that $(F_{N_0}, \ldots, F_{N_t}, F_{L_0}, \ldots, F_{L_t}) \gg 0$.

$$F_{N_{T(N,L)+1}}(N, L) > F_{N_{T(N,L)}}(N, L) \text{ or } F_{L_{T(N,L)+1}}(N, L) > F_{L_{T(N,L)}}(N, L)$$

$$(7.5.6)$$

holds. To see that $r > 0$ in equilibrium, consider the original factor, say labor, satisfying 7.5.6. From 7.5.5, $F_{N_{T+1}} \leq F_{N_T}(1 + r)$, but from 7.5.6, $F_{N_{T+1}} > F_{N_T}$. Hence, $r > 0$. Moreover, to the extent that $F_{N_{T+1}} - F_{N_T}$ is large, r must be significantly greater than 0.

We can now see formally why a positive interest rate theorem must be placed in a long-run framework. To keep matters simple, suppose that labor is the sole original factor. We also assume, not implausibly, that the ultimate vintage of each capital good is permanently fixed at the point in time it is created. Hence, in any given period, past decisions have already determined the vector of capital goods, say $(\hat{N}_2, \ldots, \hat{N}_T)$, available for production of the next period's consumption. Instead of steady-state factor usage levels, let N_0 and N_1 now indicate the quantity of next period's direct labor and this period's current labor used in the production of next period's consumption.

Now suppose that the current desire to save for next period's consumption unexpectedly increases. The rate of return earned by investments of current labor, N_1, in next period's consumption is

$$\frac{F_{N_1}(N_0, N_1, \hat{N}_2, \ldots, \hat{N}_T)}{F_{N_0}(N_0, N_1, \hat{N}_2, \ldots, \hat{N}_T)} - 1.$$

We have effectively returned to Wicksell's original two-vintage model. If N_0 is small—due, for example, to next period's savers also wanting to increase their savings—the rate of return can be negative for large N_1. Wicksell's positive interest rate conclusion is assured only when increases in the desire to save have time to translate into sufficiently lengthy investments of labor.

The Wicksell model can be broadened in a number of directions. If there were other sectors in the economy, the above argument would apply to steady-state equilibria as long as at least one sector satisfies 7.5.6. If produced inputs not reducible to original factors were added to the model, additional first-order conditions for the new factors would be necessary, but the positive interest rate argument as applied to the original factors would be unaffected. Indeed, the same reasoning could be extended to the produced factors if they can be used at multiple time periods and satisfy a condition analogous to 7.5.6; the Austrian reduction of output to a stream of original factors is therefore inessential and can be eliminated. In a similar vein, firms could produce multiple outputs. The above argument can then be reinterpreted as implicitly holding those additional outputs fixed at their optimal levels.

These extensions continue to use differentiable production functions and to suppose that lengthier vintage inputs are, at a zero usage level, more productive than all shorter-lived inputs. As I show in the appendix, however, even these assumptions are needlessly strong. Only the supposition that time can always augment the productivity of any given set of inputs is pivotal; the remaining idiosyncrasies riddling Austrian capital theory can be excised.[35]

The significance of formalizations of Austrian theory should not be over-stated. The model described here fleshes out the logic of how the productivity of time can lead to a positive interest rate; but to claim that positive interest rates arise as a matter of mathematical necessity misrepresents the Austrian stance. Even Böhm-Bawerk, when pressed, admitted that the amount of time that can be used fruitfully is bounded (1909, 1912, chap. 1). The success of the Austrian case hinges on a looser assertion that opportunities to lengthen production processes productively are so abundant that even a large supply of savings will not exploit them all.

To be sure, one can always just assert a priori that savings happen to be small enough that further expansions of capital always earn a positive net return. For instance, in the overlapping-generations example at the end of section 7.4 the model's parameters may generate a positive interest rate. The virtue of the Austrian approach is that it provides theoretical grounds for such an assertion. In Wicksell's model, for instance, the expansion of the number of capital goods (relative to a single capital good model) provides reasons why the impact of the diminishing marginal productivity of capital on the interest rate can be deferred, if not unconditionally evaded. Of course, the Böhm-Bawerk–Wicksell case still depends on the empirical claim that productive time-consuming techniques abound.

The credibility of this claim was not squarely assessed in the early neo-classical era (or a fortiori later). Although numerous Anglo-American critics challenged the link between time and productivity, their criticisms were interwoven with less fundamental attacks on the period of production and other technical oddities of the Austrian system. It remains unclear therefore how the central Austrian assertions would have fared had they received undiluted attention. Fisher's position on the abundance of productive time-consuming processes approximated Böhm-Bawerk's, but this one congruity does not guarantee that any broader consensus might have developed. Indeed, the unavoidably empirical nature of the Austrian view of technology suggests that dispute would have persisted.

7.6 Land and interest

So far our treatment of land has only considered the direct productive services and capital goods that land generates. Land is also an asset with a price. If an owner of land is entitled to the infinite future stream of rental payments that land earns—p_L per period in the above models—then the price of land must equal the discounted value of this infinite stream.

---

35. The current model and the appendix only bring out the positive interest rate dimension of Austrian capital theory. For other aspects of the Austrian system, see Dorfman's two classic papers (1959a, 1959b), and Faber (1979), which discusses the more recent German literature.

Suppose, furthermore, that the per-period rental payment always lies above some strictly positive amount; then, in order for the price of land to be finite, a positive interest rate is required. This point is particularly easy to grasp in a steady state. The current price of land as an asset, say π_L, must equal the discounted value of the sum of next period's expected rental payment and the land's price next period. In a steady state, the price of land remains constant through time; hence

$$\pi_L = \frac{p_L + \pi_L}{1 + r}$$

and $r = p_L/\pi_L$. A positive r therefore follows from the positivity of π_L and p_L.

Schumpeter analyzed this argument in some detail (1912, pp. 164–167). He hoped to establish that in the absence of a steady inflow of dynamic new entrepreneurs, the interest rate of the resulting "static" economy would be zero; he therefore needed to refute the land rationale for interest. But Schumpeter's reasoning, that land (as an asset with the right to an infinite flow of rental income) need not be traded actively, is not persuasive. Agents who want to consume their wealth prior to death will sell all their assets, including any land holdings.[36] The true difficulty with land as an explanation of interest is that it cannot account for why interest rates should be substantially positive. To this end, distinct arguments—for example, substantial impatience in the infinite-horizon model or the Austrian description of technology—are necessary.[37]

7.7 Conclusion

The transformation of interest theory differs from the other transitions we have considered. In contrast to its principled and highly visible rejections of utilitarianism and the differentiable production function, contemporary theory has mostly just ignored the postulates of early neoclassical interest theory. Current-day intertemporal theory is distinguished by its reformulation of the traditional agenda: inquiry into the sign and magnitude of interest rates has ceased.

Indeed, the drawbacks of the early neoclassical arguments for why interest rates should be substantially positive and the challenge of constructing

---

36. Samuelson (1943) was strangely sympathetic to Schumpeter's argument. He argued that in models with infinite-lived consumers land can have an infinite price. But small amounts of land would then exchange for unbounded amounts of consumption, leading to disequilibrium in consumption goods markets. Böhm-Bawerk (1889, p. 335) implicitly criticized the land argument for positive interest on the grounds that models incorporating an infinite future are inherently implausible ("literal infinity is 'out of bounds' in human affairs").

37. The link between land and positive interest rates has appeared in contemporary literature as an argument for the Pareto efficiency of equilibria in the overlapping-generations model; in the absence of population growth, $r > 0$ guarantees efficiency. See Muller and Woodford (1988) for a brief mention of this point.

a convincing contemporary replacement demonstrate the difficulty of the early neoclassical project: microeconomic theory appears to be unable to provide a pure theory of positive interest rates. A more contemporary reaction to the positivity of interest (see the end of section 7.5) is simply to assert that economic life happens to generate the phenomenon; but such an approach only restates the absence of a theoretical explanation.

Appendix

I now construct a more general, and simpler, model of the link between the productivity of time and positive interest. Defining F as in section 7.5, assume that F is continuous and that each (N, L) has a finite absolute production period $T(N, L)$. The profits earned from (N, L) are given by

$$\frac{1}{(1+r)^T} F(N, L) - \sum_{i=0}^{T} \frac{1}{(1+r)^i}(wN_{T-i} + p_L L_{T-i}). \qquad (7.A.1)$$

An equilibrium for producers occurs at a $(N, L) \geq 0$, $(w, p_L) \geq 0$, and $r \geq -1$ such that 7.A.1 reaches a maximum. Factor markets clear if $\Sigma_{i=0}^{T} N_i \leq \bar{N}$ ($=$ if $w > 0$) and $\Sigma_{i=0}^{T} L_i \leq \bar{L}$ ($=$ if $p_L > 0$).

Consider the maximum output obtainable from $\bar{N}$ and $\bar{L}$, subject to the constraint that the absolute production period is less than some arbitrary $\bar{T}$. That is, maximize $F(N, L)$ s.t.

$$\sum_{i=0}^{\bar{T}} N_i \leq \bar{N},$$

$$\sum_{i=0}^{\bar{T}} L_i \leq \bar{L},$$

$$T(N, L) \leq \bar{T}$$

This problem always has a solution, which I denote as $(N^*(\bar{T}), L^*(\bar{T}))$. Let $m(\bar{T}) = F(N^*(\bar{T}), L^*(\bar{T}))$. Depending on r, producers may well choose a level of output less than $m(\bar{T})$; when $r > 0$, for example, it may be more profitable to produce less than $m(\bar{T})$ if $m(\bar{T})$ requires a concentration of inputs early in the production process.

Consider the following condition.

Productivity of Time Assumption. The function $m(\bar{T})$ has no upper bound.

With this assumption, r must be strictly positive in producer equilibrium. To see why, note first that $F(N^*(\bar{T}), L^*(\bar{T})) - (wN_0^*(\bar{T}) + p_L L_0^*(\bar{T}))$, seen as a function of $\bar{T}$, has no upper bound; $\Sigma_{i=0}^{\bar{T}-1} (wN_{\bar{T}-i}(\bar{T}) + p_L L_{\bar{T}-i}(\bar{T}))$ in contrast is bounded above.

Rewrite profits as

$$\left(\frac{1}{1+r}\right)^T (F(N, L) - (wN_0 + p_L L_0)) - \sum_{i=0}^{T-1}\left(\frac{1}{1+r}\right)^i (wN_{T-i} + p_L L_{T-i}).$$

If $r \leq 0$,

$$\left(\frac{1}{1+r}\right)^T \geq \left(\frac{1}{1+r}\right)^i, \text{ for } i = 0, \ldots, T-1.$$

Consequently, for any (N, L), the profit earned by (N, L) must be at least as great as

$$\left(\frac{1}{1+r}\right)^T \left(F(N, L) - (wN_0 + p_L L_0) - \sum_{i=0}^{T-1}(wN_{T-i} + p_L L_{T-i}) \right).$$

Hence, the profit earned by choosing $(N, L) = (N^*(\overline{T}), L^*(\overline{T}))$ has no upper bound. Maximum profits are therefore also unbounded, and thus $r \leq 0$ is inconsistent with equilibrium.

If a positive lower bound for the interest rate is desired, the productivity of time assumption must be strengthened somewhat. If an $\varepsilon > 0$ exists such that for all T', there is a $\overline{T} > T'$ with $m(\overline{T}) > (1 + \varepsilon)^T$, then r can be no smaller than ε.

Both the weak and the strong versions of the productivity of time assumption place no upper bound on potential output. As long as we wish to establish only that r is positive, we can instead assume (1) that m is strictly increasing, that is, $m(\overline{T} + 1) > m(\overline{T})$ for all $\overline{T}$, and (2) that output can be stored, that is, for all (N, L), $F((N, 0), (L, 0)) \geq F(N, L)$. Then, if producers are in equilibrium and factor markets clear, $r > 0$. Storage immediately precludes the possibility that $r < 0$. If $r = 0$ and producers choose (N', L'),

$$F(N, L) - w\left(\sum_{i=0}^{T(N,L)} N_i\right) - p_L\left(\sum_{i=0}^{T(N,L)} L_i\right) \qquad (7.A.2)$$

must reach a maximum at (N', L'). But our definition of factor market clearing implies that profits would be greater at $(N^*(\overline{T}), L^*(\overline{T}))$, for any $\overline{T} > T(N', L')$, than at (N', L'). Note, however, that this combination of assumptions does not imply that r has a strictly positive lower bound.

8

Conclusion

8.1 Anomaly versus norm in theoretical models

Economists do not believe that the world works as general equilibrium models of perfect competition predict. Individual agents and firms influence market prices; agents do not hold to fixed goals, act with complete consistency, or form probabilities of all eventualities. Yet perfect competition and the traditional theory of rationality still form the core of neoclassical economics. They are said to describe the enduring tendencies of economic activity, or to be benchmarks against which real-world deviations can be measured.

This book has argued that some aspects of the completely rational agent and the frictionless market are misunderstood. Even in the long run, self-interested agents with no impairments in their powers of calculation need not possess complete preferences; and even when large numbers of agents come together to trade, factor markets need not be determinate or operate competitively.

Once markets are reconceived, some common features of economic life look different. Nonmarket factor price determination no longer appears as a fringe phenomenon. While bargaining models of wage determination, for example, have become familiar sights [see, e.g., Diamond (1982) and Mortenson (1982)], they portray wage bargaining as the by-product of search frictions or bilateral monopoly. Chapter 2 demonstrates that factor markets falter as price determination mechanisms even in completely competitive environments. Neither small numbers of market participants or frictions are key: point-in-time indeterminacy is in the nature of markets and technology. A similar reordering of expectations applies to many so-called decision-making irrationalities. Unlike intransitivity, incompleteness inflicts no harm on individuals. Agents who cling to the status quo are not exhibiting a foolishness that they will reason themselves out of, or that evolution

191

will ultimately weed out. The appearance of inconsistency that accompanies incomplete preferences is only an artifact of the ordinalist equation of choice and preference.

8.2 Form and content

Postwar economics discards many of the specific claims about psychology and technology that once made neoclassical economics so distinctive—and such an easy target of criticism. There is no pitfall in experimentally dropping these postulates in order to establish the minimal set of assumptions necessary for certain propositions. For example, hedonism, marginal productivity, and Austrian capital theory have no bearing on the existence of competitive equilibrium. Constructing a model without these premises therefore illuminates the relationship between assumption and inference.

The sticking point comes when the assumptions of early neoclassicism are rejected on principle but the conclusions tied to those assumptions are tacitly (or even explicitly) maintained. Completeness of preferences, determinacy of factor prices, and the positivity of interest rates now lack the substantive backing they once enjoyed; yet they are still presumed to rule in the normal state of standard models.

Does it follow that economic theory has not progressed? It may seem that contemporary theory has taken a step backward from the early twentieth century. But even putting its technical deficiencies aside, early neoclassical economics had its own internal weaknesses. Though they appreciated the conceptual trade-offs in factor price theory, early neoclassical theorists did not own up to the drawbacks of hedonism—or if they did, to the holes in utility theory that resulted—or to the difficulty of extracting meaningful policy advice from utilitarianism. The Austrians appreciated the dilemmas of interest rate theory, but their technological answer is hardly superior to the psychological discounting solutions they were trying to supplement. Hence, even if there were some purpose to drawing up a balance sheet of evaluation, a bottom line would be elusive.

Recognizing the flaws of contemporary theory renders it more, not less, powerful. A historically aware factor price theory would better understand the forces governing factor pricing and could allow for the messy possibility that supply and demand can sometimes leave prices indeterminate. Such a theory may seem less ambitious but would prove far more useful; the true complexity of economic life would emerge. Similarly, preference theory could build a more accurate and variegated picture of which of the putative axioms of rationality in fact characterize agents' interests. Rather than inviting cynical relativism, historical analysis can enable economics to benefit from its mistakes.

References

Abel, A., 1987, "Operative gift and bequest motives," *American Economic Review* 77:1037–1047.

Allen, R., 1933, "The nature of indifference curves," *Review of Economic Studies* 1:110–121.

Anand, P., 1993, *Foundations of rational choice under risk*, Oxford: Clarendon.

Anderson, E., 1993, *Value in ethics and economics*, Cambridge: Harvard University Press.

Anscombe, F., and R. Aumann, 1963, "A definition of subjective probability," *Annals of Mathematical Statistics* 34:199–205.

Appleyard, D., and J. Ingram, 1979, "A reconsideration of the additions to Mill's 'Great Chapter,' " *History of Political Economy* 11:459–476.

Arrow, K., 1951a, "An extension of the basic theorems of classical welfare economics," in *Proceedings of the second Berkeley symposium on mathematical statistics and probability* (J. Neyman, ed.), Berkeley: University of California Press.

Arrow, K., 1951b, *Social choice and individual values*, New York: Wiley, 1963.

Arrow, K., 1952, "Le principe de rationalité dans les décisions collectives," reprinted in K. Arrow, *Social choice and justice*, Cambridge: Harvard University Press, 1983.

Arrow, K., 1977, "Extended sympathy and the possibility of social choice," *American Economic Review* 67:219–225.

Arrow, K., and G. Debreu, 1954, "Existence of equilibrium for a competitive economy," *Econometrica* 22:265–290.

Arrow, K., and D. Starrett, 1973, "Cost-theoretical and demand-theoretical approaches to the theory of price determination," in *Carl Menger and the Austrian school of economics* (J. Hicks and W. Weber, eds.), Oxford: Clarendon.

Barro, R., 1974, "Are government bonds net wealth?" *Journal of Political Economy* 82:1095–1117.

Basu, K., 1982, "Determinateness of the utility function: revisiting a controversy of the thirties," *Review of Economic Studies* 49:307–311.

Becker, G., 1993, "The economic way of looking at behavior," *Journal of Political Economy* 101:385–409.

Bergson, A., 1938, "A reformulation of certain aspects of welfare economics," *Quarterly Journal of Economics* 52:310–334.

Bewley, T., 1972, "Existence of equilibria in economies with infinitely many commodities," *Journal of Economic Theory* 4:514–540.

Bewley, T., 1982, "An integration of equilibrium theory and turnpike theory," *Journal of Mathematical Economics* 10:233–268.

Bishop, R., 1946, "Professor Knight and the theory of demand," *Journal of Political Economy* 54:141–169.

Böhm-Bawerk, E. von, 1889, *Positive theory of capital*, South Holland: Libertarian Press, 1959.

Böhm-Bawerk, E. von, 1909, 1912, *Further essays on capital and interest*, South Holland: Libertarian Press, 1959.

Cairnes, J. E., 1874, *Some leading principles of political economy*, London: Macmillan.

Cass, D., 1965, "Optimal growth in an aggregative model of capital accumulation," *Review of Economic Studies* 32:233–240.

Cassel, G., 1918, *The theory of social economy*, New York: Harcourt, 1924.

Chipman, J., 1979, "Mill's 'superstructure': how well does it stand up?" *History of Political Economy* 11:477–500.

Chipman, J., 1987, "Compensation principle," in *The new Palgrave* (J. Eatwell, M. Milgate, and P. Newman, eds.), London: Macmillan.

Chipman, J., and J. Moore, 1971, "The compensation principle in welfare economics," in *Papers in quantitative economics*, vol. 2 (A. Zarley, ed.), Lawrence, KS: University Press of Kansas.

Chipman, J., and J. Moore, 1978, "The new welfare economics 1939–1974," *International Economic Review* 19:547–584.

Chipman, J., and J. Moore, 1980, "Compensating variation, consumer's surplus, and welfare," *American Economic Review* 70:933–949.

Clark, J. B., 1899, *The distribution of wealth*, New York: Macmillan, 1924.

Cooter, R., and P. Rapoport, 1984, "Were the ordinalists wrong about welfare economics?" *Journal of Economic Literature* 22:507–530.

Cummings, R., D. Brookshire, and W. Schulze, 1986, *Valuing environmental goods: an assessment of the contingent valuation method*, Totowa, NJ: Rowman and Allanheld.

Dantzig, G., 1963, *Linear programming and extensions*, Princeton: Princeton University Press.

Debreu, G., 1951, "The coefficient of resource utilization," *Econometrica* 19:273–292.

Debreu, G., 1959, *Theory of value*, New York: Wiley.

Debreu, G., 1960, "Topological methods in cardinal utility theory," in *Mathematical methods in the social sciences, 1959* (K. Arrow, S. Karlin, and P. Suppes, eds.), Stanford: Stanford University Press.

Debreu, G., 1970, "Economies with a finite set of equilibria," *Econometrica* 38:387–392.

Diamond, P., 1965, "National debt in a neoclassical growth model," *American Economic Review* 55:1126–1150.

Diamond, P., 1982, "Wage determination and efficiency in search equilibrium," *Review of Economic Studies* 49:217–227.

Dorfman, R., 1959a, "A graphical exposition of Böhm-Bawerk's interest theory," *Review of Economic Studies* 26:153–158.

Dorfman, R., 1959b, "Waiting and the period of production," *Quarterly Journal of Economics* 73:351–372.

Downey, E., 1910, "The futility of marginal utility," *Journal of Political Economy* 18:253–268.

Drazen, A., 1978, "Government debt, human capital, and bequests in a lifecycle model," *Journal of Political Economy* 86:505–516.

Edgeworth, F., 1881, *Mathematical psychics*, London: London School of Economics, 1932.

Edgeworth, F., 1897, "The pure theory of taxation," reprinted in F. Edgeworth, *Papers relating to political economy*, vol. 2, London: Macmillan, 1925.

Edgeworth, F., 1904, "The theory of distribution," *Quarterly Journal of Economics* 18:159–218.

Ekelund, R., and S. Thommesen, 1989, "Disequilibrium theory and Thornton's assault on the laws of supply and demand," *History of Political Economy* 21:567–592.

Faber, M., 1979, *Introduction to modern Austrian capital theory*, Berlin: Springer.

Fawcett, H., 1865, *The economic position of the British labourer*, London: Macmillan.

Fisher, I., 1892, *Mathematical investigations in the theory of value and price*, New Haven: Yale University Press, 1925.

Fisher, I., 1907, *The rate of interest*, New York: Macmillan.

Fisher, I., 1927, "A statistical method for measuring 'marginal utility' and testing the justice of a progressive income tax," in *Economic essays contributed in honor of John Bates Clark* (J. Hollander, ed.), New York: Macmillan.

Fisher, I., 1930, *The theory of interest*, New York: Macmillan.

Forget, E., 1992, "J. S. Mill and the Tory school: the rhetorical value of the recantation," *History of Political Economy* 24:31–59.

Fuchs, G., 1974, "Private ownership economies with a finite number of equilibria," *Journal of Mathematical Economics* 1:141–158.

Gale, D., 1967, "The existence of optimal programmes of accumulation for an infinite time horizon," *Review of Economic Studies* 32:85–104.

Gale, D., 1973, "Pure exchange equilibrium of dynamic economic models," *Journal of Economic Theory* 6:12–36.

Garegnani, P., 1976, "On a change in the notion of equilibrium in recent work on value and distribution," in *Essays in modern capital theory* (M. Brown, K. Sato, and P. Zarembka, eds.), Amsterdam: North Holland.

Garegnani, P., 1990, "Quantity of capital," in *Capital theory* (J. Eatwell, M. Milgate, and P. Newman, eds.), New York: Norton.

George, H., 1879, *Progress and poverty*, New York: Sterling.

Gordon, S., 1973, "The wage-fund controversy: the second round," *History of Political Economy* 5:14–35.

Grandmont, J.-M., 1982, "Temporary general equilibrium theory," in *Handbook of mathematical economics*, vol. 2 (K. Arrow and M. Intriligator, eds.), Amsterdam: North Holland.

Green, J., 1987, "Making book against oneself: the independence axiom and non-linear utility theory," *Quarterly Journal of Economics* 102:785–796.

Grodal, B., 1974, "Convexity of preference," in *Mathematical Models in Economics* (J. Los and M. Los, eds.), Warsaw: Polish Scientific Puslishers.

Hahn, F., 1982, "The neo-Ricardians," *Cambridge Journal of Economics* 6:353–374.

Hammond, P., 1983, "Ex-post optimality as a dynamically consistent objective for collective choice under uncertainty," in *Social choice and welfare* (P. Pattanaik and M. Salles, eds.), Amsterdam: North Holland.

Hanemann, W., 1991, "Willingness to pay and willingness to accept: how much can they differ?" *American Economic Review* 81:635–647.

Harcourt, G., 1974, "The Cambridge controversies: the afterglow," in *Contemporary issues in economics* (M. Parkin and A. Nobay, eds.), Manchester: Manchester University Press.

Harrod, R., 1938, "Scope and method of economics," *Economic Journal* 48:383–412.

Harsanyi, J., 1953, "Cardinal utility in welfare economics and in the theory of risk-taking," *Journal of Political Economy* 63:434–435.

Harsanyi, J., 1955, "Cardinal welfare, individualistic ethics, and interpersonal comparisons of utility," *Journal of Political Economy* 63:309–321.

Harsanyi, J., 1977, *Rational behavior and bargaining equilibrium in games and social situations*, Cambridge: Cambridge University Press.

Hayek, F. von, 1928, "Das intertemporale Gleichgewichtssystem der Preise und die Bewegungen des 'Geldwerthes,'" *Weltwirtschaftliches Archiv* 28:33–76.

Hicks, J., 1932, "Marginal productivity and the principle of variation," *Economica* 25:79–88.

Hicks, J., 1933, "Equilibrium and the cycle," reprinted in J. Hicks, *Money, interest and wages*, Cambridge: Harvard University Press, 1982.

Hicks, J., 1939a, "The foundations of welfare economics," *Economic Journal* 49:696–712.

Hicks, J., 1939b, *Value and capital*, Oxford: Clarendon, 1946.

Hicks, J., 1940, "The valuation of social income," *Economica* 7(n.s.):104–124.

Hicks, J., 1941, "The rehabilitation of consumers' surplus," *Review of Economic Studies* 8:108–116.

Hicks, J., 1942, "Consumers' surplus and index-numbers," *Review of Economic Studies* 9:126–137.

Hicks, J., 1943, "The four consumer's surpluses," *Review of Economic Studies* 11:31–41.

Hicks, J., 1946, "The generalized theory of consumer's surplus," *Review of Economic Studies* 13:68–74.

Hicks, J., 1956, *A revision of demand theory*, Oxford: Oxford University Press.

Hicks, J., 1973, "The Austrian theory of capital and its rebirth in modern economics," in *Carl Menger and the Austrian school of economics* (J. Hicks and W. Weber, eds.), Oxford: Clarendon.

Hicks, J., 1976, "Marshall," reprinted in J. Hicks, *Classics and moderns*, Cambridge: Harvard University Press, 1983.

Hicks, J., 1981, *Wealth and welfare*, Cambridge: Harvard University Press.

Hicks, J., and R. Allen, 1934, "A reconsideration of the theory of value," *Economica* 1(n.s.):52–76, 196–219.

High, J., and H. Bloch, 1982, "On the history of ordinal utility theory: 1900–32," *History of Political Economy* 21:351–365.

Hobson, J. A., 1900, *The economics of distribution*, New York: Macmillan.

Hobson, J. A., 1909, *The industrial system*, London: Longmans.

Hollander, S., 1979, *The economics of David Ricardo*, Toronto: Toronto University Press.

Hollander, S., 1985, *The economics of John Stuart Mill*, Oxford: Blackwell.

Hotelling, H., 1938, "The general welfare in relation to problems of taxation and of railway and utility rates," *Econometrica* 6:242–269.

Ingrao, I., and G. Israel, 1987, *The invisible hand: economic equilibrium in the history of science*, Cambridge: MIT Press, 1990.

Jaffé, W., 1976, "Menger, Jevons and Walras de-homogenized," *Economic Inquiry* 14:511–524.

Jenkin, F., 1868, "Trade-unions: how far legitimate," reprinted in F. Jenkin, *The graphic representation of the laws of supply and demand and other essays on political economy*, London: London School of Economics, 1931.

Jenkin, F., 1870, "The graphic representation of the laws of supply and demand, and their application to labour," reprinted in F. Jenkin, *The graphic representation of the laws of supply and demand and other essays on political economy*, London: London School of Economics, 1931.

Jevons, W., 1871, *The theory of political economy*, London: Macmillan.

Kahneman, D., J. Knetsch, and R. Thaler, 1990, "Experimental tests of the endowment effect and the Coase theorem," *Journal of Political Economy* 98: 1325–1348.

Kaldor, N., 1939, "Welfare propositions in economics and interpersonal comparisons of utility," *Economic Journal* 49:549–551.

Kehoe, T., 1980, "An index theorem for general equilibrium models with production," *Econometrica* 48:1211–1232.

Knight, F., 1934, "Capital, time, and the interest rate," *Economica* 1(n.s.):257–286.

Knight, F., 1936, "The quantity of capital and the rate of interest, II," *Journal of Political Economy* 44:612–642.

Knight, F., 1941, "Professor Mises and the theory of capital," *Economica* 8(n.s.):409–427.

Knight, F., 1944, "Realism and relevance in the theory of demand," *Journal of Political Economy* 52:289–318.

Knight, F., 1946, "Comment on Mr. Bishop's article," *Journal of Political Economy* 54:170–176.

Koopmans, T., 1951a, ed., *Activity analysis of production and allocation*, New Haven: Yale University Press.

Koopmans, T., 1951b, "Introduction," in *Activity analysis of production and allocation* (T. Koopmans, ed.), New Haven: Yale University Press.

Koopmans, T., 1965, "On the concept of optimal economic growth," in *The econometric approach to development planning*, Amsterdam: North Holland.

Kreps, D., 1988, *Notes on the theory of choice*, Boulder, CO: Westview.

Kuenne, R., 1963, *The theory of economic equilibrium*, Princeton: Princeton University Press.

Lange, O., 1934, "The determinateness of the utility function," *Review of Economic Studies* 1:218–235.

Lange, O., 1942, "The foundations of welfare economics," *Econometrica* 10:215–228.

Lerner, A., 1934, "The concept of monopoly and the measurement of monopoly power," *Review of Economic Studies* 1:157–175.

Levi, I., 1986, *Hard choices*, Cambridge: Cambridge University Press.

Lewin, S., 1996, "Economics and psychology: lessons for our own day, from the early twentieth century," *Journal of Economic Literature* 34:1293–1323.

Lipsey, R., and K. Lancaster, 1956, "The general theory of second best," *Review of Economic Studies* 24:11–32.

Longe, F., 1866, *A refutation of the wage-fund theory of modern political economy*, London: Longmans.

Luce, D., and H. Raiffa, 1957, *Games and decisions*, New York: Wiley.

Magill, M., 1981, "Infinite horizon programs," *Econometrica* 49:679–711.

Malinvaud, E., 1953, "Capital accumulation and efficient allocation of resources," *Econometrica* 21:233–268.

Mandler, M., 1995, "Sequential indeterminacy in production economies," *Journal of Economic Theory* 66:406–436.

Mandler, M., 1996a, "Interpersonal comparisons of utility and the policy paralysis problem," forthcoming, *Social Choice and Welfare*.

Mandler, M., 1996b, "Policy paralysis in general equilibrium theory," mimeo, Harvard University.

Mandler, M., 1997, "Sraffian indeterminacy in general equilibrium," forthcoming, *Review of Economic Studies*.

Mandler, M., 1998, "Incomplete preferences and rational intransitivity of choice," mimeo, Harvard University.

Marcet, J., 1816, *Conversations on political economy*, Philadelphia: Moses Thomas, 1817.

Marshall, A., 1879, *The pure theory of foreign trade*, reprinted in *The early writings of Alfred Marshall, 1867–1890* (J. Whitaker, ed.), London: Macmillan, 1975.

Marshall, A., 1890, *Principles of economics*, London: Macmillan.

Marshall, A., 1891, *Principles of economics*, 2nd ed., London: Macmillan.

Marshall, A., 1895, *Principles of economics*, 3rd ed., London: Macmillan.

Marshall, A., 1920, *Principles of economics*, 8th ed., London: Macmillan.

Marshall, A., and M. P. Marshall, 1879, *The economics of industry*, London: Macmillan, 1881.

Marx, K., 1867, *Capital*, vol. 1, New York: International Publishers, 1967.

Mas-Colell, A., 1975, "On the continuity of equilibrium prices in constant-returns production economies," *Journal of Mathematical Economics* 2:21–33.

Mas-Colell, A., 1985, *The theory of general economic equilibrium: a differentiable approach*, Cambridge: Cambridge University Press.

McColluch, J., 1825, *The principles of political economy*, Edinburgh: Tait, 1925.

McKenzie, L., 1954, "On equilibrium in Graham's model of world trade and other competitive systems," *Econometrica* 22:147–161.

McKenzie, L., 1986, "Optimal economic growth, turnpike theorems, and comparative dynamics," in *Handbook of mathematical economics*, vol. 3 (K. Arrow and M. Intriligator, eds.), Amsterdam: North Holland.

Milgate, M., 1979, "On the origin of the notion of 'intertemporal equilibrium,'" *Economica* 46(n.s.):1–10.

Mill, J. S., 1844, "On the definition of political economy," in J. S. Mill, *Essays on some unsettled question in political economy*, Clifton, NJ: Kelley, 1974.

Mill, J. S., 1848, *Principles of political economy*, London: Longmans, 1909.

Mill, J. S., 1852, *Principles of political economy*, 3rd ed., London: Longmans, 1909.

Mill, J. S., 1865, *Principles of political economy*, 6th ed., London: Longmans, 1909.

Mill, J. S., 1869, "Thornton on labour and its claims," reprinted in J. S. Mill, *Essays on economics and society*, Toronto: University of Toronto Press, 1967.

Milnor, J., 1954, "Games against nature," in *Decision processes* (R. Thrall, C. Coombs, and R. Davis, eds.), New York: Wiley.

Mirowski, P., 1991, "The when, the how and the why of mathematical expression in the history of economic analysis," *Journal of Economic Perspectives* 5:145–157.

Mirrlees, J., 1969, "The dynamic non-substitution theorem," *Review of Economic Studies* 36:67–76.

Mises, L. von, 1949, *Human action: a treatise on economics*, New Haven: Yale University Press.

Mitchell, W., 1916, "The role of money in economic theory," *American Economic Review* 16:140–161.

Morishima, M., 1964, *Equilibrium, stability, and growth*, Oxford: Clarendon.

Mortenson, D., 1982, "The matching process as a noncooperative bargaining game," in *The economics of information and uncertainty* (J. McCall, ed.), Chicago: University of Chicago Press.

Muller, W., and M. Woodford, 1988, "Determinacy of equilibrium in stationary economies with both finite and infinite lived consumers," *Journal of Economic Theory* 46:255–290.

Negishi, T., 1986, "Thornton's criticism of equilibrium theory and Mill," *History of Political Economy* 18:567–577.

Negishi, T., 1989a, *History of economic theory*, Amsterdam: North Holland.

Negishi, T., 1989b, "On equilibrium and disequilibrium: a reply to Ekelund and Thommesen," *History of Political Economy* 21:593–600.

Neisser, H., 1932, "Lohnhöhe und Beschäftigungsgrad im Marktgleichgewicht," *Weltwirtschaftliches Archiv* 36:413–455.

Neisser, H., 1942, " 'Permanent' technological unemployment," *American Economic Review* 32:50–71.

Neumann, J. von, 1936, "A model of general economic equilibrium," reprinted in *Review of Economic Studies* 13:1–9, 1945–1946.

Pareto, V., 1897, *Cours d'économie politique*, Lausanne: Rouge.

Pareto, V., 1909, *Manual of political economy*, New York: Augustus Kelley, 1971.

Peleg, B., and M. Yaari, 1970, "Markets with countably many commodities," *International Economic Review* 11:369–377.

Pigou, A., 1932, *The economics of welfare*, 4th ed., London: Macmillan.

Putnam, H., 1986, "Rationality in decision theory and ethics," reprinted in *Rationality in question: on Eastern and Western views of rationality* (S. Biderman and B.-A. Scharfstein, eds.), Leiden: Brill, 1989.

Ramsey, F., 1928, "A mathematical theory of saving," *Economic Journal* 38:543–559.

Raiffa, H., 1968, *Decision analysis*, Reading, MA: Addison-Wesley.

Raz, J., 1986, *The morality of freedom*, Oxford: Clarendon.

Ricardo, D., 1817, *Principles of political economy*, Cambridge: Cambridge University Press, 1951.

Ricardo, D., 1822, "On protection to agriculture," in *Works and correspondence of David Ricardo*, vol. 4 (P. Sraffa, ed.), Cambridge: Cambridge University Press, 1951.

Robbins, L., 1932, *An essay on the nature and significance of economic science*, London: Macmillan.

Robbins, L., 1935, *An essay on the nature and significance of economic science*, 2nd ed., London: Macmillan.

Robbins, L., 1938, "Interpersonal comparisons of utility: a comment," *Economic Journal* 43:635–641.

Robertson, D., 1931, "Wage grumbles," in D. Robertson, *Economic fragments*, London: P. H. King.

Robertson, D., 1951, "Utility and all that," reprinted in D. Robertson, *Utility and all that*, London: Allen & Unwin, 1952.

Robertson, D., 1957, *Lectures on economic principles*, vol. 1, London: Staples.

Salter, W., 1960, *Productivity and technical change*, Cambridge: Cambridge University Press.

Samuelson, P., 1938a, "A note on the pure theory of consumer's behaviour," *Economica* 5(n.s.):61–72.

Samuelson, P., 1938b, "The numerical representation of ordered classifications and the concept of utility," *Review of Economic Studies* 6:65–70.

Samuelson, P., 1943, "Dynamics, statics, and the stationary state," *Review of Economics and Statistics* 25:58–68.

Samuelson, P., 1947, *Foundations of economic analysis*, Cambridge: Harvard University Press.

Samuelson, P., 1950, "Evaluation of real national income," *Oxford Economic Papers* 2:1–29.

Samuelson, P., 1958, "An exact consumption-loan model of interest, with or without the social contrivance of money," *Journal of Political Economy* 66:467–482.

Samuelson, P., 1961, "A new theorem on nonsubstitution," reprinted in P. Samuelson, *Collected papers of Paul A. Samuelson*, vol. 1, Cambridge: MIT Press.

Samuelson, P., 1962, "Parable and realism in capital theory: the surrogate production function," *Review of Economic Studies* 29:193–206.

Samuelson, P., 1976, *Economics*, 10th ed., New York: McGraw-Hill.

Savage, L., 1954, *The foundations of statistics*, New York: Wiley.

Schlesinger, K., 1935, "On the production equations of economic value theory," reprinted in *Precursors in mathematical economics* (W. Baumol and S. Goldfeld, eds.), London: London School of Economics, 1968.

Schumpeter, J., 1912, *The theory of economic development*, New York: Oxford University Press, 1978.

Schumpeter, J., 1954, *History of economic analysis*, New York: Oxford University Press, 1986.

Scitovsky, T., 1941, "A note on welfare propositions in economics," *Review of Economic Studies* 9:77–88.

Sen, A., 1970, *Collective choice and social welfare*, San Francisco: Holden-Day.

Sen, A., 1973, "Behaviour and the concept of preference," *Economica* 40(n.s.):241–259.

Sen, A., 1993, "Internal consistency of choice," *Econometrica* 61:495–521.

Senior, N., 1836, *An outline of the science of political economy*, London: Clowes.

Shafer, W., and H. Sonnenschein, 1982, "Market demand and excess demand functions," in *Handbook of mathematical economics*, vol. 2 (K. Arrow and M. Intriligator, eds.), Amsterdam: North Holland.

Sidgwick, H., 1883, *The principles of political economy*, London: Macmillan.

Smale, S., 1974, "Global analysis and economics, IV," *Journal of Mathematical Economics* 1:119–127.

Smith, A., 1759, *The theory of moral sentiments*, Oxford: Oxford University Press, 1976.

Smith, A., 1776, *An inquiry into the nature and causes of the wealth of nations*, Indianapolis: Liberty Classics, 1979.

Solow, R., 1962, "Substitution and fixed proportions in the theory of capital," *Review of Economic Studies* 29:207–218.

Sraffa, P., 1960, *Production of commodities by means of commodities*, Cambridge: Cambridge University Press.

Stackelberg, H. von, 1933, "Zwei kritische Bemerkungen zur Preistheorie Gustav Cassel," *Zeitschrift für Nationalökonomie* 4:456–472.

Stigler, G., 1941, *Production and distribution theories*, New York: Macmillan.

Stigler, G., 1950, "The development of utility theory," reprinted in G. Stigler, *Essays in the history of economics*, Chicago: University of Chicago Press, 1965.

Taussig, F., 1896, *Wages and capital*, New York: Appletons.

Thornton, W., 1867, "What determines the price of labour or rate of wages?" *Fortnightly Review* 1(n.s.):551–566.

Thornton, W., 1869, *On labour*, London: Macmillan.

Thornton, W., 1870, *On labour*, 2nd ed., London: Macmillan.

Tversky, A., and D. Kahneman, 1990, "Loss aversion in riskless choice: a reference-dependent model," *Quarterly Journal of Economics* 106:1039–1061.

Varian, H., 1984, *Microeconomic analysis*, 2nd ed., New York: Norton.

Walker, F., 1875, "The wage-fund theory," *North American Review* 120 (January): 84–119.

Walker, F., 1876, *The wages question*, New York: Holt, 1886.

Walker, F., 1883, *Political economy*, New York: Holt.

Walras, L., 1874, *Elements of pure economics*, London: Allen & Unwin, 1954.

Weil, P., 1987, "Love thy children: reflections on the Barro debt neutrality theorem," *Journal of Monetary Economics* 19:377–391.

Weintraub, E. R., 1985, *General equilibrium analysis*, Cambridge: Cambridge University Press.

Weintraub, E. R., 1991, *Stabilizing dynamics: constructing economic knowledge*, New York: Cambridge University Press.

Weizsäcker, C. von, 1965, "On optimal economic development in a multi-sectoral economy," *Review of Economic Studies* 34:1–18.

Whitaker, J., 1975, *The early writings of Alfred Marshall, 1867–1890*, London: Macmillan.

Wicksell, K., 1901, *Lectures on political economy*, vol. 1, London: Routledge, 1934.

Wicksteed, P., 1894, "Degree of utility," reprinted in *Palgrave's dictionary of political economy* (H. Higgs, ed.), London: Macmillan, 1925.

Wicksteed, P., 1910, *The common sense of political economy*, London: Macmillan.

Wieser, F., 1884, *Über den Ursprung und die Hauptgesetze des Wirtschaftwerthes*, Vienna: Alfred Hölder.

Wieser, F., 1888, *Social economics*, New York: Greenberg, 1927.

Zeuthen, F., 1933, "Das Prinzip der Knappheit, technische Kombination und ökonomische Qualität," *Zeitschrift für Nationalökonomie* 7:1–24.

INDEX